YOU'RE PROBABLY WONDERING what we are trying to do. It's hard to say: sort of a magazine and sort of a newspaper. The name of it is ROLLING STONE, which comes from an old saying: "A rolling stone gathers no moss." Muddy Waters used the name for a song he wrote; the Rolling Stones took their name from Muddy's song; and "Like a Rolling Stone" was the title of Bob Dylan's first rock & roll record.

We have begun a new publication reflecting what we see are the changes in rock & roll and the changes related to rock & roll. Because the trade papers have become so inaccurate and irrelevant, and because the fan magazines are an anachronism, fashioned in the mold of myth and nonsense, we hope that we have something here for the artist and the industry, and every person who "believes in the magic that can set you free."

ROLLING STONE is not just about music, but also about the things and attitudes that the music embraces. We've been working quite hard on it, and we hope you can dig it. To describe it any further would be difficult without sounding like bullshit, and bullshit is like gathering moss.

~JANN S. WENNER

[RS 1, NOVEMBER 9TH, 1967]

Rolling Stone

THE COMPLETE COVERS

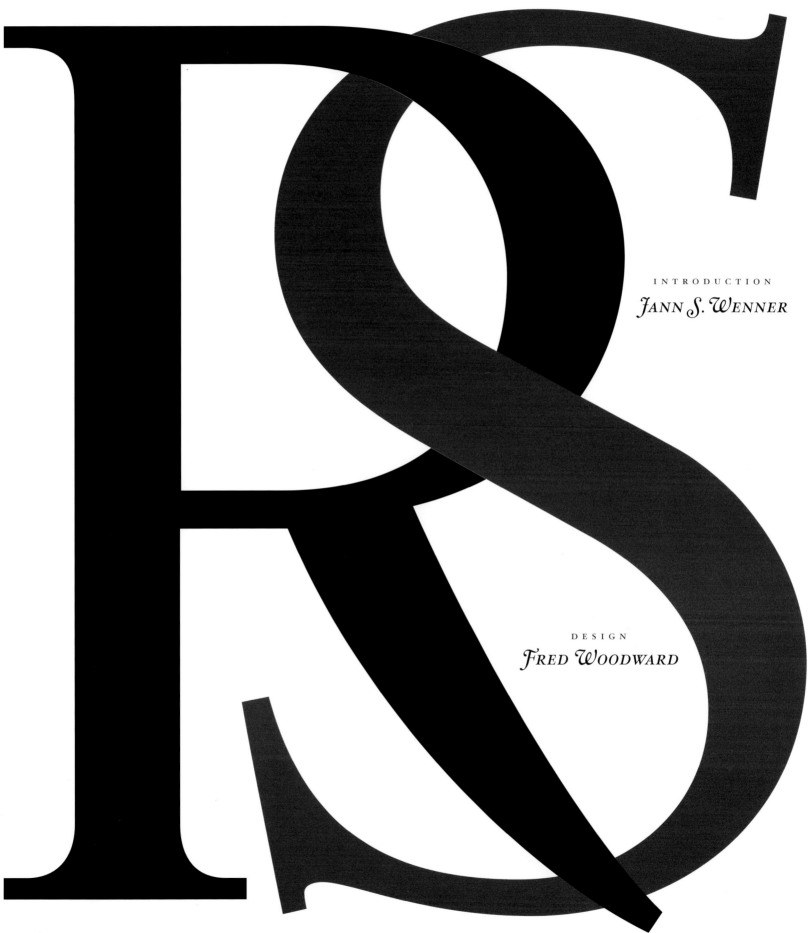

INTRODUCTION
Jann S. Wenner

DESIGN
Fred Woodward

HARRY N. ABRAMS, INC., PUBLISHERS

*To Jane, Alex, Theo and Gus
and the dear friends and
great talents – especially
Annie and Fred – who helped
make this happen.*

~JSW

*   *   *   *   *

A ROLLING STONE PRESS BOOK

Editor HOLLY GEORGE-WARREN
Associate Editor SHAWN DAHL
Editorial Assistant ANN ABEL
Editorial Consultant ROBERT LOVE

Designer FRED WOODWARD
Design Associate JESPER SUNDWALL
Design Assistants FREDRIK SUNDWALL,
YOOMI CHONG, ERIC SIRY

*   *   *   *   *

Library of Congress Cataloging-in-Publication Data
Rolling Stone: the complete covers / introduction by
Jann S. Wenner; designed by Fred Woodward.
p.   cm.
Includes index.
ISBN 0-8109-3797-2 (cloth) / ISBN 0-8109-2754-3 (qpb)
1. Rolling stone (San Francisco, Calif.).
2. Magazine covers—California—San Francisco.
I. Woodward, Fred.
NC974.4.R66R67 1998
741.6'52'097461—dc21
97-41724

ROLLING STONE covers © 1998 Straight Arrow
Publishers Company, L.P.

Copyright © 1998 Rolling Stone Press

Published in 1998 by Harry N. Abrams,
Incorporated, New York

Printed and bound in Hong Kong

Harry N. Abrams, Inc.
100 Fifth Avenue
New York, NY 10011
www.abramsbooks.com

1967

THIS BOOK, the complete collection of ROLLING STONE's covers from 1967 to 1997, represents not just the evolution of a magazine but a record of our times. For three decades, no surer sign has heralded the arrival of a performer, artist or personality than a cover of ROLLING STONE. Virtually every important rock musician and movie star, as well as many celebrated public figures, has appeared on one of the seven hundred twenty-eight covers reproduced here.

Many of them willingly have turned up time and again: Mick Jagger, with nineteen covers – some alone and others with the band or Keith – claims the all-time cover-boy crown. Among the people we have chosen to celebrate, the shrewdest collaborated with us in the creation and refinement of their public images. Many of those powerful images have since grown to define an era. When I started ROLLING STONE in November 1967, the magazine's initial charter was to cover rock & roll music with intelligence and respect. Even then, we knew that the fervor sweeping our generation encompassed more than just music. And so we gradually broadened the charter to include everything the music touched, embraced or informed: politics, movies, television, journalism, sports, Super Bowls, crime, kidnappings, astronauts, gurus, groupies, hippies, Jesus freaks, health clubs, narcs,

pimps, drugs and all the other forms of American social behavior, pathological and otherwise.

These events and personalities were captured for the cover of ROLLING STONE by some of the finest photographers of the last three decades. A partial list would include Annie Leibovitz, Mark Seliger, Richard Avedon, Anton Corbijn, Albert Watson, Herb Ritts, Francesco Scavullo, Matt Mahurin and Matthew Rolston. In addition, a great roster of illustrators and cartoonists has conjured and invented for the cover: Matt Groening, Mike Judge, Garry Trudeau, Gottfried Helnwein, Ralph Steadman, Maurice Sendak, Paul Davis, Milton Glaser, Robert Grossman, Daniel Maffia, Andy Warhol and Anita Kunz, among others.

Many of these covers have been controversial, even shocking, so here now is fair warning to those who are offended by flesh. Plenty of flesh has been artfully arranged and displayed beneath our

ROLLING STONE

November 9, 1967
VOL. I, No. I

OUR PRICE:
TWENTY-FIVE CENTS

MFP

IN THIS ISSUE:

DONOVAN: An incredible Rolling Stone Interview, with this manchild of magic ....Page 14

GRATEFUL DEAD: A photographic look at a rock and roll group after a dope bust ....Page 8

BYRD IS FLIPPED: Jim McGuinn kicks out David Crosby ....Page 4

RALPH GLEASON: The color bar on American television ....Page 11

Tom Rounds Quits KFRC

Tom Rounds, KFRC Program Director, has resigned. No immediate date has been set for his departure from the station. Rounds quit to assume the direction of Charlatan Productions, an L.A. based film company experimenting in the contemporary pop film.

Rounds spent seven years as Program Director of KPOI in Hawaii before coming to San Francisco in 1966. He successfully effected the tight format which made KFRC the number one station in San Francisco.

Les Turpin, former program director of KGB in San Diego will replace Tom Rounds at KFRC. Turpin has spent the last year as a consultant in the Drake-Chenault programming service. The new appointment could mean a tightening up of programming policies. Rounds liberalization of KFRC's play-list may well become more restricted.

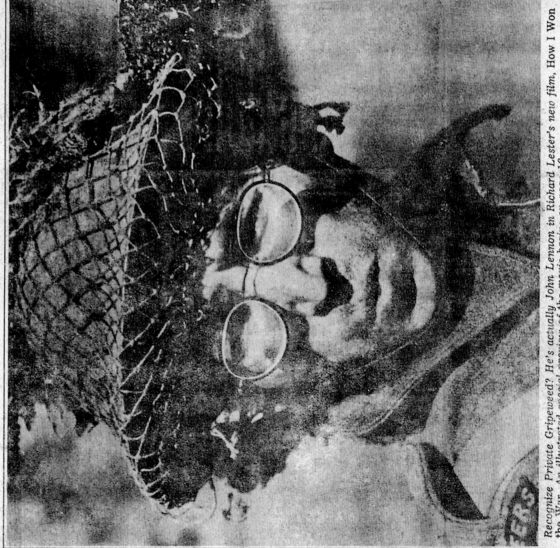

Recognize Private Gripeweed? He's actually John Lennon in Richard Lester's new film, How I Won the War. An illustrated special preview of the movie begins on page 16.

Airplane high, but no new

THE HIGH COST OF MUSIC AND LOVE:

Under the art direction of John Williams, ROLLING STONE makes its debut as an 11-by-17-inch magazine, printed on newsprint and folded in half. The cover/first page is black and white with a publicity photograph of John Lennon from the film 'How I Won the War.' The ROLLING STONE logo is a draft of a design by psychedelic poster artist Rick Griffin, who wants to refine it, but isn't given the chance.

BY MICHAEL LYDON

A weekend of "music, love, and flowers" can be done for a song (plus cost) or can be done at a cost (plus songs). The Monterey International Pop Festival, a non-profit, charity event, was, despite its own protestations, of the second sort: a damn extravagant three days.

The Festival's net profit at the end of August, the last date of accounting, was $211,451. The costs of the weekend were $290,233. Had it not been for the profit from the sale of television rights to ABC-TV of $288,843, the whole operation would have ended up a neat $77,392 in the red.

The Festival planned to have all the artists, while in Monterey, submit ideas for use of the proceeds.

In the confusion the plan miscarried and the decision on where the profits should go has still not been finally made.

So far only $50,000 has definitely been been allocated to

York City Youth Board which will set up classes for many ghetto children to learn music on guitars donated by Fender. Paul Simon, a Festival governor, will personally over see the program.

Plans to give more money to the Negro College Fund for college scholarships is now being discussed; another idea is a sum between ten and twenty thousand for the Monterey Symphony.

However worthy these plans, they are considerably less daring and innovative than the projects mentioned in the spring: the Diggers, pop conferences, and any project which would "tend to further national interest in and knowledge and enjoyment of popular music." The present plans suggest that the Board of Governors, unable or unwilling to make their grandiose schemes reality, fell back on traditional charity.

The Board of Governors did decide that the money would be given out in a small number of

instance, that the John Edwards Memorial Foundation, a folk music archive at the University of California at Los Angeles, had its small request overlooked.

In ironic fact, what happened at the Festival and its financial affairs looks in many ways like the traditional Charity Ball in hippie drag.

The overhead was high and the net was low. "For every dollar spent, there was a reason," says Derek Taylor, the Festival's PR man and one of its original officers.

Yet many of the Festival's expenses, however reasonable to Taylor, seem out of keeping with its announced spirit. The Festival management, with amateurish good will, lavished generosity on their friends.

• Producer Lou Adler was able to find a spot in the show for his own property, Johnny Rivers; Paul Simon for his friend, English folk singer Beverly; John Phillips for the Group Without A Name and Scott MacKenzie. None of them had the musical

taking more than a month to record their new album for RCA Victor. In a recording period of five weeks only five sides have been completed. No definite release date has been set.

Their usual recording schedule in Los Angeles begins at 11:00 p.m. in the evening and extends through six or seven in the morning. When they're not in the studios, they stay at a fabulous pink mansion which rents for $5,000 a month. The Beatles stayed at the house on their last American tour.

The house has two swimming pools and a variety of recreational facilities. It's a small small little paradise in the hills above Hollywood. Maybe suntans and guitars don't make it together.

status for an international pop music festival.

It is ironic that the Rivers and the rest appeared "free," but the money it cost the Festival to get them to Monterey and back, feed them, put them up (Beverly
—Continued on Page 7

famous logo. ROLLING STONE probably pioneered the trend of nude "star" covers with John Lennon and Yoko Ono's full-body shots in November 1968. At the time, nudity was a political statement, health clubs were for the weird and obsessed, and I had yet to fully appreciate readers' insatiable curiosity about the naked bodies of their heroes and heroines.

John and Yoko's self-portraits were taken in their London flat for the front and back covers of their *Two Virgins*, the album that Apple's distributor issued wrapped in brown paper – despite John's status as the leader of the Beatles. At the suggestion of ROLLING STONE's cofounder, writer Ralph J. Gleason, I telexed our friend Derek Taylor, the Beatles' publicist and soul mate, in London with an offer to print said pictures in ROLLING STONE. The photo wound up on the cover of our first anniversary issue (RS 22). This was the first sellout issue of ROLLING STONE and the first time we went back to press. Although it may seem tame from today's perspective, the idea of someone so famous and so physically average standing stark naked for all the world to see was quite extraordinary – shocking to be sure, but above all, deeply revolutionary and deeply moving.

Magazine making is a collaborative art, and I have worked with the most dedicated and talented people in publishing, including editors whose duties included writing the lines of text that tease the newsstand browser into a purchase. If you have the time and the patience to read the tiny lines of type on these collected miniatures, you will find some amusing footnotes to late-twentieth-century history.

"Dial Om for Murder," the headline for an account of criminal behavior in a religious sect, and "He's Hot, He's Sexy and He's Dead," the headline for a story on Jim Morrison's posthumous success, are among my favorites. In these thousands of cover headlines, you'll catch clever literary allusions and puns of all colors and stripes, along with ideas ranging from the naive to

"THE LOGO was an unfinished draft of a design by San Francisco psychedelic poster artist Rick Griffin, who was planning to refine it until I ripped it from his desk to get it to the printer on time."

the profound. Looking back, most of what we put on the cover remains important, but some of it may seem as pointless, trivial and ephemeral as it gets. In seven hundred–plus covers, you're bound to strike out more than once.

* * * * *

IN 1967, when I started the magazine, I didn't understand the importance of a cover and all the things that a cover could do. I didn't understand that the cover not only defined a magazine's identity but greatly determined sales and also conferred a very special status to the cover subject. It wasn't until midway through year one that Danny Fields, an editor of the early and influential pop-music magazine *16,* led me to see some of these possibilities.

The cover of RS 1, November 9th, 1967, was a wonderful, revealing accident. The photograph of John Lennon is a publicity still from a mostly forgotten film called *How I Won the War.* (The logo was an unfinished draft of a design by San Francisco psychedelic poster artist Rick Griffin, who was planning to refine it until I ripped it from his desk to get it to the printer on time.) In hindsight, it was terribly prescient of me and ROLLING STONE to have John Lennon on the first cover. That one little photograph speaks volumes about the marriage of music and movies and politics that came to define ROLLING STONE.

Back in those days, there was no tradition of rock photography. In London some good photographers – Sir Cecil Beaton, among them – had shot the Stones, the Beatles and a few other bands. In San Francisco, New York and Los Angeles, however, that hadn't happened yet. Photographs of rock stars were often bad publicity stills, snapshots or stage shots with a microphone in the performer's face. I decided to do better than that and took on a professional, Baron Wolman, as our first staff photographer. Bringing Baron into the mix, along with the

feisty Jim Marshall and a few other West Coast photographers who were doing good work, instantly distinguished our tabloid. They didn't create a particular look or impose a particular style on the bands as much as produce clean, crisp photography, well composed and artfully lit, and, perhaps most valuably, they lived the life, knew the bands and understood what they wanted to say.

Our first full-time art director was Robert Kingsbury, a wood sculptor and teacher who had never worked for a publication. Bob turned out to be brilliant at sifting through all the black and white stills we were accumulating to find a striking image. For the cover, he developed an alchemist's touch, transforming a dull photograph into something visually interesting: He'd turn it, crop it, shrink it, blow it up, silhouette it against a bold background or add a duotone color. It was still a few years before we were shooting photographs especially for covers, and he did wonders with what we had on hand.

Those covers were done on the fly, without much deliberation, and yet many of them are spirited and good. The blue solarized cover of Eric Clapton (RS 10) was taken by Linda Eastman, later to become Linda McCartney. The first woman to shoot a ROLLING STONE cover, Linda went on to take many memorable early shots, including some of Jimi Hendrix and Janis Joplin.

* * * * *

THE REMARKABLE IMAGE of Bob Dylan reaching for a crucifix (RS 12), I tore out of a publication called *Salut les Copains,* a French rock magazine. To this day, the photographer remains unknown. The Band sent us their own photos, taken by Elliott Landy, one depicting them seated on a bench with their backs to the camera. We ran that one as the cover of our sixteenth issue in August 1968, thinking ourselves pretty hip.

Another of our early lessons in publishing is that death draws people to the newsstand. When Janis Joplin and Jimi Hendrix died within weeks of each other, our staff showed their sensitivity in each case: a simple, classic portrait on the cover, with type stating only the artist's name and date of birth and death. There was nothing more to say. And that began a form of tribute that we've followed for all of our thirty years. When somebody in the magazine's purview dies, the cover is created with dignity and respect, and the coverage inside is exhaustive, sometimes highly personal and in many cases brilliant.

In 1970, a twenty-year-old art student named Annie Leibovitz came to the magazine with her portfolio. "She had just returned from a year in Israel," Bob Kingsbury remembers, "and I liked one of her pictures from the trip. I thought she showed a lot of potential, and she was just a kid. We hired her." While still attending the San Francisco Art Institute, Annie became the magazine's second staff photographer. Later that year, she went with me to New York on her first major assignment, a commissioned cover portrait of John Lennon to accompany my groundbreaking exclusive interview, "Lennon Remembers." We had fun that week, working as a team, traveling by limo and hanging with John and Yoko (who were at the time making their avant-garde film *Up Your Legs Forever*).

It turned out that the cover shot was taken during a light-meter reading. John, who was "thinking nothing," as he later recalled, looked right through the lens at Annie. For her (and the magazine), this was a defining moment, what she has called her "first encounter" with a subject. It's John's humanity that comes through in the shot, which was not what she had wanted as our cover. To me this photo was so simple and so stark that it was a natural choice. I still have the picture on my desk, in a frame. I've carried it around with me for twenty-seven years. The directness of the eye contact, the simplicity and the truth in it all presage the best of Annie's work.

Over the next three or four years, her work began to mature, and the ROLLING STONE covers became a series of portraits. Annie considered her-

self primarily a photojournalist at the time, working with a thirty-five-millimeter camera and, for the most part, natural lighting, which was the foundation for all her later work. And so for a while the covers are portrait after portrait; not all of them are Annie's pictures, but if they're not, they're in the mold we began to establish with John Lennon.

*　　*　　*　　*　　*

IN FEBRUARY 1973, we began regularly printing four-color covers, opening up new possibilities and challenges. A few months later, we went from a quarter fold to a tabloid, increasing the size of our covers from 8½ by 11 inches to 10½ by 15. As we shifted to color and a larger size, I brought in Michael Salisbury, the very imaginative and brash art director of *West,* the Sunday rotogravure magazine of the *Los Angeles Times.* He was a major score for us, our first professional art director – with a live-wire personality, raring to go.

Michael brought us smack into the world of illustration and concept covers, and we started getting a little crazier. Michael's first cover for the magazine was an illustration for a fifty-thousand-word interview I'd done with Daniel Ellsberg, of "Pentagon Papers" fame. Michael showed it to me at the last minute (which would become a habit of his), so there was no chance of changing it if I didn't like it. But it was perfect: a patriotic, sculpted profile of Ellsberg to go with the cover line we took from the Declaration of Independence: "Let facts be submitted to a candid world." The image made the point exactly.

"ROLLING STONE's identity was not only how it read, but also how it looked," Michael says. "And that was defined by the photography. The typography and newspaper format were intended to give a young publication legitimacy and credibility, but the pictures added personality and depth."

In September 1974, Tony Lane became the magazine's third full-time art director. Tony, who came from *Holiday* and *Harper's Bazaar,* had a vision and a style, and he wanted badly to work with Annie. Tony proceeded to take the cover to a sparer, poster-type look. Annie was still learning, soaking up everything, getting her craft right and

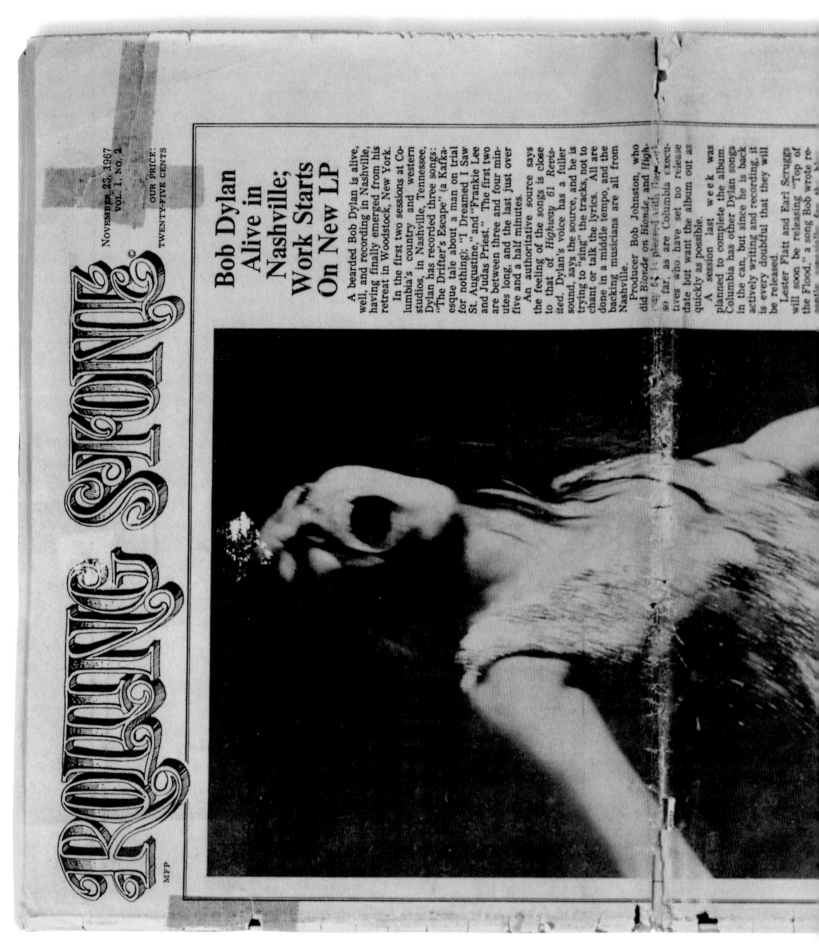

ROLLING STONE

NOVEMBER 25, 1967
VOL. 1, NO. 2

OUR PRICE:
TWENTY-FIVE CENTS

MFP

Bob Dylan Alive in Nashville; Work Starts On New LP

A bearded Bob Dylan is alive, well, and recording in Nashville, having finally emerged from his retreat in Woodstock, New York.

In the first two sessions at Columbia's country and western studios, in Nashville, Tennessee, Dylan has recorded three songs: "The Drifter's Escape" (a Kafkaesque tale about a man on trial for nothing); "I Dreamed I Saw St. Augustine," and "Frankie Lee and Judas Priest." The first two are between three and four minutes long, and the last just over five and a half minutes.

An authoritative source says the feeling of the songs is close to that of *Highway 61 Revisited*. Dylan's voice has a fuller sound, says the source, and he is trying to "sing" the tracks, not to chant or talk the lyrics. All are done in a middle tempo, and the backing musicians are all from Nashville.

Producer Bob Johnston, who did *Blonde on Blonde*, and *High-way 61*, is pleased with Dylan so far, as are Columbia executives who have set no release date but want the album out as quickly as possible.

A session last week was planned to complete the album. Columbia has other Dylan songs in the can, but since he is back actively writing and recording, it is every doubtful that they will be released.

Lester Flatt and Earl Scruggs will soon be releasing "Top of the Flood," a song Bob wrote re-

"IT WAS raunchy Tina, legs open, her red lips, her long hair. Wild! They thought I was just another of those raunchy singers 'cause no one knew the other side. Only people very close to me knew. I've always been very spiritual but my image – in terms of my work – was very far from that." ~ *TINA TURNER*

IN THIS ISSUE:

JEFFERSON AIRPLANE: Marty Balin talks about the group's n e w album .... Page 4

McNEAR'S BEACH: Big Brother and the Holding Company at an outdoor benefit — a photo-fea-
ture .... Page 10

DONOVAN: Part two of the Rolling Stone interview — the Maharishi, Gypsy Dave and Donovan's new
film .... Page 12

doing a great number of covers along the way.

The next year, I took Annie with me to lunch at the studio of the great fashion photographer Richard Avedon. I had begun discussions with him about photographic coverage of the 1976 presidential elections. I thought it would be fun for Annie to meet Dick, and I wanted her to explore new ideas and new directions for the magazine.

That day we planned the heroic black-and-white cover photograph of Mick and Keith that appeared on our July 17th, 1975, issue (RS 191). I was trying to get Annie to imitate Avedon's more formal style of working: for example, posing people in a studio against a seamless backdrop. With the Stones, I suggested, make it real simple and do the two of them as partners. It worked brilliantly; it's still one of my favorites.

It happened to be around the same time that Ralph Gleason died, and this was the cover of the issue in which he was memorialized, so the somber black-and-white cover was appropriate.

In 1975, the story that put us on the map nationally was the Patty Hearst kidnapping. I called our exclusive report the "scoop of the Seventies." ROLLING STONE had the story of her abduction, her travels, her conversion to "Tania." And, just as we were ready to go to press, after more than a year on the lam, she was captured.

The cover treatment I took from the *New York Times Sunday Magazine.* In the middle of Watergate, the *Times* had published a recap of the events and testimony, with the simple headline "The Story So Far," the text of which began on the cover. Tony Lane conceived "Tania's World," the cover illustration showing Patty Hearst in her terrorist garb in an homage to the famous Andrew Wyeth painting "Christina's World."

This was one of those occasions where you have a story so powerful it needs no explanation. It was international and dead on the mark, timing-wise. Our title: "The Inside Story." ROLLING STONE made head-

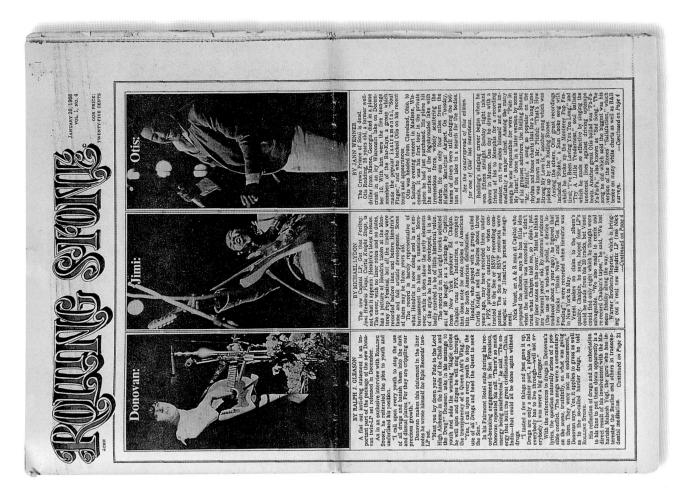

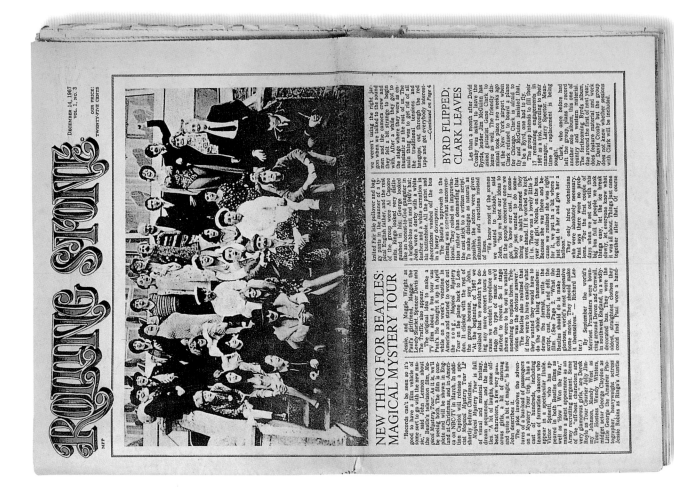

Production changes of the magazine affected the cover dramatically. The ROLLING STONE logo gets color with RS 3. Other notable changes soon follow with RS 8: an extra quarter-fold alters the cover's size, decreasing it to 8½ inches by 11 inches, and a bit more color is used. ○

RS 6 | JANIS JOPLIN, GATHERING OF THE TRIBES BE-IN
FEBRUARY 24TH, 1968
Photographs by BARON WOLMAN

RS 5 | JIM MORRISON
FEBRUARY 10TH, 1968
Photographs by BARON WOLMAN

MARCH 9, 1968
Vol. I, No. 7

OUR PRICE:
TWENTY-FIVE CENTS

ROLLING STONE

ACME

AIRPLANE FLIES!—LEAVES MANAGER, BATTLES RCA

Group Follows
Beatles Lead:
Run Own Show

SAN FRANCISCO

The Jefferson Airplane have "divorced" themselves from the personal management of Fillmore Auditorium manager Bill Graham on February 6, following the lead of the Beatles, Grateful Dead, and Quicksilver Messenger Service. Each of these groups has taken its business affairs into its own hands on a strictly cooperative basis.

Bill Thompson, long the Airplane's road manager and now their spokesman (like Rock Scully and Danny Rifkin of the Dead, he is an integral part of the group and not an autonomous individual with his own, possibly conflicting, interests) was reticent about discussing the break with Graham but definite about the band's independence.

"We might get other management," he said, "then again, the Earth might split open."

Like the other two San Francisco outfits, the first venture to interest Jefferson Airplane has been, naturally, a rock and roll show. The Great Northwest Tour undertaken by the Dead, Quicksilver and Jerry Abrams' Headlights—it was actually organized and promoted by Rifkin, Scully, Ron Rakow and attorney Brian Rohan—was a huge success, not so much financially, although it did end up in the black, as in showing that an independent group-based operation could do everything the show business professionals could do, do it (musically) better, and have a

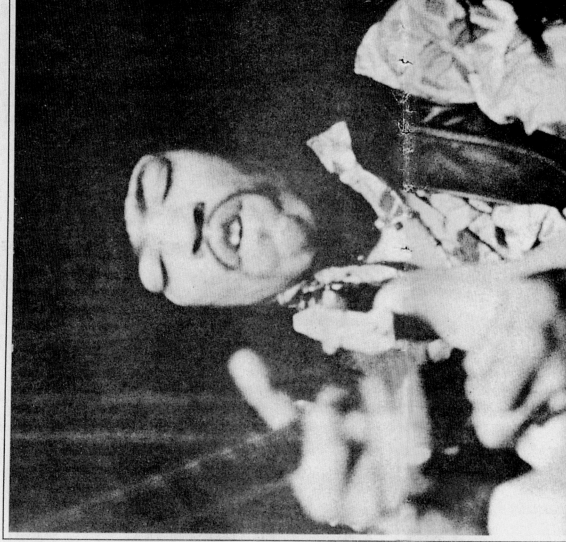

"I STARTED PLAYING the camera [shooting at concerts]. I could almost anticipate the licks. It sounds really hokey, but I got fabulous photos, one after another, becau

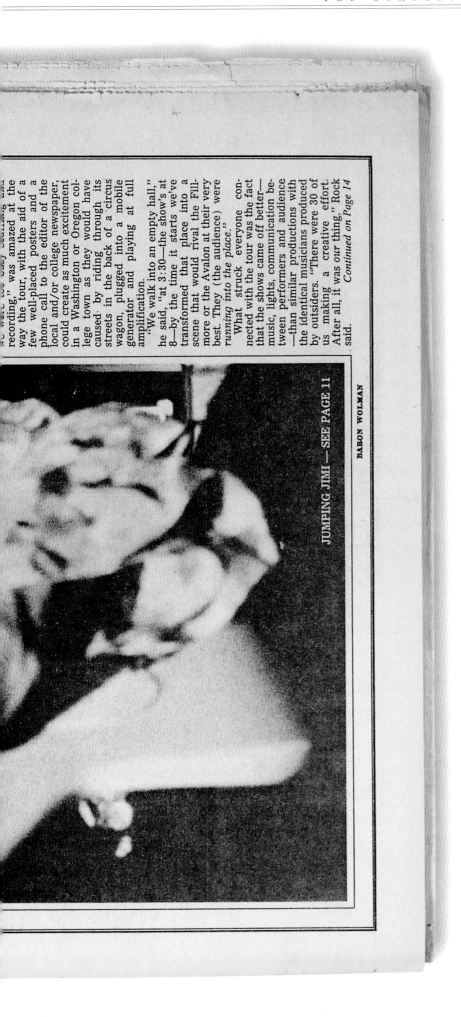

Continued on Page 14

JUMPING JIMI — SEE PAGE 11

BARON WOLMAN

was really in tune with what he was doing." ~ BARON WOLMAN

lines around the world and led all three national network news broadcasts, and that issue sold like mad.

Meanwhile, Annie busted loose with marvelous covers: Bob Marley in the throes of ecstasy (RS 219), Paul Simon in his window overlooking Central Park (RS 216), Jack Ford in front of the White House (RS 218) are all terrific. One of the most memorable to me is the portrait of Beach Boys founder Brian Wilson, reemerged after years of exile inside his house (RS 225). Annie shot a black-and-white photo of Brian as surf patriarch, in his bathrobe, holding a board. I had it hand-colored in that old pastel postcard style. It was perfect.

The late Seventies stand as a true golden age of creativity in ROLLING STONE covers, especially with Annie's work. Sometimes she and I would work on a concept, but most often she was talking with my wife, Jane. Annie was always bringing to the house books of other photographers' work, looking for new ideas, and talking, talking. Among my favorites is the Fleetwood Mac cover (RS 235). Brilliantly, Annie posed them on an unmade bed, which solved the perennial graphic problem of getting multiple group members in the frame in a new and interesting way. And Bette Midler on a bed of roses (RS 306): What a beauty.

Annie's attitude was, Give me a great idea – who cares where it comes from. Our collaboration was nearly always happy. We were working together constantly, thinking up things to do with the cover, and our work was *us*.

In 1976, ROLLING STONE published "The Family," a special issue of Avedon's portraits (RS 224), for which we won a National Magazine Award. Dick wanted to shoot the entire political and economic power structure of the United States. It was a months-long adventure, with Dick traveling around the country shooting generals, presidents, corporate bosses, politicians, labor leaders and even Rose Mary Woods and Rose Kennedy: the

"WE PUSHED deadlines back and worked around the clock, never doubting for a minute that he was worth it. Elvis was the first king we ever had."

real American establishment. It was an instant classic. I don't think any magazine had ever before done anything like it. This marked the start of Avedon's relationship with ROLLING STONE. In a few years, we had him collaborating with the likes of Prince, Eddie Murphy and Boy George.

We had the access. The world inhabited by ROLLING STONE and its subjects was tighter, smaller and, for the most part, devoid of the public-relations mavens who attend celebrities now. Those we didn't know personally, we certainly knew by reputation. And they knew us.

In 1977, we moved our entire operation from the San Francisco warehouse district to New York's Fifth Avenue. Within five days of our arrival, somebody walked into my new office and said, "Elvis is dead." Within seconds, the various editors gathered in my office to map out a strategy. We postponed the planned special issue celebrating our move to New York. We found this great picture of Elvis in his prime, an old poster none of us had ever seen, an image as American as apple pie. In the Editor's Note, I wrote: "We pushed deadlines back and worked around the clock, never doubting for a minute that he was worth it. Elvis was the first king we ever had." It became the best-selling issue in the magazine's history.

Our New York issue came next. Andy Warhol had been commissioned to do the cover of a prominent New Yorker. Once again, my left-wing instincts had overruled common sense, and we'd had Andy do a portrait of mayoral primary candidate Bella Abzug instead of her opponent Ed Koch. Bella turned our cover into a campaign poster, and gave away signed copies. Before the issue hit the stands, she'd lost the election.

In April 1976, Roger Black, who was a typographer by training, took over as art director. Suddenly, type became very important. On the cover and throughout our every page, the type assumed increasing detail and sophistication.

The Roman numeral X was Roger's idea for our Tenth Anniversary cover, which also marked the end of the funky, hand-drawn logo and the initiation of a new, bolder typeface. We kept the drop and in-line shadowing but took it from all caps to upper- and lower-case characters and eliminated the swashes and ligatures between some of the letters. (Jim Parkinson, who did the new version, became our in-house type designer.) It was the beginning of another phase, and in my Editor's Note I wrote that the new logo "symbolizes as much as anything what we are up to: respectful of our origins, considerate of new ideas and open to the times to come."

Annie's covers at this time were, as always, brilliant: The Blues Brothers painted blue seemed so clichéd but turned out to be so timeless. Annie shot Teddy Kennedy and John Travolta, Linda Ronstadt and Rodney Dangerfield. What a mix. Years later, when Annie's work was hung at the National Portrait Gallery, in Washington, D.C., outside the columned building were suspended from the arches two large images: Gilbert Charles Stuart's George Washington and Annie's cover portrait of Patti Smith before a wall of flames.

In 1980, Mick Jagger and I were having a late-night discussion about ROLLING STONE. Mick is a very serious reader; he understands how the magazine works. He didn't really like the new logo because, he said, we had taken out too much of the character, the funkiness. In his humble opinion, we ought to go back and reintegrate some of those old elements. Put the balls back on, as it were.

So we put back the curlicue at the end of the E, made the loop on the bottom of the G, restored ligatures and swashes and put the "roll" back in the R.

Mick was right: It looked perfect. We planned to unveil the logo – the Jagger revision – simultaneously with another paper-quality upgrade and a different trim size. Our first issue of 1981, it was to feature a new Annie photograph of John and

RS 8 | APRIL 6TH, 1968
MONTEREY POP FESTIVAL
PHOTOGRAPHER UNKNOWN

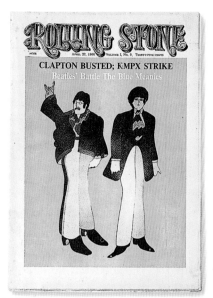

RS 9 | APRIL 27TH, 1968
JOHN LENNON & PAUL McCARTNEY
Illustration by HEINZ EDELMANN

RS 10 | MAY 11TH, 1968
ERIC CLAPTON
Photograph by LINDA EASTMAN

RS 11 | MAY 25TH, 1968
ROCK FASHION
Photograph by BARON WOLMAN

RS 12 | JUNE 22ND, 1968
BOB DYLAN
PHOTOGRAPHER UNKNOWN

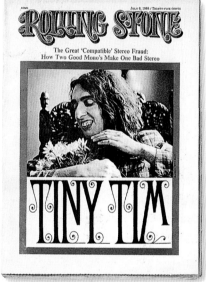

RS 13 | JULY 6TH, 1968
TINY TIM
Photograph by BARON WOLMAN

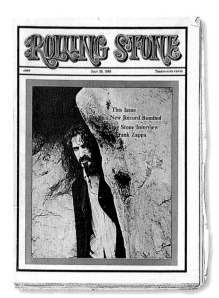

RS 14 | JULY 20TH, 1968
FRANK ZAPPA
Photograph by BARON WOLMAN

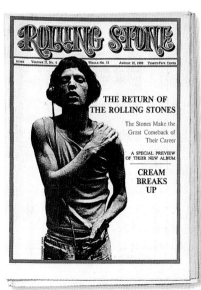

RS 15 | AUGUST 10TH, 1968
MICK JAGGER
Photograph by DEAN GOODHILL

RS 16 | AUGUST 24TH, 1968
THE BAND
Photograph by ELLIOTT LANDY

ROLLING STONE's first-ever news cover (RS 8) featured the Monterey Pop Festival and its organizers, producer Lou Adler and John Phillips of the Mamas and the Papas. ○ The first concept cover was "Rock Fashion" (RS 11). According to photographer Baron Wolman, art director John Williams didn't care for his proposed cover portraits of B.B. King and Johnny Cash, but loved a photo Wolman had taken of his wife, Julianna. Since there was a fashion story and Ms. Wolman looked very stylish, she became the cover. ○ RS 16 was the inaugural issue for the magazine's first full-time art director, sculptor Robert Kingsbury. ○

"FROM A POLAROID test shot, John and Yoko chose the image they wanted for the cover, the one that eventually did run. That night, he was assassinated, shot down outside his home."

Yoko timed with the completion of their upcoming album, *Double Fantasy*.

At this session, on December 8th, 1980, they greeted Annie like an old friend, and the work from that day shows three people working with commitment. From a Polaroid test shot, John and Yoko chose the image they wanted for the cover, the one that eventually did run. That night, he was assassinated, shot down outside his home. The haunting, spectral image of John, naked and curled around Yoko in fetal position – along with the photos inside – were the last portraits taken of him. In the wake of his death, there was no need for a headline, and for the first time in the magazine's history, we ran Annie's cover without one. I guess this is, if I had to choose, the best cover we've ever done.

In 1983, after ten years as chief photographer and one hundred forty-two covers, Annie left. Her legacy and remarkable body of work continue to influence the art of photography and the lives of young photographers. And she is one of the handful of people who can be said to have been a principal in creating what ROLLING STONE became.

We could not replace Annie, so we took the opportunity to use a wide array of photographers. Avedon shot covers, as did Albert Watson, David Bailey, Hiro, Bonnie Schiffman, Aaron Rapoport, E.J. Camp, Steven Meisel and Matthew Rolston.

Roger Black moved on; and Bea Feitler, Mary Shanahan and Derek Ungless followed him as art directors, all of them partners who left their creative mark on ROLLING STONE.

A master of celebrity portraiture, Herb Ritts captured the Eighties' glossy look in his best work; for a good stretch he was our most-featured cover photographer. He ran his sessions like a sure-handed movie director, confident in his ability to create a hip kind of beauty. Herb's covers give off an understated sexiness that flows naturally from attitude, not props or tricks. He photographed Bruce Springsteen, Tom Cruise,

Michael Jackson, David Bowie and many other notable performers of the Eighties. But it was his work with Madonna that stands apart. His series of iconographic covers traces the trajectory of a superstar over two decades: cheek to cheek with Rosanna Arquette for their starring roles in *Desperately Seeking Susan* (RS 447), a Kabuki-painted Nefertiti in three-quarter profile (RS 508), the reigning queen of pop frolicking in the surf (RS 561). Herb's Schwarzenegger in mid-stride (RS 611) conveys the energetic, fun machismo of Arnold at his most magnetic. But his cover of Cindy Crawford as a modern incarnation of Botticelli's Venus (RS 672/673) proved to be one of our best-selling covers ever. It flew off the newsstand.

By 1987, I'd become restless and wanted a new art director, a fresh collaboration. Fred Woodward, whom we had been watching set fire to *Texas Monthly,* confessed to me in our initial meeting that he had dreamed of being the art director of ROLLING STONE since he was fifteen. Fred arrived at his dream job as we were counting down to a Twentieth Anniversary special issue. It was perfect timing. He and his new staff hit the bound volumes of past issues to conduct a blitzkrieg retrospective of our design history – on deadline. "I was running on pure adrenaline, and I was scared to death," he recalls. "I wanted to do work that measured up to that twenty-year legacy."

Fred successfully reconnected the magazine's new look to its past, and in his ten years of refining that connection, he has produced an amazing body of work that not only has kept ROLLING STONE supplied with gold medals for design excellence but has earned him a place in the Art Director's Hall of Fame, its youngest member ever. As an editor, I consider the discovery of a great art director to be a historic event. And Fred is a great one. His understanding of photography, illustration, typography and concept is unparalleled among his generation. His covers have at

RS 17 | SEPTEMBER 14TH, 1968
ZAP COMIX
Illustration by RICK GRIFFIN

RS 18 | SEPTEMBER 28TH, 1968
PETE TOWNSHEND
Photograph by BARON WOLMAN

RS 19 | OCTOBER 12TH, 1968
MICK JAGGER
Photograph by ETHAN RUSSELL

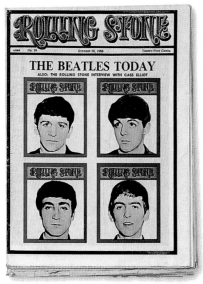

RS 20 | OCTOBER 26TH, 1968
THE BEATLES
PHOTOGRAPHER UNKNOWN

RS 21 | NOVEMBER 9TH, 1968
DRUGS IN THE ARMY
ILLUSTRATOR UNKNOWN

RS 22 | JOHN LENNON & YOKO ONO | Photograph by JOHN LENNON | NOVEMBER 23RD, 1968

"I HADN'T POSED nude for pictures before. We were just being honest – that was its strength." ~ YOKO ONO

RS 23 | DECEMBER 7TH, 1968
DOUG & SEAN SAHM
Photograph by BARON WOLMAN

RS 24 | DECEMBER 21ST, 1968
THE BEATLES
PHOTOGRAPHER UNKNOWN

RS 25 | JANUARY 4TH, 1969
ROB TYNER
PHOTOGRAPHER UNKNOWN

RS 26 | FEBRUARY 1ST, 1969
JIMI HENDRIX
Photograph by BARON WOLMAN

RS 27 | FEBRUARY 15TH, 1969
GROUPIES
Photograph by BARON WOLMAN

RS 28 | MARCH 1ST, 1969
JAPANESE ROCK
Photograph by NAOKO LASH

RS 29 | MARCH 15TH, 1969
JANIS JOPLIN
PHOTOGRAPHER UNKNOWN

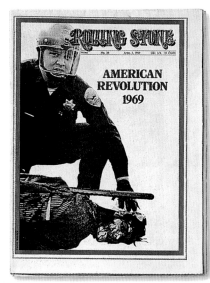

RS 30 | APRIL 5TH, 1969
AMERICAN REVOLUTION 1969
Photograph by NACIO BROWN

RS 31 | APRIL 19TH, 1969
SUN RA
Photograph by BARON WOLMAN

"American Revolution 1969" (RS 30) marked the first time ROLLING STONE *editors created a special issue of the magazine devoted to a political topic, in this case the social movements and unrest prevalent in the late Sixties. Contributors included Black Panther Party Minister of Education George Mason Murray and Berkeley Free Speech Movement leader Michael Rossman.* ◇

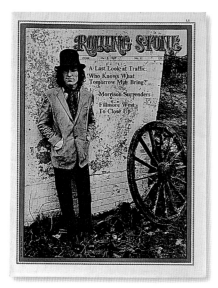

RS 32 | MAY 3RD, 1969
STEVIE WINWOOD
Photograph by DAVID DALTON

RS 33 | MAY 17TH, 1969
JONI MITCHELL
Photograph by BARON WOLMAN

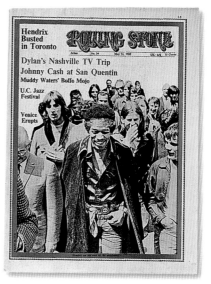

RS 34 | MAY 31, 1969
JIMI HENDRIX
Photograph by FRANZ MAIER

RS 35 | JUNE 14TH, 1969
CHUCK BERRY
Photograph by BARON WOLMAN

RS 36 | JUNE 28TH, 1969
NUDIE
Photograph by BARON WOLMAN

RS 37 | JULY 12TH, 1969
ELVIS PRESLEY
PHOTOGRAPHER UNKNOWN

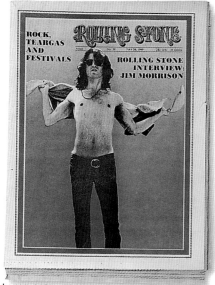

RS 38 | JULY 26TH, 1969
JIM MORRISON
PHOTOGRAPHER UNKNOWN

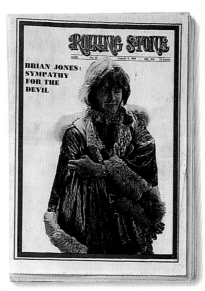

RS 39 | AUGUST 9TH, 1969
BRIAN JONES
Photograph by JIM MARSHALL

RS 40 | AUGUST 23RD, 1969
JERRY GARCIA
Photograph by BARON WOLMAN

The little cowboy on RS 36 is Nudie Cohn, the flamboyant western-wear designer responsible for the lavishly decorated outfits favored by country stars of the Fifties and Sixties. He also created Elvis Presley's famous gold lamé suit, which graces the cover of RS 643. ⊃

RS 41 | SEPTEMBER 6TH, 1969
JOE COCKER
Photograph by STEVEN SHAMES

RS 42 | SEPTEMBER 20TH, 1969
WOODSTOCK
Photograph by BARON WOLMAN

RS 43 | OCTOBER 4TH, 1969
THE UNDERGROUND PRESS
Photograph by STEVEN SHAMES

RS 44 | OCTOBER 18TH, 1969
DAVID CROSBY
Photograph by ROBERT ALTMAN

RS 45 | NOVEMBER 1ST, 1969
TINA TURNER
Photograph by ROBERT ALTMAN

RS 46 | NOVEMBER 15TH, 1969
THE BEATLES
PHOTOGRAPHER UNKNOWN

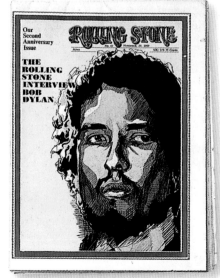

RS 47 | NOVEMBER 29TH, 1969
BOB DYLAN
ILLUSTRATOR UNKNOWN

RS 48 | DECEMBER 13TH, 1969
MILES DAVIS
PHOTOGRAPHER UNKNOWN

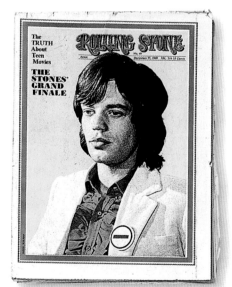

RS 49 | DECEMBER 27TH, 1969
MICK JAGGER
Photograph by BARON WOLMAN

"OUR SUBJECTS have been the most creative people of these times, presidents and poets, the outsiders and insiders with their shoulders to the wheel and their pictures beneath the logo."

one time or another violated every rule, including my personal mandate for covers showing people wearing few clothes: Only someone of Fred's idiosyncratic vision would have seen the dark graphic power of the Batman cape, which illustrated a 1992 cover story (RS 634/635), or chosen to illustrate our "Portraits" issue with a simple, stunning shot of Elvis's gold lamé Nudie suit on a hanger (RS 643). After a decade of such late-night decisions and deadlines, Fred's DNA has woven itself into the life of ROLLING STONE.

In the Nineties we hired Mark Seliger as our new chief photographer, the first since Annie and only the third in the magazine's history. Mark has told me that, from his teenage years, he was a student of ROLLING STONE, and it shows. For each assignment — and he's done more than seventy covers at last count — he prepares impeccably. He delves into an artist's history and then brainstorms with Fred and our photo editor Jodi Peckman. That's when we sometimes catch a glimpse of him between flights, wearing a backpack, Vans and something from his funky hat collection. His 1994 cover shot of actor Brad Pitt (RS 696) came to life after the two drove together from California to Mexico. Pitt wanted it to be real, according to Mark. "We hoped to model it after an old, traditional ROLLING STONE shoot where you're living with a person for a period of time, rather than it just being a two-hour experience in a studio."

For the record, Mark came up with the idea of pairing Jenny McCarthy (RS 738/739) with a hot dog ("She had incredible aim with the mustard," he says) and dressing Ice-T, the rapper behind "Cop Killer," in a policeman's uniform (RS 637).

I have always wanted to give my generation a voice in public affairs. Over the years, we have assigned many political pieces. We have interviewed senators and congressmen, but there is no more clear-cut means of getting heard than addressing your questions directly to the president of the United States. Bill Clinton has appeared on the cover twice, both times to accompany lengthy, in-depth interviews, the kind a president essentially never does. During the 1992 campaign, Hunter Thompson, Bill Greider, P.J. O'Rourke and I flew to Little Rock for a three-hour lunch at Doe's Eat Place. Later, I returned to the governor's mansion with Mark Seliger for the photo shoot. Clinton went upstairs to change clothes and came back in jeans and cowboy boots. He looked at me, and gesturing with his hands at his get-up, said, "The leader of the free world, huh?"

The next year we met for lunch and an interview in his private White House dining room. The food was better, but the lunch was shorter and only fifteen minutes were allotted for a cover shoot on the White House lawn. While Henry Kissinger and several other notables waited next door at the Treasury to discuss the passage of the North American Free Trade Agreement, Mark set up his lights and tripods. Talk about pressure. But having worked with the likes of Metallica and Nirvana, he pulled it off with style and brought home a distinguished cover image that is now an important part of our history.

* * * * *

WHAT A LONG, strange trip it's been. Our mission has taken us from the Haight-Ashbury to the Oval Office, bringing us face to face with the major cultural events and influential people of our time. Our readers have taken the journey with us, cheering us on with their love letters and advice. Our subjects have been the most creative people of these times, presidents and poets, the outsiders and insiders with their shoulders to the wheel and their pictures beneath the logo. In the end, this collection of covers will prove to be a great, sprawling archive of the three decades we've been around. We have devoted ourselves to the task with all the passion, energy and talent that we had to give. I believe that nobody has done it better.

~ JANN S. WENNER

1970

"There was a time during 1976, 1977, where the record business went crazy. That was when 'Hotel California' came out, and 'Saturday Night Fever' and also 'Rumours' by Fleetwood Mac. That was the music business at its decadent zenith. I seem to remember that the wine was the best and the drugs were good and the women were beautiful and, man, we seemed to have an endless amount of energy. Endless stores of energy. Hangovers were conquered with Bloody Marys and aspirin. You were resilient."

~ **GLENN FREY**

"I DIDN'T KNOW his name or anything, but he was standing alongside of me. You know, we were both watching Mick Jagger, and a Hell's Angel – the fat one; I don't know his name or anything – he reached over. He didn't like us being so close or something, you know, we were seeing Mick Jagger too well, or something. He was just being uptight. He reached over and grabbed the guy beside me by the ear and hair and yanked on it, thinking it was funny, you know, kind of laughing. And so this guy shook loose; he yanked away from him."

"Now this guy that you're talking about, is this the black guy that got killed?"

"Yeah, right. He shook loose, and the Hell's Angel hit him in the mouth and he fell back into the crowd, and he jumped offstage and jumped at him. And he tried to scramble, you know, through the crowd to run from the Hell's Angel, and four other Hell's Angels jumped on him."

Robert Hiatt, a medical resident at the Public Health Hospital in San Francisco, was the first doctor to reach eighteen-year-old Meredith Hunter after the fatal wounds. He was behind the stage and responded to Jagger's call from the stage for a doctor. When Hiatt got to the scene, people were trying to get Hunter up on the stage, apparently in the hope that the Stones would stop playing and help could get through quicker.

"I carried him myself back to the first-aid area," Hiatt said. "He was limp in my hands and unconscious. He was still breathing then, though quite shallowly, and he had a very weak pulse. It was obvious he wasn't going to make it, but if anything could be done, he would have to get to a hospital quickly.

"He had very serious wounds. He had a wound in the lower back, which could have gone into the lungs; a wound in the back near the spine, which could have severed a major vessel; and a fairly large wound in the left temple. You couldn't tell how deep the wounds were, but each was about three-fourths of an inch long, so they would have been fairly deep.

"It was just obvious he wasn't going to make it."

[EXCERPT FROM ALTAMONT COVER STORY REPORTED BY LESTER BANGS, RENY BROWN, JOHN BURKS, SAMMY EGAN, MICHAEL GOODWIN, GEOFFREY LINK, GREIL MARCUS, JOHN MORTHLAND, EUGENE SCHOENFELD, PATRICK THOMAS AND LANGDON WINNER]

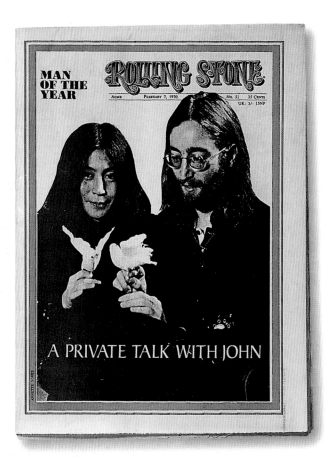

RS 51 | FEBRUARY 7TH, 1970
JOHN LENNON & YOKO ONO
Photograph by ANNETTE YORKE

Which of the John-and-Paul songs do you think were good?

I can't . . . well, you know, the early stuff like "I Wanna Hold Your Hand," "She Loves You" and stuff that was written together. I can't think of any others but things like that.

Not long ago, you told me you thought the 'Abbey Road' album was as good as 'Sgt. Pepper' and the White Album was also as good.

Yeah, yeah. I mean, I think each album since *Pepper* has been better. People just have this dream about *Pepper.* I mean, it was good for then, but it wasn't that spectacular when you look back on it. Like anything, it was great then. But I certainly prefer some of the tracks off the double album and some of the tracks off *Abbey Road* than all the tracks on *Pepper.* When you think back on *Pepper,* what do you remember? Just "A Day in the Life." You know. I go for individual songs, not for whole albums.

[EXCERPT FROM JOHN LENNON INTERVIEW BY RITCHIE YORKE]

"AS AN ENTERTAINER to his audience, I don't want anyone just going, 'I know what he's gonna say,' and then not listen. You want 'em to listen, and especially if you're gonna say something that sort of reaches beyond normal entertainment, you know. We've got enough goin' against us just because we have long hair. There's a certain element that won't listen anyway, which is a drag."

~ John Fogerty

RS 53 | MARCH 7TH, 1970
MARK FRECHETTE & DARIA HALPRIN
'ZABRISKIE POINT' FILM STILL

RS 52 | FEBRUARY 21ST, 1970
CREEDENCE CLEARWATER REVIVAL
Photograph by BARON WOLMAN

RS 54 | MARCH 19TH, 1970
SLY & THE FAMILY STONE
Photograph by STEPHEN PALEY

RS 55 | APRIL 2ND, 1970
ABBIE HOFFMAN
Photograph by BILL MYERS

RS 56 | APRIL 16TH, 1970
DENNIS HOPPER
Photograph by MICHAEL ANDERSON JR.

RS 57 | APRIL 30TH, 1970
PAUL McCARTNEY
Photograph by LINDA EASTMAN

RS 58 | MAY 14TH, 1970
CAPTAIN BEEFHEART
Photograph by JOHN WILLIAMS

RS 59 | MAY 28TH, 1970
LITTLE RICHARD
Photograph by BARON WOLMAN

"JANN WENNER . . . SUGGESTED that I and David Dalton do a story on Charles Manson. None of the editors liked the idea, including myself, but Jann figured there was a story there.

It turned out he was amazingly perceptive. Because Manson wanted his album plugged, he granted us an exclusive prison interview. Because an assistant prosecutor thought we were a cute hippie rag with a circulation of maybe 10,000 (it was then about 250,000), he gave us a detailed on-the-record account of his case before trial, enabling us to scoop the established dailies. Because the Manson family thought of us as brothers under the ground, they let us view their mercenary attempts to cash in on their leader's story. After a few weeks, we knew we had something bigger than even Jann had anticipated.

And certainly *longer* than Jann had anticipated – eventually the story took some 20,000 words and, more to the point, three months to write. And it was this *time* thing, I soon discovered, that tended to make Jann fret. I've always felt that anything worth doing is worth doing slowly. ('The Tortoise and the Hare' is one of my favorite stories, and someday I'm going to finish reading it.) But for some reason, Jann has never warmed to the idea. I remember the time I flew up to San Francisco to show him an outline for one section of the Manson story. I figured I would meet with him for about an hour, then fly home. But when I walked into Jann's office, he seemed disturbed and a little chagrined, like someone who'd just learned of a bad investment. He'd been talking to my previous employer. 'I understand,' he said with a weak smile, 'that at the *L.A. Times* they called you the Stonecutter.' With that, he forbade me to leave the office until the section was completely written. I stayed there a week, night and day, without a toothbrush or a change of clothing, a rather unpleasant situation for both me and anyone in the immediate vicinity.

That should have been the tipoff right there: clearly a violation of adult labor laws. But in fact I fell into Jann's trap again a month later while working on the introduction and was imprisoned for another week without warning or underwear. The end result was a six-part epic, which I still consider the best thing written on Manson and the culture. ROLLING STONE won a National Magazine Award for it. The assistant prosecutor was removed from the case because he talked too much."

~ DAVID FELTON

RS 60 | JUNE 11TH, 1970
ANTIWAR DEMONSTRATORS
Photograph by ANNIE LEIBOVITZ

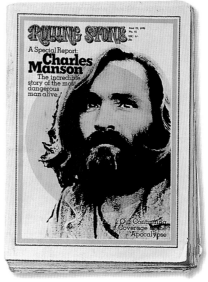

RS 61 | JUNE 25TH, 1970
CHARLES MANSON
PHOTOGRAPHER UNKNOWN

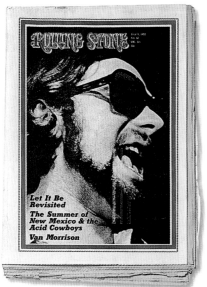

RS 62 | JULY 9TH, 1970
VAN MORRISON
PHOTOGRAPHER UNKNOWN

RS 63 | JULY 23RD, 1970
DAVID CROSBY
Photograph by ED CARAEFF

RS 66 | SEPTEMBER 17TH, 1970
THE GRATEFUL DEAD
Photograph by JIM MARSHALL

RS 64 | AUGUST 6TH, 1970
JANIS JOPLIN
Photograph by TONY LANE

RS 65 | SEPTEMBER 3RD, 1970
MICK JAGGER & ANITA PALLENBERG
'PERFORMANCE' FILM STILL

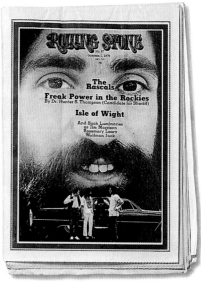

RS 67 | OCTOBER 1ST, 1970
FELIX CAVALIERE & THE RASCALS
Photograph by STEPHEN PALEY

IN 1967, HENDRIX BURST onto the rock & roll scene not initially because of his music. Sure, it was far-out, but the most significant thing was the Hendrix Presence. The sexual savage electric dandy rock & roll nigger Presence! The voodoo child run wild in electric ladyland! Fully aware that this would be Jimi's best starting image, his first LP and singles were heavy on Presence, light on his (ultimately) strongest facet. It was through live performances and the later recordings that the rock & roll audience was to discover his greatly more astounding side: He was perhaps the master virtuoso of electric guitar. It was Jimi Hendrix, more than any other guitarist, who brought the full range of sound from all the reaches of serious electronic music – a wider palette of sound than any other performing instrumentalist in the history of music ever had at his fingertips – plus the fullest tradition of black music – from Charley Patton and Louis Armstrong all the way to John Coltrane and Sun Ra – to rock & roll. Nobody could doubt that Jimi Hendrix was a rock & roll musician, yet to jazz musicians and jazz fans, he was also a jazz performer. When Jimi Hendrix took a solo, it had everything in it.

It is only three years and three months since [the Jimi Hendrix Experience made its first American appearance at the Monterey Pop Festival]. Most master musicians are granted a good deal more time to make their statement. (Charlie Parker lived thirty-five years.) The amazing thing is how rich a musical legacy Hendrix has left in so short a time.

Certainly there is a place in the chapter on rock & roll lyrics (in the *Whole History of Rock & Roll*, to be published a few years hence, when the whole trip is dead) for Jimi. It's not just that he was adept at slinging the words together. But clearly Hendrix has got to be viewed as the father of Narcotic Fantasia imagery. This was his role as a lyricist at the start of his career. It was important to the voodoo child image that his songs came off as far out as possible, and how are you going to come off farther out than by asking your listeners to " 'Scuse me while I kiss the sky . . ."? What about "Queen Jealousy, Envy, waits behind him, her fiery green gown sneers at the grassy ground"? . . .

Hendrix told interviewers that he had been scared to sing for a long time because he thought his voice wasn't up to it. Then he heard Dylan and dug what Dylan was doing and figured, What the hell, if that cat can do that much with no more voice than *he's* got, what's holding me back? In fact, he was a great singer, as distinctive as Neil Young, and a harder wailer (swinger, mover) than either of them. It was a light but rich voice, perfectly suited to the laughter-from-the-shadows insinuations, the purrs and gurgles and the high crooning shouts that were his means to a super-expressive style. . . .

On "Voodoo Child," Hendrix sang: "If I don't meet you no more in this world, I'll meet you in the next one – don't be late . . ."

There will never be another like him.

~ JOHN BURKS
[EXCERPT FROM JIMI HENDRIX TRIBUTE]

"WE USED TO get drunk and play pool together. She beat me 80 percent of the time."

~ PIGPEN
[EXCERPT FROM JANIS JOPLIN TRIBUTE]

"SHE WAS IMPULSIVE, generous, softhearted, shy and determined. She had style and class, and in a way, she didn't believe it. What did she want? It was all there for her but something that she knew wasn't fated to happen. Many people loved her a very great deal, like many people loved Billie Holiday, but somehow that was not enough.

We'll never know and it doesn't matter, in a sense, because that brightly burning candle made an incredibly strong light in its brief life.

They heard Janis Joplin 'round the world, loud and clear, and they will continue to hear her. I am only sorry for those who never had the flash of seeing her perform.

Janis and Big Brother sang hymns at Monterey. It never seemed to me to be just music. I hope now that she's freed herself of that ball and chain, that she is at rest. She gave us a little piece of her heart and all of her soul every time she went onstage.

Monterey, 1967. Otis, Jimi, Brian, Janis. Isn't that enough?

Little girl blue, with the floppy hats and the brave attempt to be one of the guys. She took a little piece of all of us with her when she went. She was beautiful. That's not corny. It's true."

~ RALPH J. GLEASON
[EXCERPT FROM JANIS JOPLIN TRIBUTE]

"JANIS WAS like a *real person*, man. She went through all the changes we did. She went on the same trips. She was just like the rest of us – fucked up, strung out, in weird places. Back in the old days, the pre-success days, she was using all kinds of things, just like anybody, man.

When she went out after something, she went out after it really hard, harder than most people ever think to do, ever conceive of doing.

She was on a real hard path. She picked it, she chose it, it's okay. She was doing what she was doing as hard as she could, which is as much as any of us could do. She did what she had to do and closed her books. I don't know whether it's *the* thing to do, but it's what she had to do."

~ JERRY GARCIA

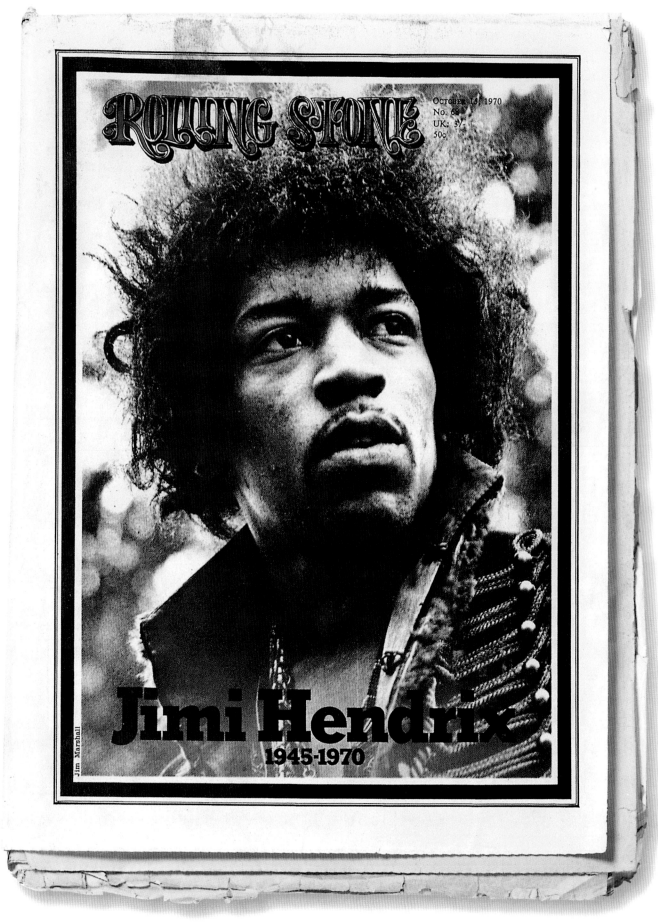

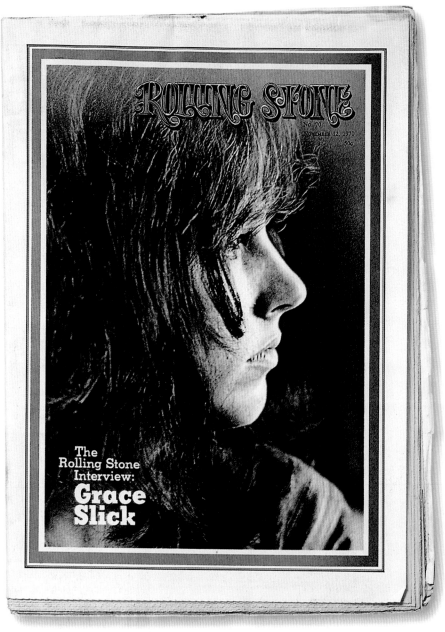

"**JOHN LENNON** was one of my first covers for ROLLING STONE [it was her first commissioned portrait]. And at the time – I was still in school – I felt the cover shot was like, you know, the mediocre picture, the secondary consideration. A photograph to me was not a portrait – anyone can do that. I was addicted to hardcore journalism, newspaper stuff, capture the moment in time, Cartier-Bresson. I liked to combine the composition with the action. I carried a camera every second, and I was constantly framing life into little thirty-five-millimeter squares.

So when I shot Lennon I was carrying three thirty-five-millimeter cameras, and on one of them I kept a 105 lens, which I used for light-meter readings. It was a long lens, I came in close on Lennon's face, and while I was taking the light-meter reading, he looked at me, and I just snapped one picture. And then I did all my other pictures. But I got back to ROLLING STONE, and Jann Wenner went through the contact sheets and immediately pulled out that picture for a cover. I said, 'Oh Jann, ughhhh!' I couldn't understand why he liked that picture. I think it took me ten, twelve years to come to an understanding of what that picture was. Maybe I was a little bit reluctant to have somebody look back at me. It was the first encounter. And that shooting, at the very beginning of my career, set a precedent for my work with anyone of any notoriety or fame after that. Lennon was honest and straightforward and cooperative; he made me feel human right away. I wish there was a more elegant way to talk about this, because it really meant so much to me at the time to be treated well by someone who was so famous, who stood out as a legend in my mind. He made me realize we were all people and we were all here on earth, and it was the basis of how I was to approach everyone from then on."

~ *Annie Leibovitz*

RS 70 | NOVEMBER 12TH, 1970
GRACE SLICK
Photograph by ANNIE LEIBOVITZ

RS 71 | NOVEMBER 26TH, 1970
MEHER BABA
PHOTOGRAPHER UNKNOWN

RS 72 | DECEMBER 10TH, 1970
LEON RUSSELL
Photograph by ED CARAEFF

RS 73 | DECEMBER 24TH, 1970
ROD STEWART
Photograph by ANNIE LEIBOVITZ

Just why was Meher Baba on the cover of ROLLING STONE *– and who was he, again? He was a sort of peace-extolling mystical personal-actualization cult leader. The Who's Pete Townshend followed him (remember "Baba O'Riley" from* Who's Next*?) and wrote the accompanying cover story.* ○

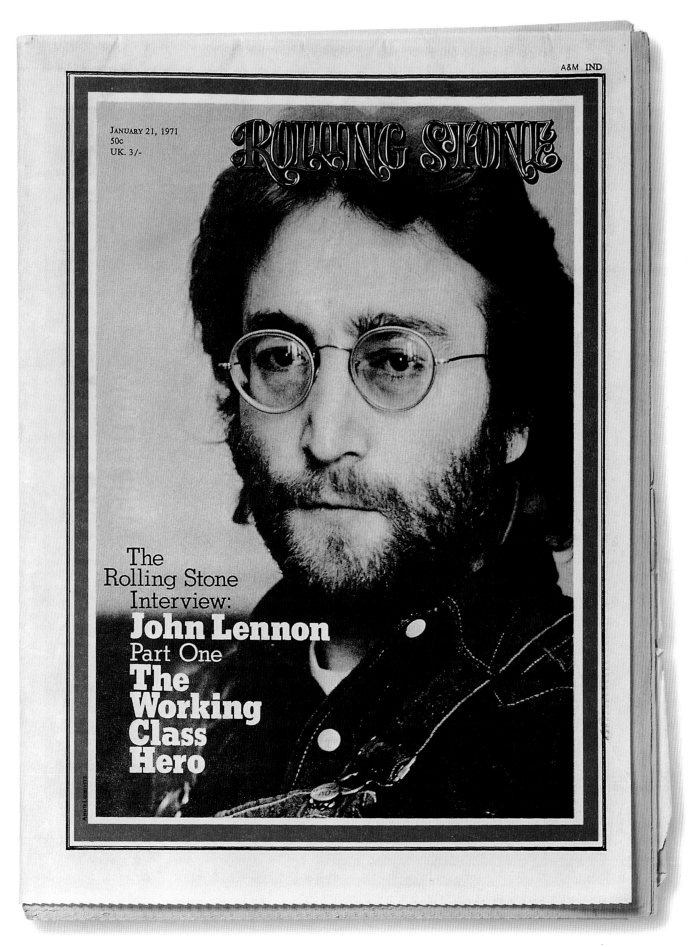

A&M IND

JANUARY 21, 1971
50c
UK. 3/-

ROLLING STONE

The
Rolling Stone
Interview:
John Lennon
Part One
**The
Working
Class
Hero**

ANNIE LEIBOVITZ

RS 75 | FEBRUARY 4TH, 1971
JOHN LENNON & YOKO ONO
Photograph by ANNIE LEIBOVITZ

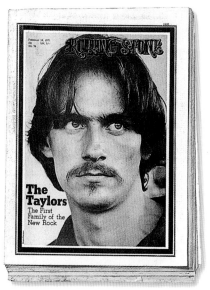

RS 76 | FEBRUARY 18TH, 1971
JAMES TAYLOR
Photograph by BARON WOLMAN

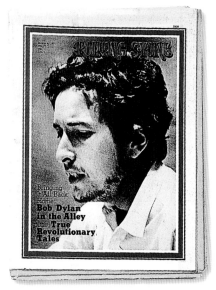

RS 77 | MARCH 4TH, 1971
BOB DYLAN
PHOTOGRAPHER UNKNOWN

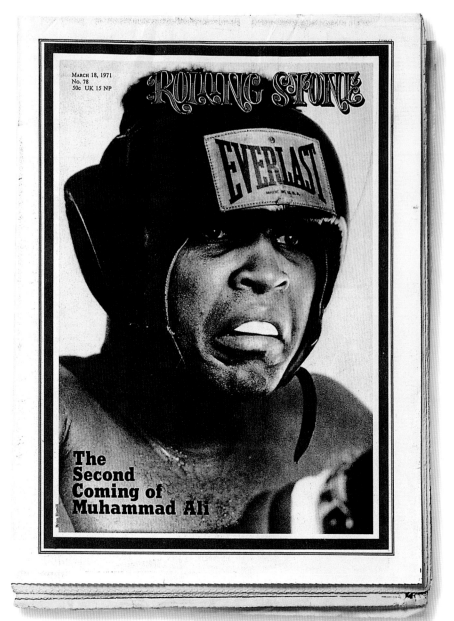

RS 78 | MARCH 18TH, 1971
MUHAMMAD ALI
Photograph by BRIAN HAMILL

RS 79 | APRIL 1ST, 1971
NICHOLAS JOHNSON
Photograph by ANNIE LEIBOVITZ

RS 80 | APRIL 15TH, 1971
JOE DALLESANDRO
Photograph by ANNIE LEIBOVITZ

Muhammad Ali was the first athlete to grace the cover of ROLLING STONE. He remains the athlete with the most cover appearances, three. Brian Hamill's photo shows the then-undefeated champ as unscratched (the only scar on his face came from running his bicycle into a wall as a child). ○

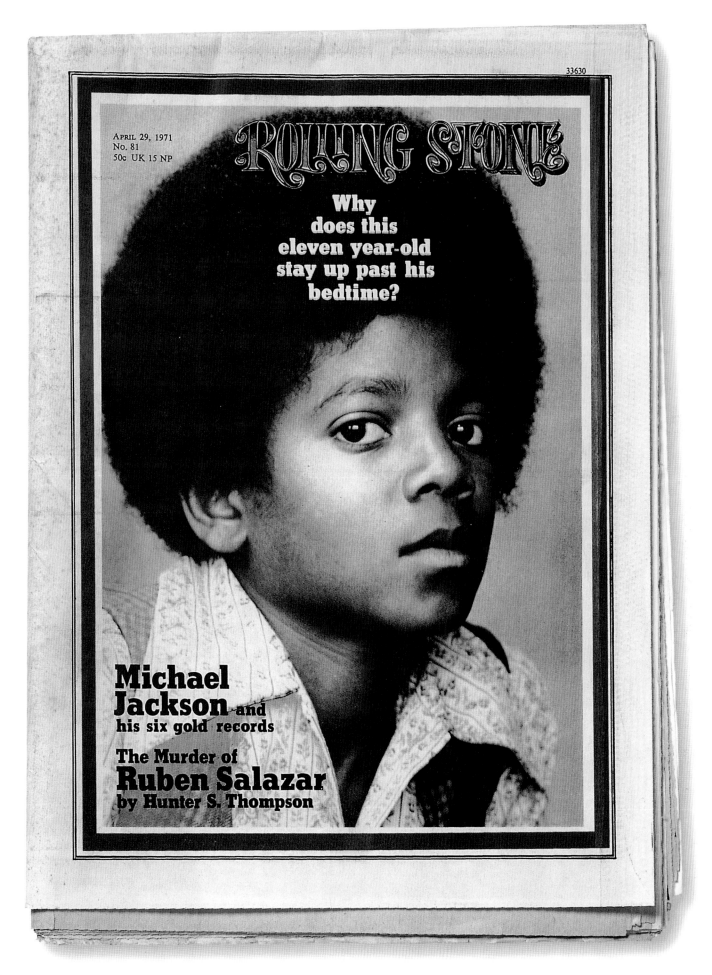

33630

APRIL 29, 1971
No. 81
50¢ UK 15 NP

ROLLING STONE

Why does this eleven year-old stay up past his bedtime?

Michael Jackson and his six gold records

The Murder of Ruben Salazar by Hunter S. Thompson

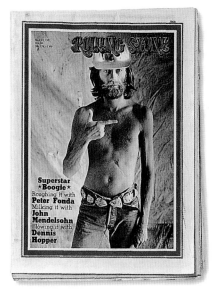

RS 82 | MAY 13TH, 1971
PETER FONDA
Photograph by ANNIE LEIBOVITZ

RS 83 | MAY 27TH, 1971
COUNTRY JOE McDONALD &
ROBIN MENKEN
Photograph by ANNIE LEIBOVITZ

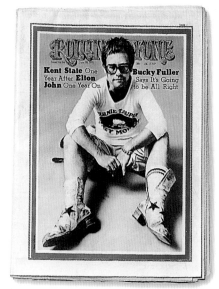

RS 84 | JUNE 10TH, 1971
ELTON JOHN
Photograph by ANNIE LEIBOVITZ

RS 85 | JUNE 24TH, 1971
TRICIA NIXON
PHOTOGRAPHER UNKNOWN

RS 86 | JULY 8TH, 1971
DOUG SAHM
Photograph by BARON WOLMAN

RS 87 | JULY 22ND, 1971
IAN ANDERSON
Photograph by ANNIE LEIBOVITZ

I WOKE UP one morning, pretty hung over, and started poking around the apartment looking for something to read, and I found Jim's poetry manuscript. I sat down and read it and thought, Holy smoke, this is fantastic, and I was just sort of like ragingly delighted to find such a beautiful first book of poetry. When Jim came down later, I told him what I thought, and we talked about it a bit, and he was interested in what to do with it. He wanted to be known as a poet, he didn't want to be . . . in other words . . . Jim was very serious about being a poet, and he didn't want to come in on top of being Jim-Morrison-the-big-rock-singer. . . .

Later, when the book had been published and the first copies arrived by mail in L.A., I found Jim in his room, crying. He was sitting there, holding the book, crying, and he said, "This is the first time I haven't been fucked." He said that a couple of times, and I guess he felt that that was the first time he'd come through as himself. . . .

I think that any two people who know each other closely probably influence each other. If I influenced him, he influenced me as well. It's hard to have a friend whose work you like where there's not some kind of mutual feedback. It's perfectly obvious in reading his book that Jim already had his own style and that he was already his own person. As to his potential for growth – well, he started out so good that I don't know how much better he could've gotten. He started off like a heavyweight.

[EXCERPT FROM TRIBUTE
TO JIM MORRISON BY MICHAEL McCLURE]

RS 89 | AUGUST 19TH, 1971
KEITH RICHARDS
Photograph by ROBERT ALTMAN

RS 90 | SEPTEMBER 2ND, 1971
GEORGE HARRISON
Photograph by ANNIE LEIBOVITZ

RS 91 | SEPTEMBER 16TH, 1971
THE INCREDIBLE HULK
Illustration by HERB TRIMPE

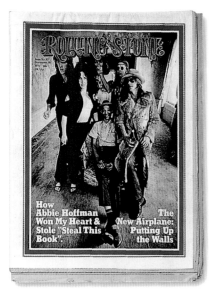

RS 92 | SEPTEMBER 30TH, 1971
JEFFERSON AIRPLANE
Photograph by ANNIE LEIBOVITZ

RS 94 | OCTOBER 28TH, 1971
THE BEACH BOYS
Photograph by ANNIE LEIBOVITZ

RS 93 | OCTOBER 14TH, 1971
IKE & TINA TURNER
Photograph by ANNIE LEIBOVITZ

IND 33630

No. 95
November 11, 1971
60¢
UK 15p

Our Fourth
Anniversary Issue:

**Fear and
Loathing in
Las Vegas: A
Savage Journey
to the Heart
of the American
Dream
by Raoul
Duke**

Beach Boys:
Part Two of A
California Saga

**The Band: "It's
The Restless Age"
by Jon Landau**

**C, S, N & Y Come
Together Again**

**At Work with
Fellini On His
Next Epic**

**From Texas: The
Young Americans
For Freedom in
Congress**

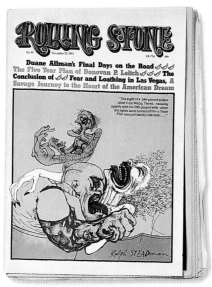

RS 96 | NOVEMBER 25TH, 1971
FEAR AND LOATHING IN LAS VEGAS
Illustration by RALPH STEADMAN

RS 97 | DECEMBER 9TH, 1971
PETE TOWNSHEND
Photograph by NEVIS CAMERON

RS 98 | DECEMBER 23RD, 1971
EVANGELIST MEL LYMAN
Photograph by DAVID GAHR

RS 99 | JANUARY 6TH, 1972
CAT STEVENS
Photograph by ANNIE LEIBOVITZ

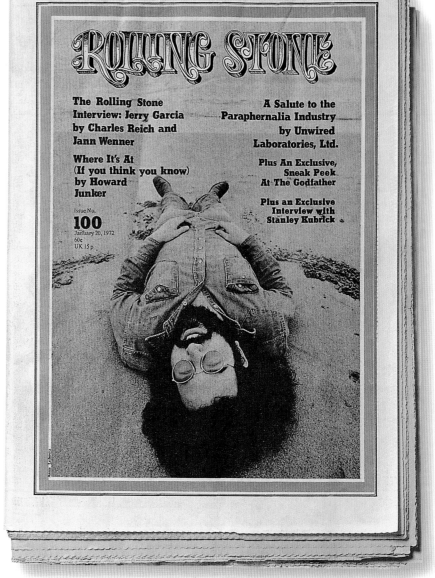

RS 101 | FEBRUARY 3RD, 1972
THE GRATEFUL DEAD
Photograph by ANNIE LEIBOVITZ

RS 100 | JANUARY 20TH, 1972
JERRY GARCIA
Photograph by ANNIE LEIBOVITZ

The name the Lyman Family (RS 98) doesn't ring a bell? Its leader Mel Lyman was yet another "spiritual" leader prominent in the early Seventies. He was a sort of death-extolling quasi-mystical personal-actualization cult leader and author of 'Mirror at the End of the Road.' He had some interesting ideas: "I am going to turn ideals to shit. I am going to shove hope up your ass." Ditto infrastructure renovations: "I am going to burn down the world, and then I am going to burn the rubble." This cover assignment, reportedly, was a day in the park for David Felton, coauthor of the six-part Charles Manson exposé. ○

RS 102 | FEBRUARY 17TH, 1972
NARC AGENT GERRITT VAN RAAM
PHOTOGRAPHER UNKNOWN

RS 103 | MARCH 2ND, 1972
BOB DYLAN
Illustration by MILTON GLASER

RS 105 | MARCH 30TH, 1972
ALICE COOPER
Photograph by ANNIE LEIBOVITZ

RS 104 | MARCH 16TH, 1972
BOB DYLAN
Illustration by ROBERT GROSSMAN

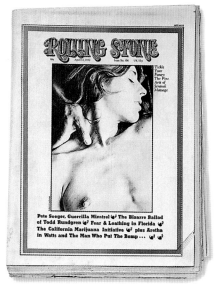

RS 106 | APRIL 13TH, 1972
THE ART OF SENSUAL MASSAGE
Photograph by ROBERT FOOTHORAP

RS 107 | APRIL 27TH, 1972
VARIOUS
Photographs by ANNIE LEIBOVITZ

RS 108 | MAY 11TH, 1972
DAVID CASSIDY
Photograph by ANNIE LEIBOVITZ

RS 109 | MAY 25TH, 1972
JANE FONDA
Photograph by ANNIE LEIBOVITZ

RS 110 | JUNE 8TH, 1972
GEORGE McGOVERN
Illustration by EDWARD SOREL

RS 111 | JUNE 22ND, 1972
VAN MORRISON
Photograph by ANNIE LEIBOVITZ

"IT PISSED OFF everybody that was really profiting from the business of David Cassidy. I had fan letters that came to me – and there were hundreds of thousands of them, literally – in defense of me by fans of mine, that said, 'Oh David, I know that you couldn't possibly have done this because I know that you would never have posed nude for photographs.' And the fact was, I had, had willingly done so, had thought about it. I scratched my head and thought, You know, this David Cassidy business has really gotten outta hand."

~ *DAVID CASSIDY*

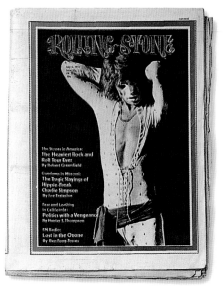

RS 112 | JULY 6TH, 1972
MICK JAGGER
Photograph by ANNIE LEIBOVITZ

RS 113 | JULY 20TH, 1972
PAUL SIMON
Photograph by PETER SIMON

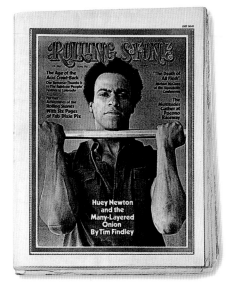

RS 114 | AUGUST 3RD, 1972
HUEY NEWTON
Photograph by ANNIE LEIBOVITZ

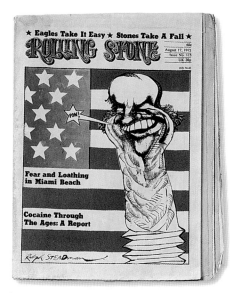

RS 115 | AUGUST 17TH, 1972
1972 DEMOCRATIC CONVENTION
Illustration by RALPH STEADMAN

RS 116 | AUGUST 31ST, 1972
RANDY NEWMAN
Photograph by ANNIE LEIBOVITZ

RS 117 | SEPTEMBER 14TH, 1972
THREE DOG NIGHT
Photograph by ANNIE LEIBOVITZ

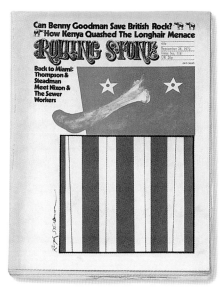

RS 118 | SEPTEMBER 28TH, 1972
1972 REPUBLICAN CONVENTION
Illustration by RALPH STEADMAN

RS 119 | OCTOBER 12TH, 1972
SALLY STRUTHERS
Photograph by MEL TRAXEL

RS 120 | OCTOBER 26TH, 1972
JEFF BECK
Photograph by HERBIE GREENE

NOVEMBER 9TH, 1972
DAVID BOWIE
Photograph by MICK ROCK

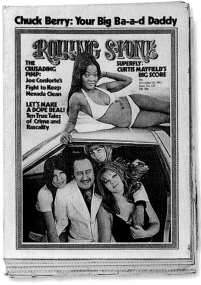

RS 122 NOVEMBER 23RD, 1972
PIMP JOE CONFORTE &
HIS WORKING GIRLS
Photograph by ANNIE LEIBOVITZ

"**SOME PEOPLE SAY** I'll do anything for the press, it's true . . . that I make meself too available. I just like to 'ave fun. There was this time Keith Altham and Chris Williams, who look after our PR, phoned me up and said I 'ad to be at their office at three o'clock for an interview. Well, you know, the pubs shut at three, so I was rather delayed, because they don't turn out until ten past, and they don't turn me out until ha' past. So it was quarter to four before I eventually started. I was back up in my office at Track [Records] and finally I remembered; I'd forgotten all about it. So uhhh, 'Oh, Christ, they're gonna be angry.' Right opposite the office is a chemist's, so I sent Dougal, me driver, over there to pick up some rolls of bandages and plaster, and I did all me leg up, strapped me arms up and purchased a stick, a walking stick. Then I went over to the office: 'Sorry I'm late, but the 'ospital delayed me.' I'd called earlier and told them I'd been run over by a bus on Oxford Street."

~ *Keith Moon*

RS 123 DECEMBER 7TH, 1972
CARLOS SANTANA
Photograph by ANNIE LEIBOVITZ

RS 124 DECEMBER 21ST, 1972
KEITH MOON
Photograph by BOB GRUEN

RS 125 JANUARY 4TH, 1973
JAMES TAYLOR & CARLY SIMON
Photograph by PETER SIMON

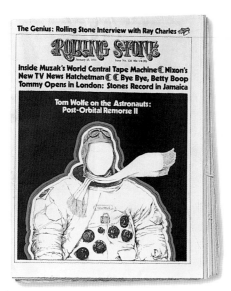

RS 126 | JANUARY 18TH, 1973
APOLLO ASTRONAUT
Illustration by DUGALD STERMER

RS 127 | FEBRUARY 1ST, 1973
DIANA ROSS
Photograph by ANNIE LEIBOVITZ

RS 129 | MARCH 1ST, 1973
MICK JAGGER
Photograph by ANNIE LEIBOVITZ

RS 128 | FEBRUARY 25TH, 1973
BETTE MIDLER
Illustration by PHILIP HAYS

"**I THINK** [I really started to enjoy shooting the cover] when ROLLING STONE went to color [RS 128]. I had to change to color, too, and it was very scary. I was glad I came from a school of black and white, because I learned to look at things in tones, highlights. ROLLING STONE was printed on newsprint, rag print, and ink sinks into the magazine. So the only thing that would make it on the cover were pictures that had two or three colors, primary colors, a very posterlike effect. In a strange way, you almost had to make the color look like black and white. So I developed a very graphic use of form and color just to survive the printing process."

~ ANNIE LEIBOVITZ

RS 130 | MARCH 15TH, 1973
ROBERT MITCHUM
Illustration by CHARLES E. WHITE III

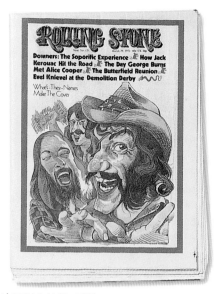

RS 131 | MARCH 29TH, 1973
DR. HOOK & THE MEDICINE SHOW
Illustration by GERRY GERSTEN

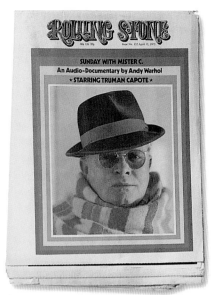

RS 132 | APRIL 12TH, 1973
TRUMAN CAPOTE
Photograph by HENRY DILTZ

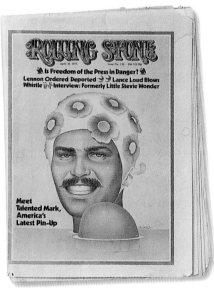

RS 133 | APRIL 26TH, 1973
MARK SPITZ
Illustration by IGNACIO GOMEZ

RS 134 | MAY 10TH, 1973
ALICE COOPER
Photograph by ANNIE LEIBOVITZ

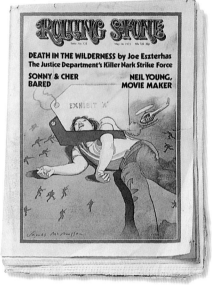

RS 135 | MAY 24TH, 1973
CRIME VICTIM DIRK DICKENSON
Illustration by JAMES McMULLAN

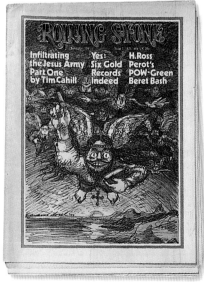

RS 136 | JUNE 7TH, 1973
JESUS FREAKS
Illustration by EDWARD SOREL

RS 137 | JUNE 21ST, 1973
ROD STEWART
Photograph by CHARLES GATEWOOD

RS 138 | JULY 5TH, 1973
PAUL NEWMAN
Photograph by STEPHEN SHUGRUE

How could ROLLING STONE not give them a cover (RS 131)? Dr. Hook & the Medicine Show's "The Cover of ROLLING STONE" hit Number Six on the 'Billboard' chart, March 17th, 1973. ○ Swimmer Mark Spitz was riding high as a record-breaking Olympian when he made the cover of ROLLING STONE (RS 133). He was also America's heartthrob, along with such fellow sex symbols as Burt Reynolds and Tom Jones. ○ One of the covers has got to have the distinction – and RS 134 is the one: the worst-selling issue in ROLLING STONE's history. ○

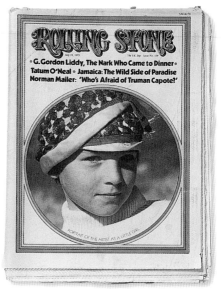

RS 139 | JULY 19TH, 1973
TATUM O'NEAL
Photograph by STEVE JAFFE

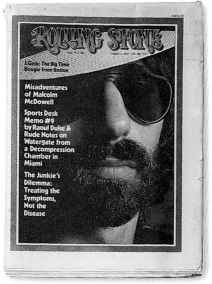

RS 140 | AUGUST 2ND, 1973
PETER WOLF
Photograph by ANNIE LEIBOVITZ

RS 141 | AUGUST 16TH, 1973
ELTON JOHN
Illustration by KIM WHITESIDES

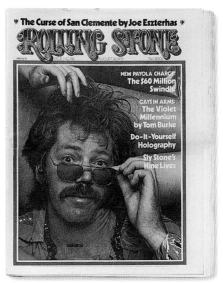

RS 142 | AUGUST 30TH, 1973
DAN HICKS
Photograph by ANNIE LEIBOVITZ

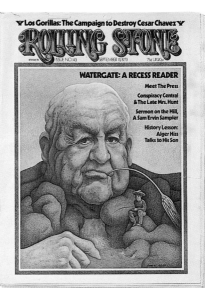

RS 143 | SEPTEMBER 13TH, 1973
SENATOR SAM ERVIN
Illustration by CHARLES SHIELDS

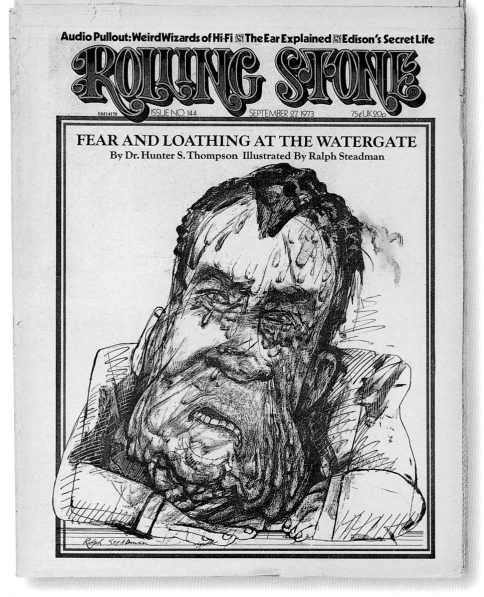

RS 144 | SEPTEMBER 27TH, 1973
RICHARD NIXON
Illustration by RALPH STEADMAN

RS 145 | OCTOBER 11TH, 1973
ART GARFUNKEL
Photograph by JIM MARSHALL

RS 146 | OCTOBER 25TH, 1973
GENE AUTRY
Illustration by GARY OVERACRE

RS 147 | NOVEMBER 8TH, 1973
DANIEL ELLSBURG
Illustration by DAVE WILLARDSON

RS 148 | NOVEMBER 22ND, 1973
JERRY GARCIA
Illustration by ROBERT GROSSMAN

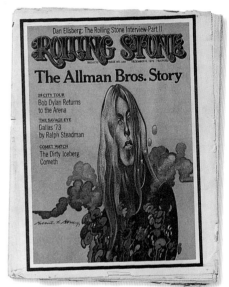

RS 149 | DECEMBER 6TH, 1973
GREGG ALLMAN
Illustration by GILBERT STONE

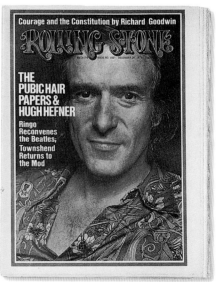

RS 150 | DECEMBER 20TH, 1973
HUGH HEFNER
Photograph by ANNIE LEIBOVITZ

Michael Salisbury, a renowned Los Angeles designer, and his associate Lloyd Ziff temporarily move into Annie Leibovitz's San Francisco loft and take over ROLLING STONE's design while Robert Kingsbury is on a leave of absence for nine covers (RS 147–RS 155). They collaborate on RS 156, with Salisbury taking the helm officially for RS 157. ◯

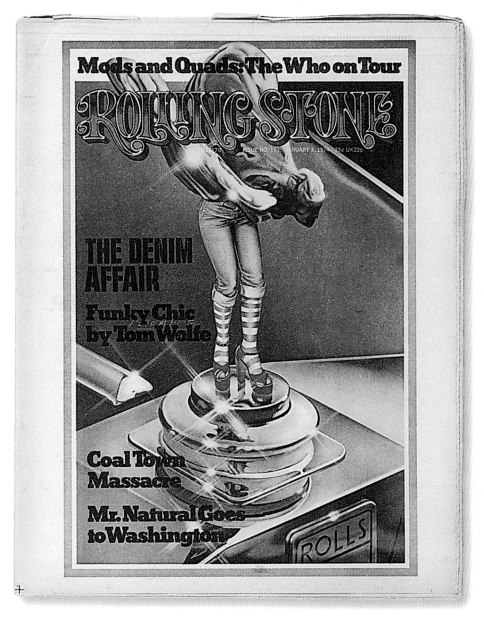

RS 151 | JANUARY 3RD, 1974
FUNKY CHIC
Illustration by PETER PALOMBI

ANTIFASHION! Terrific. Right away antifashion itself became the most raving fashion imaginable . . . also known as Funky Chic. Everybody had sworn off fashion, but somehow nobody moved to Cincinnati to work among the poor. Instead, everyone stayed put and imported the poor to the fashion pages. That's the way it happened! . . . Funky Chic evolved into its most exquisite manifestation, namely, Radical Chic, which I have had the occasion to describe elsewhere . . .

[EXCERPT FROM RS 151 COVER STORY
BY TOM WOLFE]

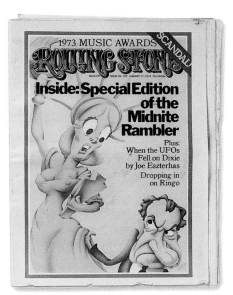

RS 152 | JANUARY 17TH, 1974
RICHARD NIXON
Illustration by ROBERT GROSSMAN

RS 153 | JANUARY 31ST, 1974
PAUL & LINDA McCARTNEY
Photograph by FRANCESCO SCAVULLO

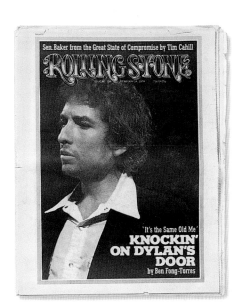

RS 154 | FEBRUARY 14TH, 1974
BOB DYLAN
Photograph by BARRY FEINSTEIN

RS 155 | FEBRUARY 28TH, 1974
FEAR AND LOATHING
AT THE SUPER BOWL
ILLUSTRATOR UNKNOWN

SM14170

Dismantle the Presidency by Richard N. Goodwin

ROLLING STONE

ISSUE NO. 156   MARCH 14, 1974   75¢ UK25p

The Poet's Poet
by Michael McClure

ROCK ME MAHARAJ JI
The Little Guru
Without A Prayer

UP FROM CBS
The Smothers Brothers
Slow Road Back

Paul Davis

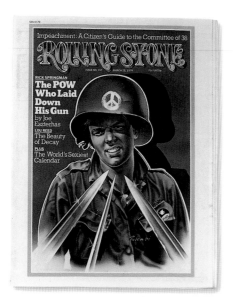

RS 157 | MARCH 28TH, 1974
P.O.W. RICK SPRINGMAN
Illustration by PETER PALOMBI

RS 158 | APRIL 11TH, 1974
MARVIN GAYE
Photograph by ANNIE LEIBOVITZ

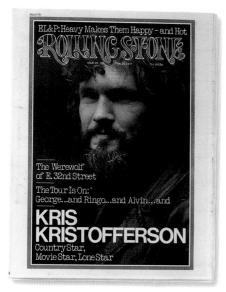

RS 159 | APRIL 25TH, 1974
KRIS KRISTOFFERSON
Photograph by ANNIE LEIBOVITZ

RS 160 | MAY 9TH, 1974
PAUL GETTY
Photograph by ANNIE LEIBOVITZ

RS 161 | MAY 23RD, 1974
JACKSON & ETHAN BROWNE
Photograph by ANNIE LEIBOVITZ

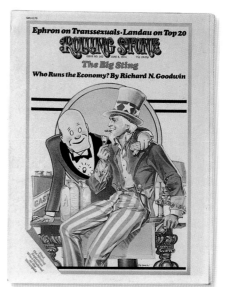

RS 162 | JUNE 6TH, 1974
THE ECONOMY
Illustration by PETER PALOMBI

RS 163 | JUNE 20TH, 1974
JAMES DEAN
Illustration by JOHN VAN HAMERSVELD

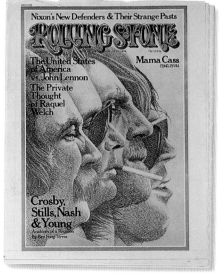

RS 164 | JULY 4TH, 1974
KAREN & RICHARD CARPENTER
Photograph by ANNIE LEIBOVITZ

RS 165 | JULY 18TH, 1974
ERIC CLAPTON
Illustration by PHILIP HAYS

RS 166 | AUGUST 1ST, 1974
MARIA MULDAUR
Photograph by ANNIE LEIBOVITZ

RS 167 | AUGUST 15TH, 1974
STEELY DAN
Illustration by DAVE WILLARDSON

RS 168 | AUGUST 29TH, 1974
CROSBY, STILLS, NASH & YOUNG
Illustration by DUGALD STERMER

Though ROLLING STONE has raised eyebrows over many of its covers, most have been more overtly controversial than the illustration for the Steely Dan cover (RS 167). Is the bathing-suit-clad cover girl riding a silver vibrator? Yes, the concept was this: Walter Becker and Donald Fagen named their group after a vibrator called Steely Dan in William S. Burroughs's 'Naked Lunch.' Apparently, when Dave Willardson completed his airbrushed image, art director Michael Salisbury hid it from the rest of the staff until the issue was running on press – just in case there was any nay-saying.

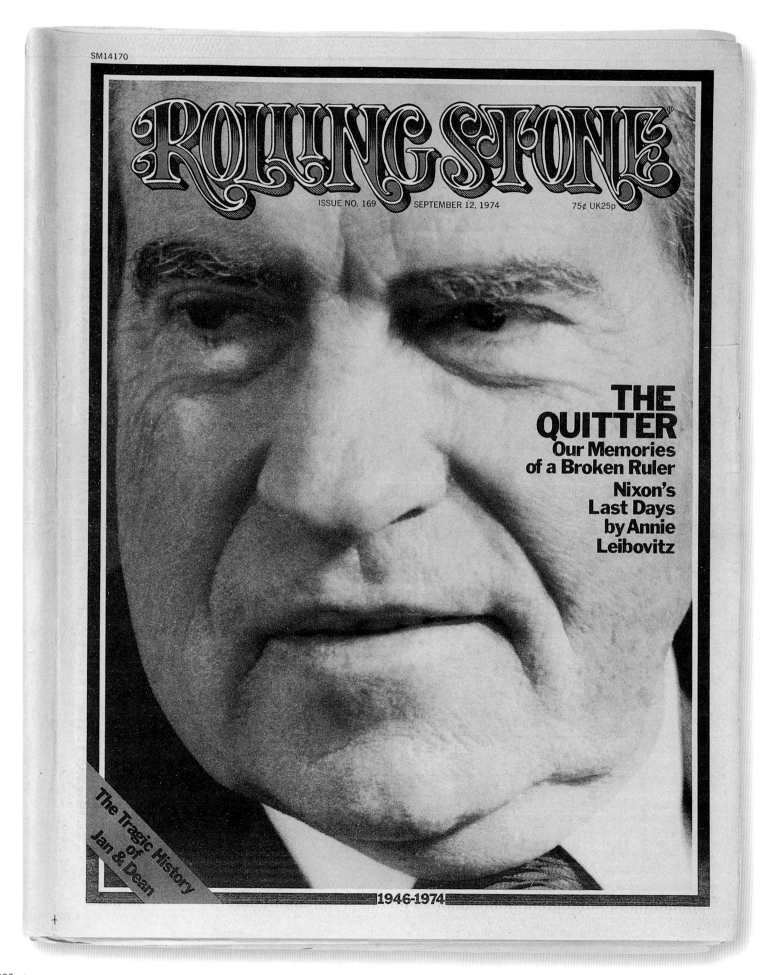

SM14170

ROLLING STONE

ISSUE NO. 169   SEPTEMBER 12, 1974   75¢ UK25p

THE QUITTER
Our Memories of a Broken Ruler

Nixon's Last Days by Annie Leibovitz

The Tragic History of Jan & Dean

1946-1974

When Richard Nixon resigned in 1974, Rolling Stone had been around only slightly longer than Nixon had been president. From time to time, the magazine commented on the former president and his actions. For RS 169, seven editors read over the preceding 168 issues to see what had been written about Nixon. They looked for "bright, breezy material as well as the kind of vicious, distorted, hysterical reporting that got Rolling Stone banned from the White House for all but the last months, when the pit began to open up at Nixon's feet."

Meanwhile, writer Richard Goodwin and Annie Leibovitz had been busy with, respectively, an essay on Nixon and a photo record of his last days. Goodwin had been in Washington setting up the Rolling Stone operation there. Leibovitz appeared twice on television: once in San Clemente climbing the podium of Nixon's Special Counsel James St. Clair and the other time shooting the former president's long and lachrymose walk from the Oval Office to the waiting helicopter. ○

*   *   *   *   *

DICK AND PAT THOUGHT that China was a very funny place. Everywhere they went, they found things to laugh at. Dick especially liked to make jokes.

They visited a place called the Forbidden City. Their new friend Chou showed them a pretty room in an old palace. Once, Chou told them, a child emperor ruled the country in this room. His mother hid behind the screen to tell him what to do.

"It's the same today," joked Dick. "The women are always the backseat drivers!"

Then Chou showed Dick a pair of ear stoppers. Emperors used to put them in their ears. That way they could not hear when people said bad things about them.

"Give me a pair of those. Then you can only hear the questions you want to!" said clever Dick.

[RS WHITE HOUSE CORRESPONDENTS, MARCH 30TH, 1972]

WE URGE the Congress to vote impeachment proceedings before Nixon can escape through resignation. And, in either event, we then want a trial to determine innocence or a conviction.

And that is just the first step.

~ *THE EDITORS*
[JUNE 7TH, 1973]

SIX MONTHS AGO, Richard Nixon was the most powerful political leader in the history of the world, more powerful than Augustus Caesar, when he had his act rolling full bore – six months ago.

Now, with the passing of each sweaty afternoon, into what history will call "the Summer of '73," Richard Nixon is being dragged closer and closer – with all deliberate speed, as it were – to disgrace and merciless infamy. His place in history is already fixed: He will go down with Grant and Harding as one of democracy's classic mutations.

~ *HUNTER S. THOMPSON*
[SEPTEMBER 27TH, 1973]

HE ATE A LOT of cornmeal and pumped gas for his father's gas station. His father bought a Quaker meeting-house across the road and expanded the gas station into a grocery store. The boy took to studying in the bell-tower of the church/store. He was devoted to his mother. He once wrote her a letter that began: "My Dear Master" and ended "Your Good Dog, Richard." He had a habit of sitting in a big chair and staring into space . . .

He mixed with few people and hardly ever dated. When he did date, he asked the girls intimate questions: What would have happened to the world if Persia had conquered Greece? What would have happened if Plato had never lived?

~ Joe Eszterhas

[AUGUST 30TH, 1973]

RS 170 | SEPTEMBER 26TH, 1974
TANYA TUCKER
Photograph by DOUG METZLER

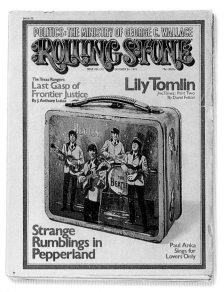

RS 172 | OCTOBER 24TH, 1974
THE BEATLES
Photograph by TOM ROSE

RS 171 | OCTOBER 10TH, 1974
LILY TOMLIN & RICHARD PRYOR
Photograph by ANNIE LEIBOVITZ

RS 173 | NOVEMBER 7TH, 1974
EVEL KNIEVEL
Illustration by RAY DOMINGO

RS 174 | NOVEMBER 21ST, 1974
ELTON JOHN
Photograph by ANNIE LEIBOVITZ

"I LOVE LILY. I have this thing about her, a little crush. She's so good I get embarrassed, I get in awe of her. I'd seen her on *Laugh-In* and shit, and something about her is very sensual. You know, when she works, I'd like to ball her in all them different characters she does sometimes. Wouldn't you? I mean, have her around the house and have her do all that – be Ernestine one minute [*he imitates Ernestine, Lily's telephone operator*]: 'Oh [*snort, snort*], just put it in the proper place. Thank you [*snort, snort*].'"

~RICHARD PRYOR

RS 175 | DECEMBER 5TH, 1974
DUSTIN HOFFMAN
Photograph by STEVE SCHAPIRO

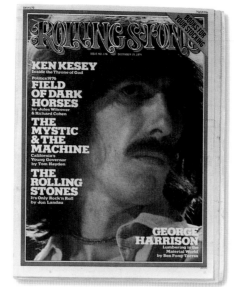

RS 176 | DECEMBER 19TH, 1974
GEORGE HARRISON
Photograph by MARK FOCUS

RS 177 | JANUARY 2ND, 1975
SUZI QUATRO
Photograph by PETER GOWLAND

RS 178 | JANUARY 16TH, 1975
GREGG ALLMAN
Photograph by PETE TURNER

RS 179 | JANUARY 30TH, 1975
FREDDIE PRINZE
Photograph by DON PETERSON

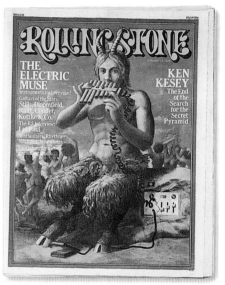

RS 180 | FEBRUARY 13TH, 1975
THE ELECTRIC MUSE
Illustration by PHIL CARROLL

RS 181 | FEBRUARY 27TH, 1975
KENNY LOGGINS & JIM MESSINA
Photograph by ANNIE LEIBOVITZ

RS 182 | MARCH 13TH, 1975
JIMMY PAGE & ROBERT PLANT
Photograph by NEAL PRESTON

RS 183 | MARCH 27TH, 1975
LINDA RONSTADT
Photograph by ANNIE LEIBOVITZ

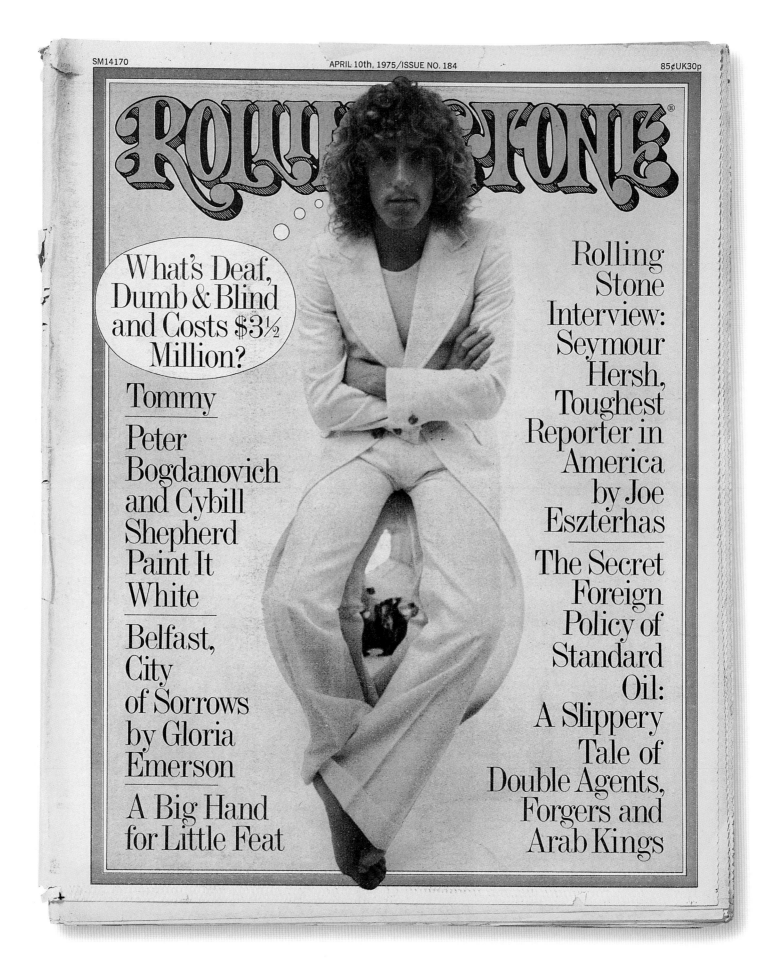

RS 184 | ROGER DALTREY | PHOTOGRAPHER UNKNOWN | APRIL 10TH, 1975

"THE CHASM between the original record album and the film is a great one. But everything [director] Ken Russell has done with the story and the music has my full blessing. As a gag, when we were working on it, we started to call it a rock opera, knowing full well it wasn't a true opera at all. I didn't need the music critics to tell me it wasn't an opera – I've probably listened to as much straight opera as any of them. But the tag stuck, and we realized it was maybe a bit fanciful, but in spite of that we quite liked the idea."

~ PETE TOWNSHEND

* * * * *

"ROGER DALTREY is a natural performer, and he has a good sense of cinema. He didn't know anything of the technique, but he suggested some good cinematic ideas."

~ KEN RUSSELL

* * * * *

DALTREY was transformed by *Tommy*. . . . Gone were his short mod hairstyles and frilly clothes. Now he wore his curly golden locks as tresses, swooping to his shoulders and framing a face from which blue eyes glared. . . . Bronzed from hours in the sun, always fit as an athlete, Daltrey stood in the full heat of the white spots and defined a new kind of rock star: sensual, rugged but with the macho aspects eliminated. . . . Townshend had written an opera that gave Daltrey the opportunity to become the pop star he had dreamed of being.

[EXCERPT FROM 'BEFORE I GET OLD' BY DAVE MARSH]

RS 185 | APRIL 24TH, 1975
PETER FALK
Photograph by ANNIE LEIBOVITZ

RS 186 | MAY 8TH, 1975
JOHN DENVER
Photograph by FRANCESCO SCAVULLO

RS 187 | MAY 22ND, 1975
CARLY SIMON
Photograph by TONY LANE

RS 188 | JUNE 5TH, 1975
PHOEBE SNOW
Photograph by ANNIE LEIBOVITZ

RS 189 | JUNE 19TH, 1975
STEVIE WONDER
Illustration by MILTON GLASER

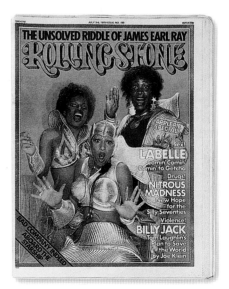

RS 190 | JULY 3RD, 1975
LABELLE
Photograph by HIRO

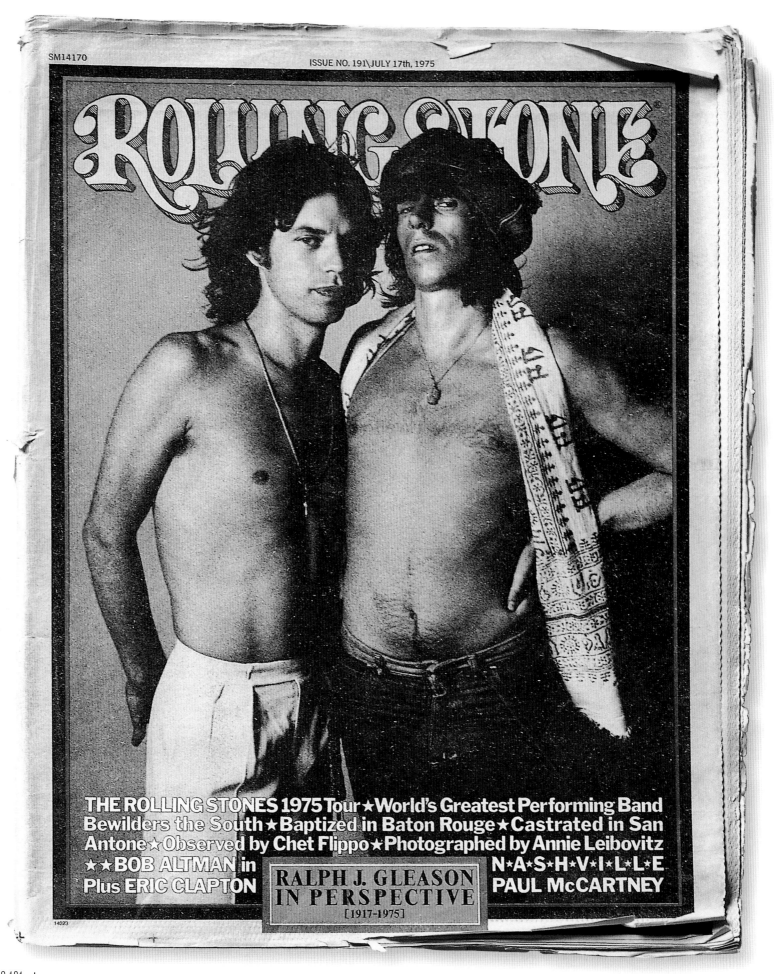

"**ANNIE** always likes to get your shirt off by the end of the shoot." ~ *Mick Jagger*

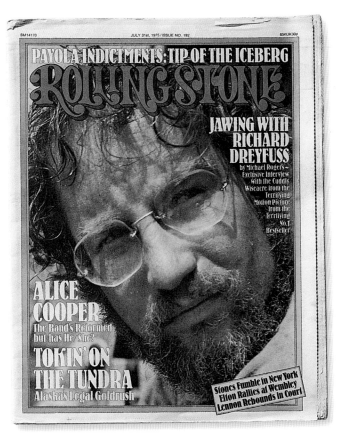

RS 192 | JULY 31ST, 1975
RICHARD DREYFUSS
Photograph by BUD LEE

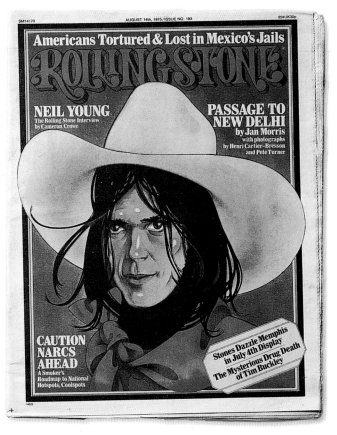

RS 193 | AUGUST 14TH, 1975
NEIL YOUNG
Illustration by KIM WHITESIDES

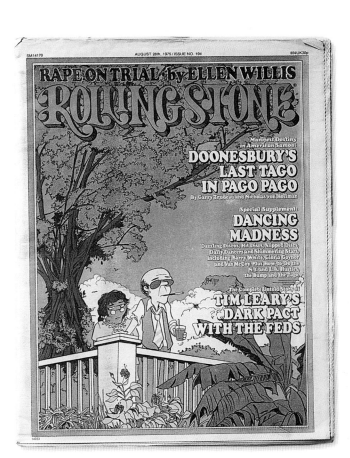

RS 194 | AUGUST 28TH, 1975
DOONESBURY'S UNCLE DUKE
Illustration by GARRY TRUDEAU

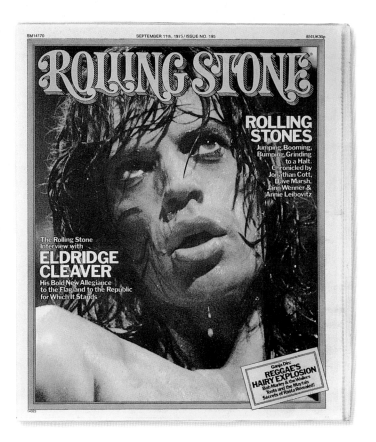

RS 195 | SEPTEMBER 11TH, 1975
MICK JAGGER
Photograph by ANNIE LEIBOVITZ

RS 194 is the first of three covers that Pulitzer Prize–winning cartoonist Garry Trudeau has illustrated for ROLLING STONE. Doonesbury's gonzoid Uncle Duke arrived on the cover after he'd been appointed governor of American Samoa. The character infuriated the real Raoul Duke, Hunter S. Thompson, on whom the character is directly based. (Thompson had once claimed that Democratic party chairman Larry O'Brien had offered him the governorship.) Thompson said of Trudeau, characteristically, "If I ever catch that little bastard, I'll rip his lungs out."

SM14170

OCTOBER 23rd, 1975/ISSUE NO. 198

85¢UK30p

ROLLING STONE

THE INSIDE STORY

By Howard Kohn and David Weir

PATTY HEARST and Emily Harris waited on a grimy Los Angeles street, fighting their emotions as they listened to a radio rebroadcasting the sounds of their friends dying. On a nearby corner Bill Harris dickered over the price of a battered old car.

Only blocks away, rifle cartridges were exploding in the dying flames of a charred bungalow. The ashes were still too hot to retrieve the bodies of the six SLA members who had died hours before on the afternoon of May 17th, 1974.

Bill Harris shifted impatiently as the car's owner patted a dented fender. "I want five bills for this mother."

The SLA survivors had only $400. Reluctantly Harris offered $350. The man quickly pocketed the money.

Minutes later Bill picked up Patty and Emily and steered onto a freeway north to San Francisco. They drove all night

—the Harrises in the front seat of the noisy car and Patty in back, hidden under a blanket. They were too tense to sleep, each grappling with the aftershock of the fiery deaths.

They exited twice at brightly lit service station clusters that flank Interstate 5, checking out each before picking what looked like the safest attendant. They made no other stops and reached San Francisco in the predawn darkness.

The three fugitives drove to a black ghetto with rows of ramshackle Victorians—and sought out a friend. Bill and Emily's knocks brought the man sleepy-eyed to the door.

"You're alive!" Then he panicked. "You can't stay here. The whole state is gonna be crawling with pigs looking for you." He gave them five dollars and shut the door. "Don't come back."

The Harrises returned to the car and twisted the ignition key. Patty poked her head out from under the blanket. "What's the matter? Why won't it start?"

The fugitives had no choice —to continue fiddling with the dead battery might attract attention—so they abandoned the car. Walking the streets, however, was a worse alternative.

"C'mon Tania," said Emily. "You better bring the blanket." Bill and Emily both carried duffel bags. Inside were weapons, disguises and tattered books.

A few blocks away, under a faded Victorian, they spotted a crawl space, a gloomy cave for rats and runaway dogs. As Patty and the Harrises huddled in the dirt under the old house, the noise of a late-night party began in the living room above. Patty gripped her homemade machine gun. "The pigs must have found the car!"

"Shhh," came a whispered response. "Shut up, goddamnit. Please shut up!"

[Continued on page 41]

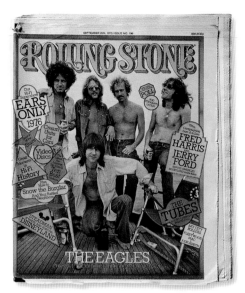

RS 196 | SEPTEMBER 25TH, 1975
THE EAGLES
Photograph by NEAL PRESTON

RS 197 | OCTOBER 9TH, 1975
MUHAMMAD ALI
Illustration by BRUCE WOLFE

RS 199 | NOVEMBER 6TH, 1975
ROD STEWART & BRITT EKLAND
Photograph by Annie Leibovitz

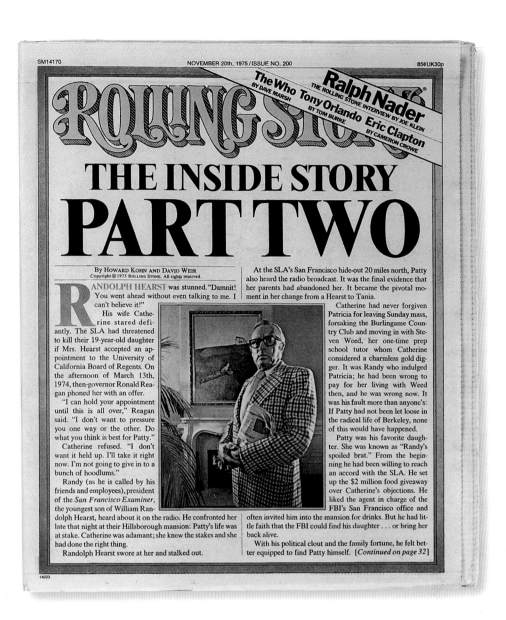

RS 200 | NOVEMBER 20TH, 1975
THE PATTY HEARST STORY, PART TWO
Photograph by TONY LANE

About this groundbreaking scoop (RS 198 and RS 200), the editors wrote: "To obtain the interviews, Howard Kohn and David Weir had to promise they would go to jail before revealing the names of their sources (a promise they would have made in any case). They were not allowed to tape the interviews, so to keep things as accurate as possible, separate notes were taken by the two journalists and Alison Weir, an editor of 'Womensports.' The material was then checked with independent outside sources. The entire process – negotiations, interviews, research and writing – took four months, during which time Kohn and Weir retraced Patty's trail across America, including a visit to the farmhouse rented by Jack and Micki Scott in Pennsylvania. Ironically, as the layouts were being readied for the printer, Patty Hearst and the Harrises were apprehended in San Francisco. But the narrative remains a scoop in itself – the first detailed account of Tania's conversion, her paranoid flights across the country, her hiding out with the Scotts. Part Two will cover her life leading up to the bust, secret meetings between her friends and her parents and how the FBI finally broke the case. You might want to send $1 (for the issue plus postage) to Inside Story, ROLLING STONE, 625 Third Street, San Francisco, CA 94107, and get Part Two before the FBI."

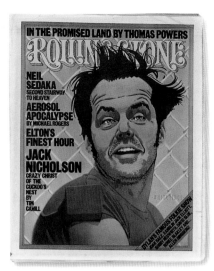

RS 201
DECEMBER 4TH, 1975
JACK NICHOLSON
Illustration by KIM WHITESIDES

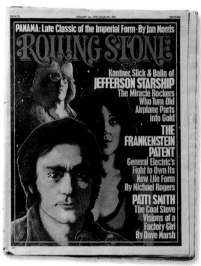

RS 203
JANUARY 1ST, 1976
JEFFERSON STARSHIP
Illustration by GREG SCOTT

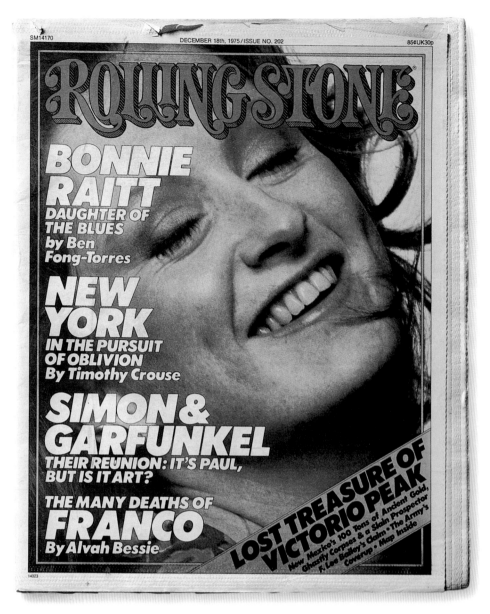

RS 202
DECEMBER 18TH, 1975
BONNIE RAITT
Photograph by BILL KING

RS 204
JANUARY 15TH, 1976
JOAN BAEZ & BOB DYLAN
Photograph by KEN REGAN

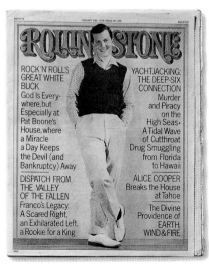

RS 205
JANUARY 29TH, 1976
PAT BOONE
Photograph by BRUNO OF HOLLYWOOD

"THE CAMERA never lies. In this case [RS 206], it only tells half the story. With a small target set up a few yards away, [I'd been] taking pot-shots with an oversized pistol. The gun was a present from one of my mid-Seventies 'friends.' I was definitely under the impression that I was merely 'passing through this world.' I didn't care where I came from and cared less where I was going; the present was futile and surreal. I ate little, but ingested a critically unfair amount of chemicals...."

~ DAVID BOWIE

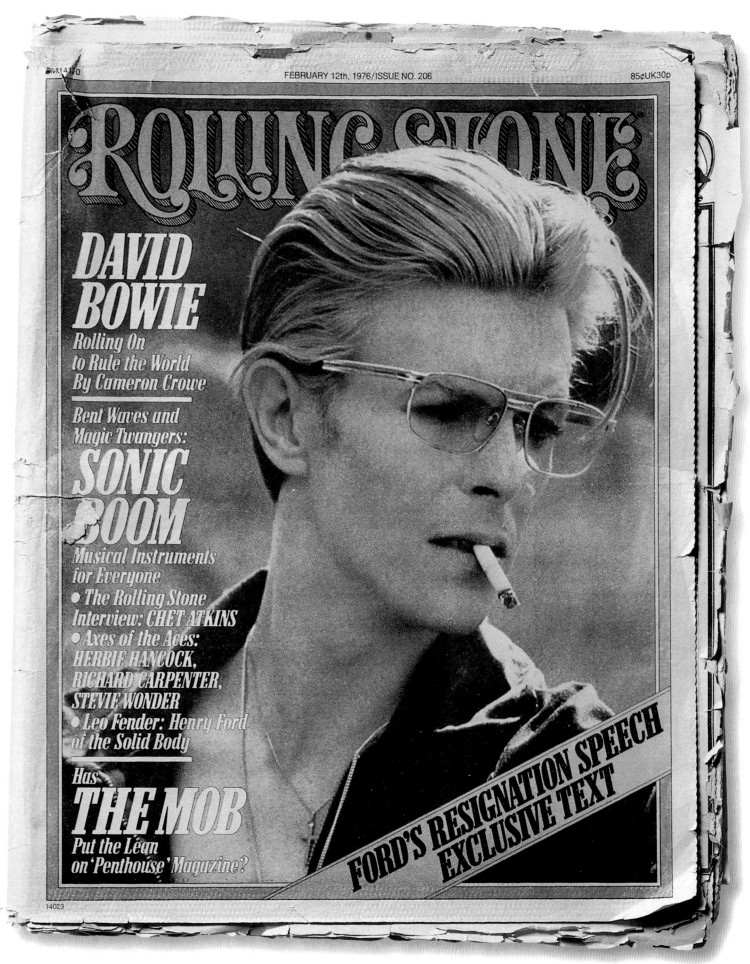

FEBRUARY 12th, 1976/ISSUE NO. 206   85¢UK30p

ROLLING STONE

DAVID BOWIE

*Rolling On
to Rule the World
By Cameron Crowe*

*Bent Waves and
Magic Twangers:*

**SONIC
BOOM**

*Musical Instruments
for Everyone*
*• The Rolling Stone
Interview: CHET ATKINS*
*• Axes of the Aces:
HERBIE HANCOCK,
RICHARD CARPENTER,
STEVIE WONDER*
*• Leo Fender: Henry Ford
of the Solid Body*

Has
THE MOB
*Put the Lean
on 'Penthouse' Magazine?*

**FORD'S RESIGNATION SPEECH
EXCLUSIVE TEXT**

RS 206 | DAVID BOWIE | Photograph by STEVE SCHAPIRO | FEBRUARY 12TH, 1976

RS 207 | FEBRUARY 26TH, 1976
SAN FRANCISCO ROCKERS
Photograph by JIM MARSHALL

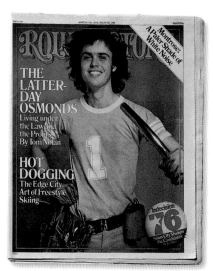

RS 208 | MARCH 11TH, 1976
DONNY OSMOND
Photograph by ANNIE LEIBOVITZ

RS 209 | MARCH 25TH, 1976
LOUISE LASSER
Photograph by BILL EPPRIDGE

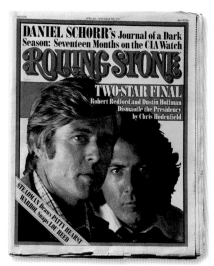

RS 210 | APRIL 8TH, 1976
ROBERT REDFORD & DUSTIN HOFFMAN
Photograph by STANLEY TRETICK

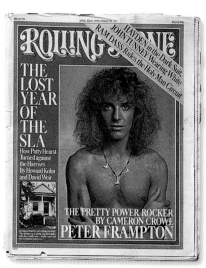

RS 211 | APRIL 22ND, 1976
PETER FRAMPTON
Photograph by FRANCESCO SCAVULLO

RS 211 | APRIL 22ND, 1976
PETER FRAMPTON
Photograph by BUD LEE

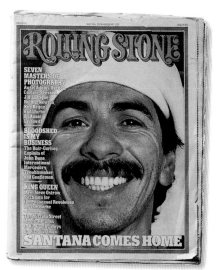

RS 212 | MAY 6TH, 1976
CARLOS SANTANA
Photograph by ANNIE LEIBOVITZ

IT'S LIKE STEPPING INTO a scene from *Blow-Up*. The white walls of Francesco Scavullo's Manhattan studio are covered with black and white portraits of blank-expressioned models. Young male assistants scurry around, each of them trying to act more hassled than the next.

In another room, looking very much out of place, twenty-five-year-old Peter Frampton waits to have his picture taken for the cover of ROLLING STONE. He squirms while a makeup man dabs colors on his cheeks and eyelids, readying him for a session with one of the world's most renowned fashion photographers. It's all happening so fast. Three months ago, Frampton was just another hardworking British rocker, crisscrossing the country with a four-album repertoire. Today, he is the brightest new star of '76.

Frampton pries himself away from the makeup man to greet his visitor. "You mean you still recognize me?" he jokes a little uneasily. "I'm in such a daze. Do you believe all that's happened? Number One? Do you believe it? What a giggle." He is quickly led before the camera and the blitz-clicking is on.

[EXCERPT FROM RS 211 COVER STORY BY CAMERON CROWE]

For RS 211, Jann Wenner commissioned two photographs of Peter Frampton by two different photographers, was talked into using one image, then changed his mind and insisted on the other shot the day the cover was due to the printer. Different photographs appeared on early and later shipments. ○

SM14170

MAY 20th, 1976/ISSUE NO. 213

85¢UK30p

THE HUGHES-NIXON-LANSKY CONNECTION: THE SECRET ALLIANCES OF THE CIA FROM WWII TO WATERGATE·BY HOWARD KOHN

ROLLING STONE

BRANDO
The Method
of His Madness
A Portrait By
Chris Hodenfield

BRAVE NEW WEED
Three Spaced-Age Tales of Dope Utopia · By Theodore Sturgeon, Michael Rogers and Thomas M. Disch

GAMBLE AND HUFF
Their Solid Gold Gospel

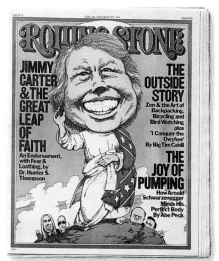

| JUNE 3RD, 1976
JIMMY CARTER
Illustration by GREG SCOTT

I HAVE SPENT enough time with Carter in the past two years to feel I have a pretty good sense of his candidacy. I went down to Plains, Georgia, to spend a few days with him on his own turf and to hopefully find out who Jimmy Carter really was before the campaign shroud came down on him and he started talking like a candidate instead of a human being. Once a presidential aspirant gets out on the campaign trail and starts seeing visions of himself hunkered down behind that big desk in the Oval Office, the idea of sitting down in his own living room and talking openly with some foul-mouthed, argumentative journalist carrying a tape recorder in one hand and a bottle of Wild Turkey in the other is totally out of the question. . . .

Both Carter and his wife have always been amazingly tolerant of my behavior, and on one or two occasions they have had to deal with me in a noticeably bent condition. I have always been careful not to commit any felonies right in front of them, but other than that I have never made much of an effort to adjust my behavior around Jimmy Carter or anyone else in his family – including his seventy-eight-year-old mother, Miss Lillian, who is the only member of the Carter family I could comfortably endorse for the presidency, right now, with no reservations at all.

[EXCERPT FROM COVER STORY
BY HUNTER S. THOMPSON]

No one seems perturbed that the leader of Wings is not on the loose, the way a Robert Plant or Roger Daltrey or Mick Jagger seems to be. And even if they're married, they don't display their wives up onstage with them.

I used to think of that, when we first got together, had Linda in the group. Oh, oh, we've had it with the groupies now! Everyone's gonna think we're real old squares – *blimey!* Married! God, at least we could have just lived together or something – that would have been a bit hip. Then you realize it doesn't matter. They really come for the music. At first it did seem funny to be up there with a wife instead of just friends or people associated with the game. But I think the nice thing that's happened is it seems to be part of a trend anyway, where women are getting in a bit more, families are a bit cooler than they were. Things change.

[EXCERPT FROM PAUL McCARTNEY INTERVIEW BY BEN FONG-TORRES]

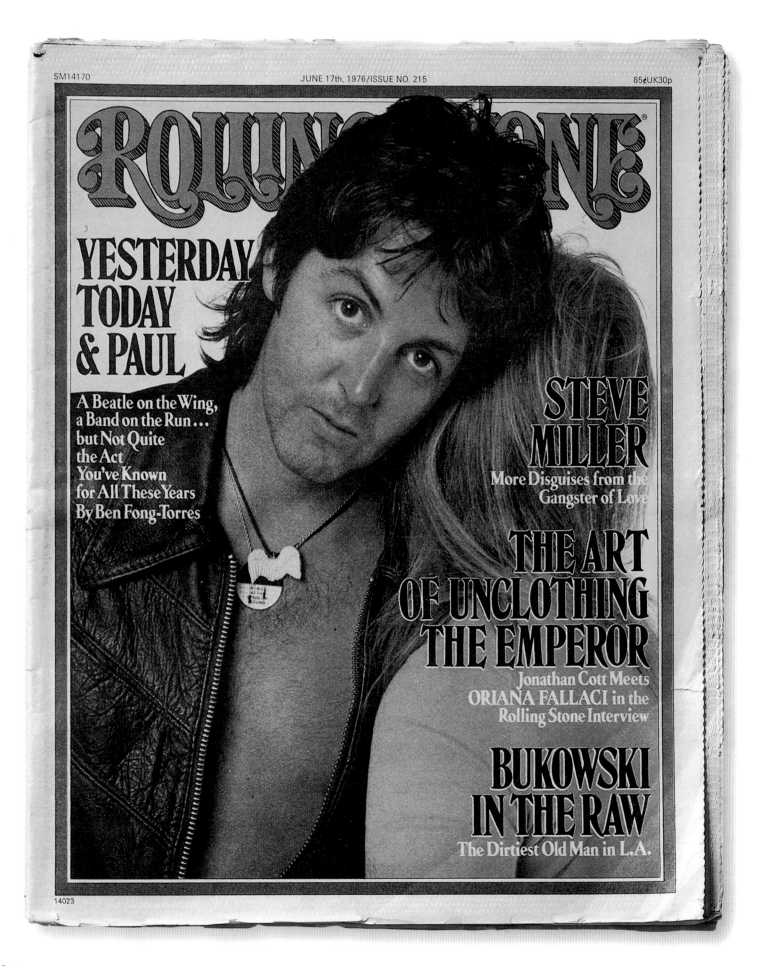

SM14170

JUNE 17th, 1976/ISSUE NO. 215

85¢/UK30p

ROLLING STONE

YESTERDAY TODAY & PAUL

A Beatle on the Wing,
a Band on the Run...
but Not Quite
the Act
You've Known
for All These Years
By Ben Fong-Torres

STEVE MILLER

More Disguises from the
Gangster of Love

THE ART OF UNCLOTHING THE EMPEROR

Jonathan Cott Meets
ORIANA FALLACI in the
Rolling Stone Interview

BUKOWSKI IN THE RAW

The Dirtiest Old Man in L.A.

14023

RS 215 | PAUL & LINDA McCARTNEY | Photograph by ANNIE LEIBOVITZ | JUNE 17TH, 1976

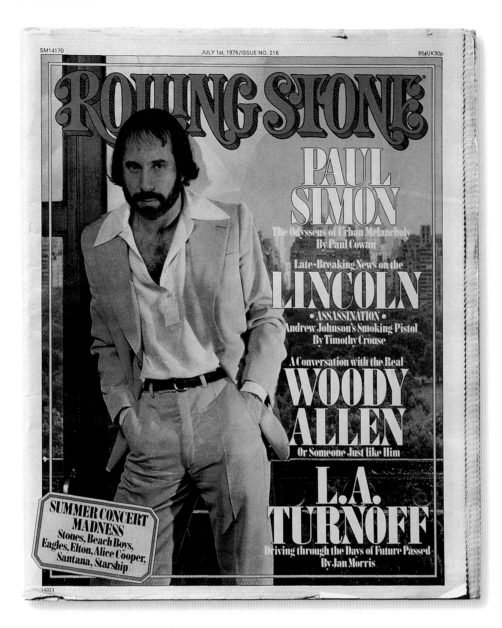

RS 216 | JULY 1ST, 1976
PAUL SIMON
Photograph by ANNIE LEIBOVITZ

"**I STARTED** to follow musical examples, not sociological examples. I realized that how you dressed or how you looked or what you said wasn't as important as whether you had the musical goods.

I could certainly see George Gershwin as somebody to measure against. Leonard Bernstein is somebody to measure against. Which is not to say that I aspire to write songs like Leonard Bernstein or George Gershwin. But there was an excellence they achieved that was right for their time....

I don't feel that it is truly significant that my record goes to Number One or that I win a Grammy. Those things are pleasant rewards.... But I understand there's a higher standard that can be applied to the work. And then there's a higher standard even than that. When you get to be Gershwin that doesn't make you Bartók."

~ *PAUL SIMON*

* * * * *

"**MOS' TIME** me no see nobody but I brethren, I family. Mos' time me no see nobody but dem, an' jus' stay heah an' wit I music an' I meditatin', mon. But sometime I like to talk to scribes for dem dat slow to catch onto I message, mon. Sometime it good for I and I to talk, 'cause sometime it cleah de air, mon. De only t'ing me no like is when dem get I message wrong, mon. Me hafta laugh sometime when dem scribes seh me like Mick Jagger or some superstar t'ing like dat. Dem hafta listen closeh to de music, 'cause de message not de same . . . noooo, mon, de reggae not de twist, mon!"

~ *BOB MARLEY*

RS 217 | JULY 15TH, 1976
THE BEATLES
Photograph by JOHN ZIMMERMAN

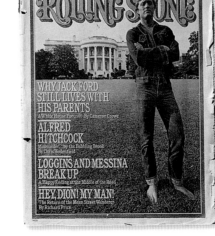

RS 218 | JULY 29TH, 1976
JACK FORD
Photograph by ANNIE LEIBOVITZ

AUGUST 12th, 1976 · ISSUE NO. 219

85¢ UK30p

ROLLING STONE

Bob Marley
Rastaman with a Bullet
By Ed McCormack

THE BEACH BOYS TEST THE WATER
BY JIM MILLER

JAMAICA AT WAR
Stalking the Beast of Babylon By Michael Thomas

PAT MOYNIHAN
Ruling-Class Hero By Timothy Crouse

JIMMY PAGE
Beats the Devil By Cameron Crowe

14023

"**I FOUND** that by taking the studio to the person, it looked like they posed for our cover and it built our credibility. With Bob Marley I set up a studio in his dressing room and waited around. After two nights he started to feel sorry for me and posed for the cover shot." ~ *ANNIE LEIBOVITZ*

RS 220 | AUGUST 26TH, 1976
STEVEN TYLER
Photograph by ANNIE LEIBOVITZ

RS 221 | SEPTEMBER 9TH, 1976
DOONESBURY'S GINNY SLADE &
JIMMY THUDPUCKER
Illustration by GARRY TRUDEAU

RS 222 | SEPTEMBER 23RD, 1976
NEIL DIAMOND
Photograph by ANNIE LEIBOVITZ

RS 223 | OCTOBER 7TH, 1976
ELTON JOHN
Photograph by DAVID NUTTER

"BEING ON THE COVER of ROLLING STONE? You know, the old kiss of death. It's like *whoops*, wait a minute. It's great, no it isn't. *It is*, no it isn't."

~STEVEN TYLER
[OF AEROSMITH]

EARLY THIS YEAR we asked Richard Avedon – one of the world's greatest photographers – to cover America's bicentennial presidential election. Our original idea was to publish a chronicle of the campaign – the candidates and the conventions – from beginning to end.

Shortly after accepting our commission, Mr. Avedon called to say that there was more to the election than met the eye; that the real story was not simply the candidates, but a broad group of men and women – some of whom we had never heard of before – who constitute the political leadership of America.

Thus began a special issue of ROLLING STONE, a collection of seventy-three portraits. This project was edited by Renata Adler, author of *Toward a Radical Middle* and the recently published novel *Speedboat*. Aside from the accompanying *Who's Who* biographies, there is no text; we think the portraits speak for themselves.

[RS 224 EDITORS' NOTE]

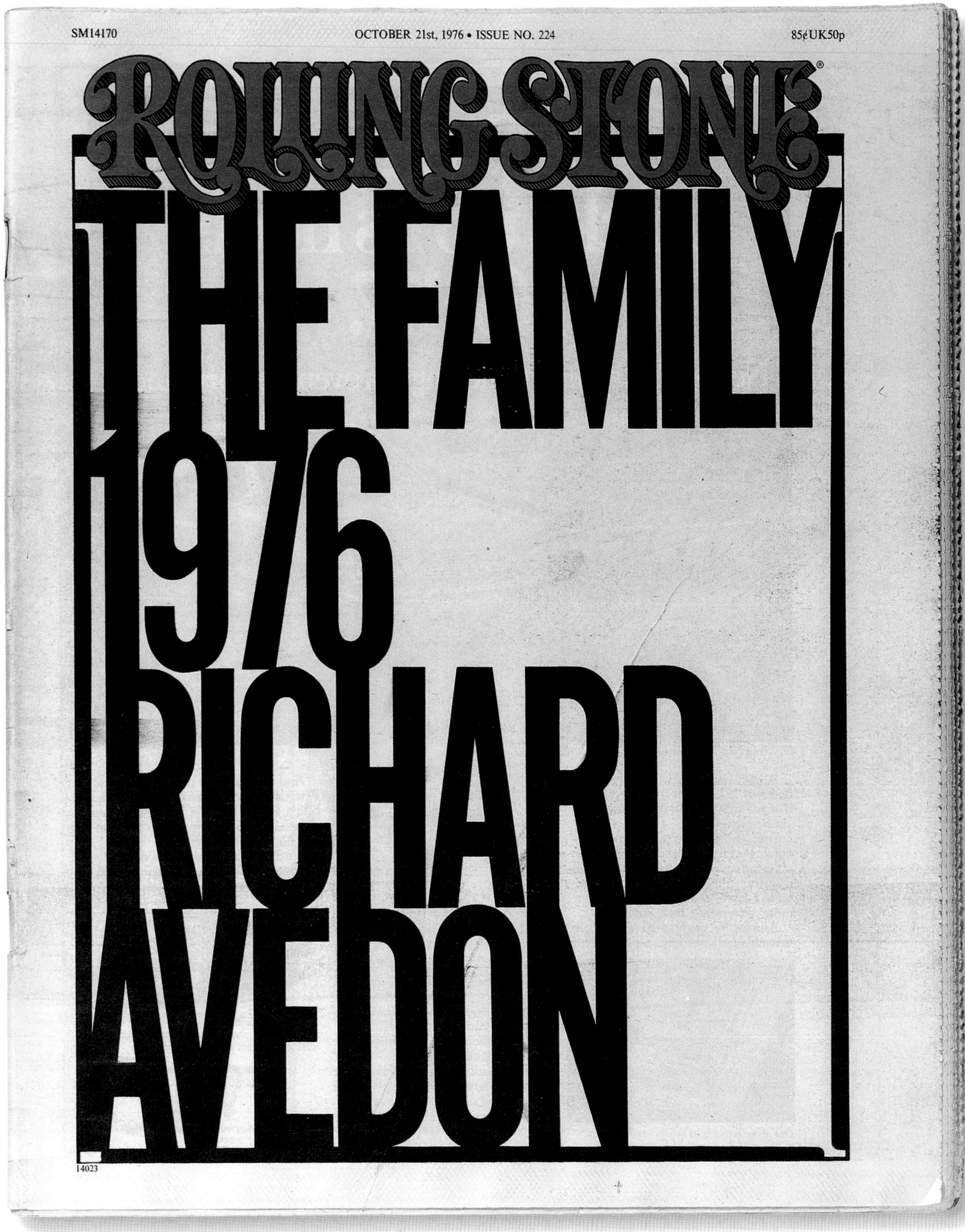

SM14170   OCTOBER 21st, 1976 • ISSUE NO. 224   85¢ UK50p

ROLLING STONE

THE FAMILY 1976 RICHARD AVEDON

14023

RS 224 | RICHARD AVEDON'S PORTFOLIO "THE FAMILY 1976" | Typography by ELIZABETH PAUL | OCTOBER 21ST, 1976

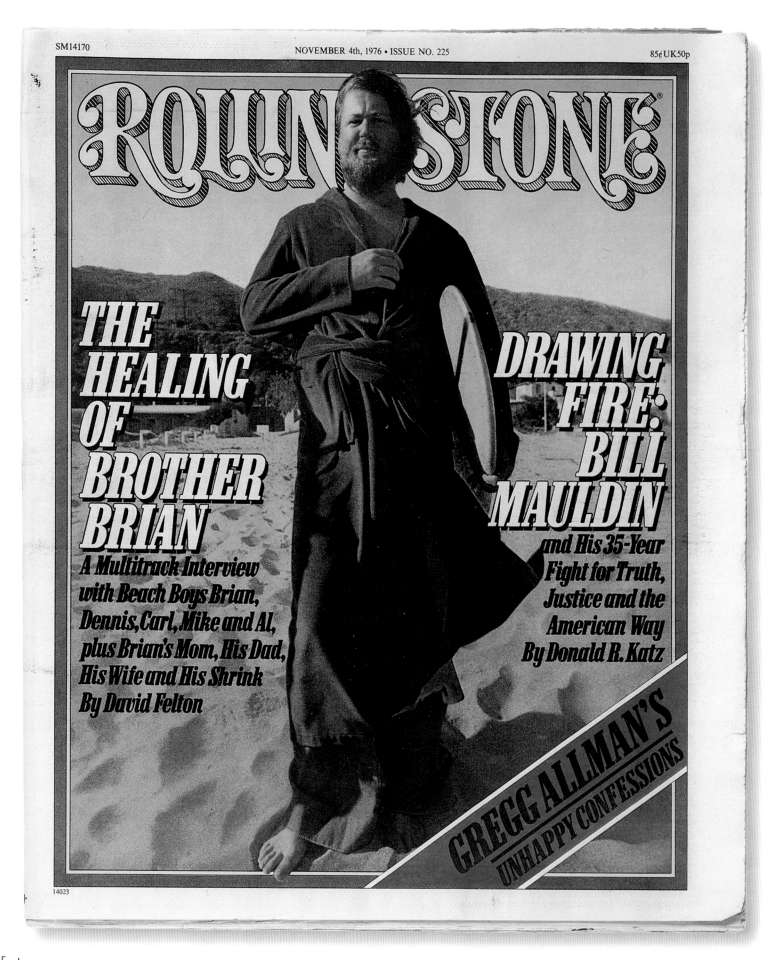

SM14170   NOVEMBER 4th, 1976 • ISSUE NO. 225   85¢ UK 50p

ROLLING STONE

THE HEALING OF BROTHER BRIAN

A Multitrack Interview with Beach Boys Brian, Dennis, Carl, Mike and Al, plus Brian's Mom, His Dad, His Wife and His Shrink By David Felton

DRAWING FIRE: BILL MAULDIN

and His 35-Year Fight for Truth, Justice and the American Way By Donald R. Katz

GREGG ALLMAN'S UNHAPPY CONFESSIONS

14023

RS 225 | BRIAN WILSON | Photograph by ANNIE LEIBOVITZ | NOVEMBER 4TH, 1976

"BRIAN SEEMS TO BE ON ACID all the time . . . except when he's in his room, where he's completely normal." ~*ANNIE LEIBOVITZ*

"I HAVE a writing block right now. Even today I started to sit down to write a song, and there was a block there. God knows what that is. Unless it's *supposed* to be there. I mean, it's not something you just kick and say, 'Come on, let's go, let's get a song writ.' If the block is there, it's there.

I believe that writers run out of material, I really do. I believe very strongly in the fact that when the natural time is up, writers actually do run out of material. To me, it's black and white. When there's a song, there's a song; when there's not, there's not. Of *course*, you run out, maybe not indefinitely, but everybody that writes runs out of some material for a while. And it's a very frightening experience....

Another thing, too, is that I used to write on pills. I used to take uppers and write, and I used to like that effect. In fact, I'd like to take uppers now and write, because they give me, you know, a certain lift and a certain outlook. And it's not an unnatural thing. I mean, the pill might be unnatural and the energy, but the song itself doesn't turn out unnatural on the uppers. The creativity flows through. I'm thinking of asking the doctor if I can go back to those, yeah."

~ Brian Wilson

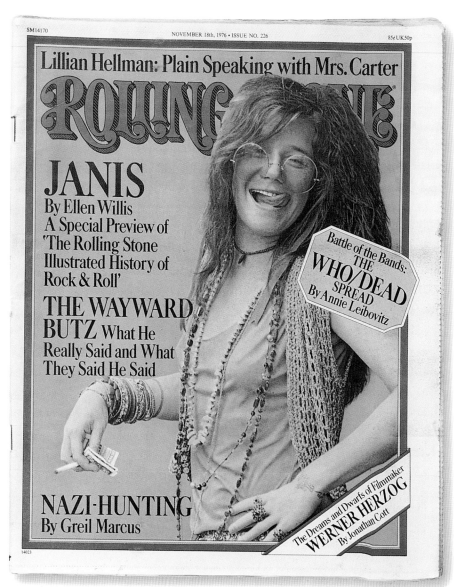

RS 226 | NOVEMBER 18TH, 1976
JANIS JOPLIN
Photograph by DAVID GAHR

JANIS JOPLIN BELONGED to that select group of pop figures who matter as much for themselves as for their music; among American rock performers she was second only to Bob Dylan in importance as a creator/recorder/embodiment of her generation's history and mythology. She was also the only woman to achieve that kind of stature in what was basically a male club, the only Sixties culture hero to make visible and public women's experience of the quest for individual liberation, which was very different from men's. If Janis's favorite metaphors – singing as fucking (a first principle of rock & roll) and fucking as liberation (a first principle of the cultural revolution) – were equally approved by her male peers, the congruence was only on the surface. Underneath – just barely – lurked a feminist (or prefeminist) paradox.

[EXCERPT FROM RS 226 COVER STORY BY ELLEN WILLIS]

SM14170   DECEMBER 2nd, 1976 • ISSUE NO. 227   85¢ UK50p

ROLLING STONE

Linda Ronstadt
The Million-Dollar Woman
THE RAPE OF
Jimi Hendrix
A Scandal of Lawsuits and Laundered Money

THE NATURAL ACTS OF WINTER
Outside!
Adventure by Tim Cahill, Fiction by Michael Rogers, plus Hardware-Software and the Armchair Rambler

14023

SM14170

DECEMBER 16th, 1976 · ISSUE NO. 228

85¢ UK50p

ROLLING STONE

The Law Day Speech of
JIMMY
Carter
Portrait by Leibovitz

RICHARD
Helms
Survival and Sudden
Death in the CIA
By Thomas
Powers

JACKSON
Browne
Say a Prayer
for the Pretender
By Paul Nelson

DANIEL
Schorr
On the Reality of 'Network'

Maffia
76

14023

RS 228 | JACKSON BROWNE | Illustration by DANIEL MAFFIA | DECEMBER 16TH, 1976

RS 229 | DECEMBER 30TH, 1976
WILD THINGS
Illustration by MAURICE SENDAK

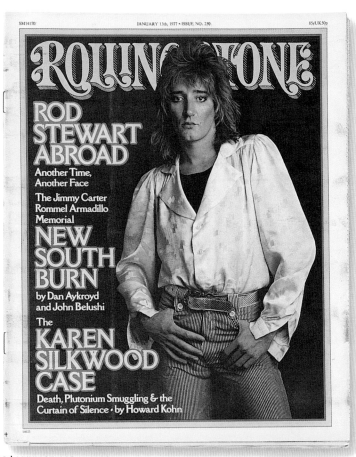

RS 230 | JANUARY 13TH, 1977
ROD STEWART
Photograph by DAVID MONTGOMERY

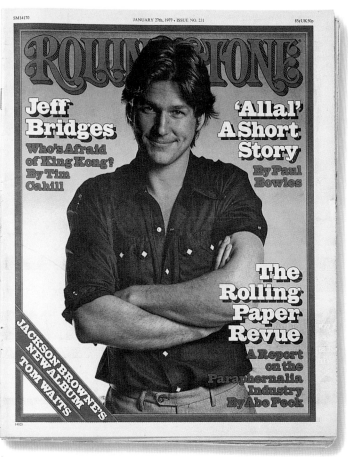

RS 231 | JANUARY 27TH, 1977
JEFF BRIDGES
Photograph by ANNIE LEIBOVITZ

RS 232 | FEBRUARY 10TH, 1977
PETER FRAMPTON
Photograph by ANNIE LEIBOVITZ

SM14170   FEBRUARY 24th, 1977, ISSUE NO. 233   85¢UK50p

ROLLING STONE

Boz Scaggs
The Slow Dancer Who Spun Platinum

Lillian Hellman
A Conversation with the Grande Dame of American Letters

My Life with the Real
King Kong
By Elliott Stein

The Unnatural Disaster of
Hurricane Carter
A Night Bob Dylan Would Rather Forget By Chet Flippo

14023   †

AS WE WRAPPED UP our new album, John McVie came up with a new title for the record: *Rumours*. It was brilliantly apt. It seemed at the time that everyone in the music business in Southern California had the exclusive inside dope about the secret lives of Fleetwood Mac, and no one hesitated to circulate the most scurrilous tales. They said that Stevie was sleeping with me; that Christine had run off with Lindsey; that Stevie was seeing both John and me on alternate Wednesdays; that violent fistfights were commonplace in the studio; that Stevie was definitely leaving the band next Friday; that Stevie had left us months ago, and this was the reason the new album had been delayed; that we were all crippled by mass quantities of alcohol and cocaine; that Stevie practiced black magic and led a coven of witches in the Hollywood Hills; that Fleetwood Mac was a burnt-out case. Tales of flamboyant infidelity and dementia circulated like polluted air. So rampant were the rumors that we sometimes heard them fifth-hand, got worried and had to call each other up to make sure we were still sane and in touch."

~ Mick Fleetwood

"[FLEETWOOD MAC] was sort of a soap opera – who was with whom, someone had just split up with another one. It was as if each one of them was sort of jumping from bed to bed. It seems like they'd all passed through each other's lives yet were still a *band.*" ~ ANNIE LEIBOVITZ

RS 236 | APRIL 7TH, 1977
LILY TOMLIN
Photograph by ANNIE LEIBOVITZ

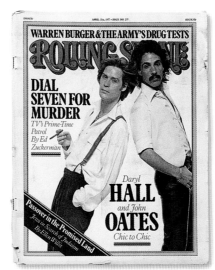

RS 237 | APRIL 21ST, 1977
DARYL HALL & JOHN OATES
Photograph by ANNIE LEIBOVITZ

RS 238 | MAY 5TH, 1977
MARK FIDRYCH
Photograph by ANNIE LEIBOVITZ

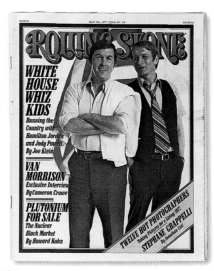

RS 239 | MAY 19TH, 1977
HAMILTON JORDAN & JODY POWELL
Photograph by ANNIE LEIBOVITZ

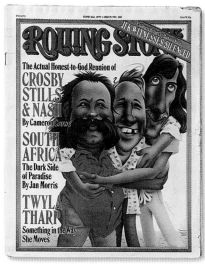

RS 240 | JUNE 2ND, 1977
CROSBY, STILLS & NASH
Illustration by ROBERT GROSSMAN

RS 241 | JUNE 16TH, 1977
ROBERT DE NIRO
Photograph by LEONARD DE RAEMY

SO CROSBY, STILLS AND NASH – CSN – are back together. It's 1977, eight years since their first and only album became a rallying point for a budding Woodstock generation. But now Richard Nixon is out of office, the war is over, marijuana is slowly being "decriminalized," and a Democrat is in the White House. Rock music is bigger business than ever, and artists like Peter Frampton and Fleetwood Mac easily outsell the entire CSN catalogue (with or without Neil Young) with a single album.

And yet Young is back with his band, Crazy Horse, and CSN are back in the studio. Another turn around the wheel...

There was a time in late 1970, with *Déjà Vu* at its peak, when CSNY were just about the American Beatles. The four of them had clear and separate, slightly adversary identities: Crosby, the former Byrd, the political voice, the California dreamer; Nash, the Briton, the former Hollie, the spiritually hungry searcher; Stills, the guitar hero from Buffalo Springfield; and Young, the brooding dark horse from Canada. They were, at once, steeped in mystique and still the guys next door.

"They always had that Judy Garland, tragic American hero aura about them," a former business associate remembers. "It's still going on. Were they strong enough to survive? Would they kill each other? Did they really like their audience? Were they leaders? Was it all for the bucks? Would they fall apart before reaching the top?"

In the end, they did fall apart. In 1970, after less than two years, CSNY shattered into four directions several months after recording the single "Ohio," backed, ironically, with "Find the Cost of Freedom." With the exception of a summer-long reunion tour in 1974, they never got together again. Apart and in partial combinations, their projects were mostly disappointing. But every year or so there was a tease. At least three times they announced attempts to record another CSNY studio album, but each one collapsed in bitterness. In their place, bands like the Eagles, whose members once idolized them, emerged.

And then, two months ago, I got a phone call and invitation from Crosby: "We're doin' it, man. It's CSN, just us this time, and it's coming out. C'mon down and have a listen." A plane flight later, I learned that he was right. For the first time since those nights in 1969, Crosby, Stills and Nash are in harmony. Only one question: Does anybody out there still care?

[EXCERPT FROM RS 240 COVER STORY BY CAMERON CROWE]

Mark Fidrych, 1976's Rookie of the Year, is the only baseball player to appear on the cover of ᚱ Rolling Stone. The six-foot-three Detroit Tigers all-star pitcher – nicknamed "the Bird" for his resemblance to Big Bird from 'Sesame Street' – failed to live up to this early promise. ⊙

SM14170　　　　JUNE 30th, 1977 • ISSUE NO. 242　　　　85¢ UK 50p

ROLLING STONE

Diane Keaton, the Next Hepburn

'Really? Do You Think So? Really? Well, La-De-Dah.' By Ben Fong-Torres

States in Siege

Rhodesia By Jan Morris

The Beatles Live

at the Hollywood Bowl

Last Notes from Home

A Work in Progress By Frederick Exley

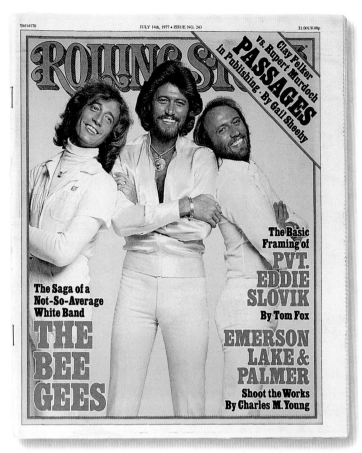

RS 243 | JULY 14TH, 1977
THE BEE GEES
Photograph by FRANCESCO SCAVULLO

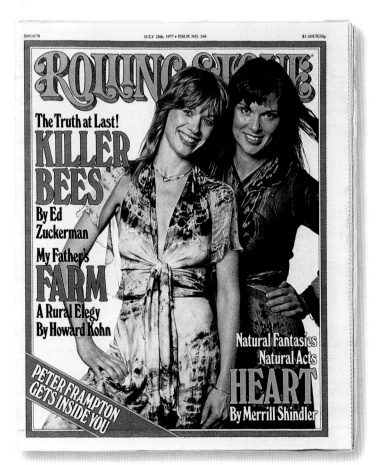

RS 244 | JULY 28TH, 1977
ANN & NANCY WILSON
Photograph by ERIC MEOLA

"**I REMEMBER** at one point glancing in the mirror and once again saying to myself, Will I have to sit in front of this mirror and spend hours putting on makeup for the rest of my life? This is what I have been doing since I was a child, putting this stuff on my face, then going onstage for two or two and a half hours, maybe three at the most and then having to undergo the misery of taking it all off again. It's not any fun, but there's no getting around it. The lights do strange things to the skin, and heavy stage makeup is necessary. So when I'm not working, I try not to wear much makeup. Particularly in the daytime...

Back to the face in the mirror. Who is this looking back at me? A woman, a mother, who with each stroke of the eyeliner, with each brush of the rouge, is transforming into a stage personality. My shoulders are tense. I breathe deeply, searching for relief from the reality in front of me. My mind wanders to distant places, anywhere but here, away from the pressure. When I travel, I love to be invited to use someone's private plane, because that way I can look funky; I don't have to dress up at all. But that isn't always possible. Sometimes I have to walk through public airports where people see me, and there is this expectation that I look a certain way. I have to be Diana Ross, the performer, the star, not Diana, the human being, the mother, the weary traveler. This makes me smile as I write. It is yet another situation where things are not as they appear, where my seemingly glamorous life is really quite difficult."

~ *DIANA ROSS*

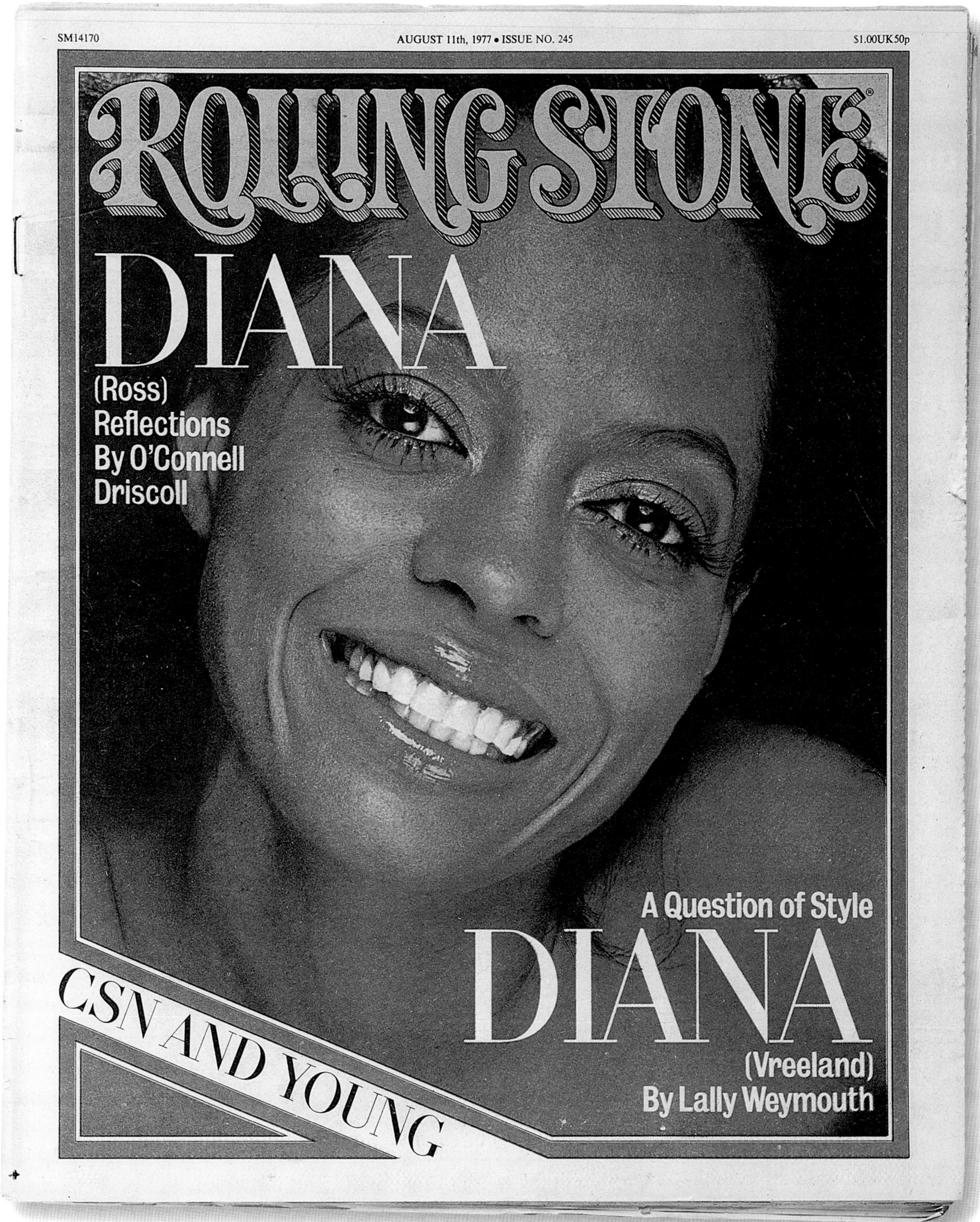

SM14170
AUGUST 11th, 1977 • ISSUE NO. 245
$1.00UK50p
ROLLING STONE
DIANA
(Ross)
Reflections
By O'Connell
Driscoll
A Question of Style
DIANA
(Vreeland)
By Lally Weymouth
CSN AND YOUNG

RS 245 | DIANA ROSS | Photograph by ANNIE LEIBOVITZ | AUGUST 11TH, 1977

SM14170   AUGUST 25th, 1977 • ISSUE NO. 246 $1.00UK.50p

ROLLING STONE

FLEETWOOD MAC Rocks Madison Garden

The Wizard of STAR WARS

An Interview with George Lucas By Paul Scanlon

TED NUGENT'S Bloodlust Rock By Charles Young

DOLLY PARTON

By Chet Flippo

Plus:

Dolly Meets Mr. Universe By Annie Leibovitz

SM14170 SEPTEMBER 8th 1977 • ISSUE NO. 247 $1.00 UK 50p

ROLLING STONE

THE JUICE
OJ Simpson
A Man for
All Seasons
By Tim Cahill

HI-FI '78
Sex Symbols &
Their Sound Effects
10 Super Systems
Betamax:
The Video Wars
Mono Nostalgia
and More

ZEPPELIN DISASTER
EMOTIONS REJOICE

RS 247 | O.J. SIMPSON | Photograph by ANNIE LEIBOVITZ | SEPTEMBER 8TH, 1977

The first football player to grace the cover of ROLLING STONE, O.J. Simpson was dabbling in film and becoming known as the TV spokesman for Hertz; his future notoriety was nearly two decades away.

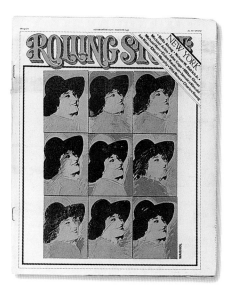

RS 249 | OCTOBER 6TH, 1977
BELLA ABZUG
Illustration by ANDY WARHOL

To celebrate Rolling Stone's relocation to New York City from San Francisco, the magazine devoted the entire feature well to New York and commissioned Andy Warhol to create a cover portrait of mayoral primary candidate Bella Abzug, who contributed her own personal guide to the city (she lost the election, by the way, to Ed Koch). Wrote the editors: "A Columbia University sociologist recently published a study which suggests that people who live in big cities appear to be mentally healthier than those who live in small towns and rural areas. At a time when mere residence in New York was thought to be hazardous to the central nervous system, this study was particularly heartening to us, poised as we were for a great leap across the country to our new offices in midtown Manhattan – after all, Rolling Stone has been coming to you from various funky offices in San Francisco for nearly ten years. . . . It occurred to us that an issue devoted to New York would help us come to grips with what some call the center of the universe and others call the pits, and at the same time announce that we were here." ○

Elvis Presley was generally considered an overweight Las Vegas nightclub throwback by many rock fans when he died on August 16th, 1977. On the other hand, Jann Wenner, determined that the man still mattered, decided to scrap an issue ready for the printer and create a brand-new one in honor of the King. His decision was the right one: The issue sold more copies than any other in the history of Rolling Stone.

E**LVIS WAS THE KING OF ROCK & ROLL** because he was the embodiment of its sins and virtues: grand and vulgar, rude and eloquent, powerful and frustrated, absurdly simple and awesomely complex. He was the King, I mean, in our hearts, which is the place where the music really comes to life. And just as rock & roll will stand as long as our hearts beat, he will always be our King: forever, irreplaceable, corrupt and incorruptible, beautiful and horrible, imprisoned and liberated. And finally, rockin' and free, free at last.

~ DAVE MARSH
[EXCERPT FROM TRIBUTE]

"**I COULD NOT IMAGINE** that guy dying. He was so incredibly important to me, to go on and do what I want to do. When I heard the news it was like somebody took a piece out of me. . . . To me, he was as big as the whole country itself, as big as the whole dream. He just embodied the essence of it and he was in mortal combat with the thing. It was horrible and, at the same time, it was fantastic. Nothing will ever take the place of that guy. Like I used to say when I introduced one of his songs: 'There have been a lotta tough guys. There have been pretenders. There have been contenders. But there is only one King.'"

~ BRUCE SPRINGSTEEN

"**I LAST SAW HIM** last December in Las Vegas. Had a *fantastic* visit, oh, almost two hours, from the time he came off to the time he went back on. We talked about the early days and the recent days. We talked about the people we admired – each other – and people who tried to really perform, from the heart, with soul, as opposed to trying to make commercial records.

I hope people remember the impact – it's not only historical fact, but it's definitely lingering fact."

~ ROY ORBISON

"**I NEVER SAW HIM** in the earlier years . . . he never played in New York until a few years ago, when I saw him at the Garden. He was in good shape, looked real good. The first time I ever heard his music, back in '54 or '55, I was in a car and heard the announcer say, 'Here's a guy who, when he appears onstage in the South, the girls scream and rush the stage.' Then he played 'That's All Right, Mama.' I thought his name was about the weirdest I'd ever heard. I thought for sure he was a black guy.

Later on I grew my hair like him, imitated his stage act – once I went all over New York looking for a lavender shirt like the one he wore on one of his albums. I did stop liking his music pretty early, though. I felt wonderful when he sang 'Bridge Over Troubled Water,' even though it was a touch on the dramatic side – but so was the song."

~ PAUL SIMON

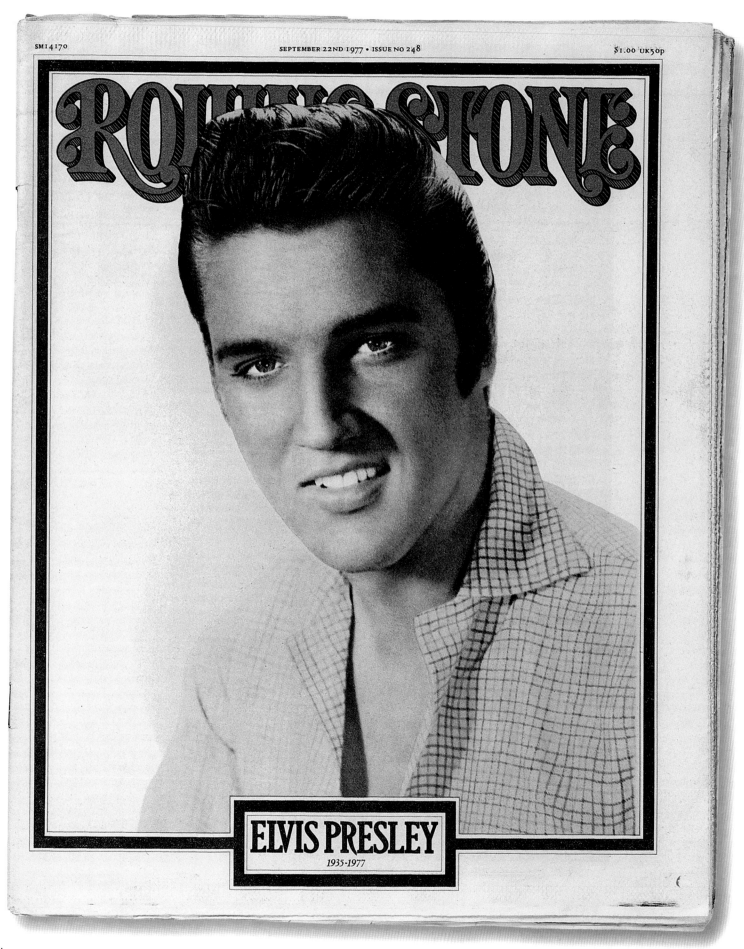

SM14170   SEPTEMBER 22ND 1977 • ISSUE NO 248 $1.00 UK30p

ROLLING STONE

ELVIS PRESLEY
1935-1977

RS 248 | ELVIS PRESLEY | PHOTOGRAPHER UNKNOWN | SEPTEMBER 22ND, 1977

RS 250 | OCTOBER 20TH, 1977
JOHNNY ROTTEN
Photographs by BOB GRUEN, DENNIS MORRIS

A LITTLE BEFORE MIDNIGHT, my taxi arrives at a club called the Vortex. Half a block away ten or twelve teenage boys dressed like horror-movie morticians jump up and down and hit each other. Their hair is short, either greased back or combed to stick straight out with a pomade of Vaseline and talcum powder. Periodically, one chases another out of the pack, grabs the other's arm and twists it until he screams with pain. Then they rush back laughing and leap about some more. Sitting oblivious against a building, a man dressed in a burlap bag nods gently as a large puddle of urine forms between his legs.

Shouting epithets at themselves in a thick proletarian accent, the boys finally bob down the street as another cab pulls up to the entrance. A man with curly, moderately long red hair, a pale face and an apelike black sweater gets out. It is Malcolm McLaren, manager of the Sex Pistols, the world's most notorious punk band, who I have flown from New York to meet and see perform. McLaren has been avoiding me for two days. I introduce myself and suggest we get together soon. He changes the subject by introducing me to Russ Meyer, the soft-core porn king of *Supervixens* and *Beyond the Valley of the Dolls* fame, who is directing the Sex Pistols' movie. "You're a journalist?" asks Meyer. "Do you know Roger Ebert? He won the Pulitzer Prize for film criticism, and he's writing the movie with me. You should talk to him. He's really into tits."

McLaren seizes the opportunity to disappear into the Vortex and is lost to me for the rest of the evening. The dense crowd inside consists of a few curiosity seekers and four hundred to five hundred cadaverous teenagers dressed in black or gray. Often their hair is dyed shades of industrial pink, green and yellow. Several blacks, also drably dressed and with rainbow stripes dyed into their short Afros, speckle the audience. The music over the loudspeakers is about two-thirds shrieking New Wave singles and one-third reggae tunes, which the kids respond to with almost as much enthusiasm as the punk rock. The dancing is frantic as a band called the Slits sets up. The style is called pogo dancing – jumping up and down and flailing one's arms around. It is as far as one can get from the Hustle, and it is the only way one can dance if one is wearing bondage pants tied together at the knees. Most are pogoing alone. Those with partners (usually of the same sex) grasp each other at the neck or shoulders and act like they are strangling each other. Every four or five minutes, someone gets an elbow in the nose and the ensuing punch-out lasts about thirty seconds amid a swirling mass of tripping bodies.

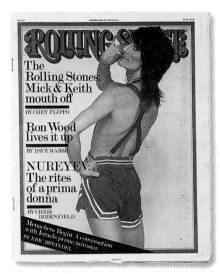

RS 251 | NOVEMBER 3RD, 1977
RON WOOD
Photograph by ANNIE LEIBOVITZ

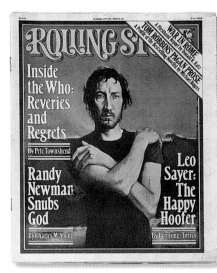

RS 252 | NOVEMBER 17TH, 1977
PETE TOWNSHEND
Illustration by DANIEL MAFFIA

[EXCERPT FROM RS 250 COVER STORY
BY CHARLES M. YOUNG]

"I THINK THE SEX PISTOLS have copped out. Now they're on the front of ROLLING STONE. That's a real cop-out. I mean, if I were Johnny Rotten . . . I wouldn't even talk to ROLLING STONE. I'd tell them to go fuck themselves." ~ *MICK JAGGER*

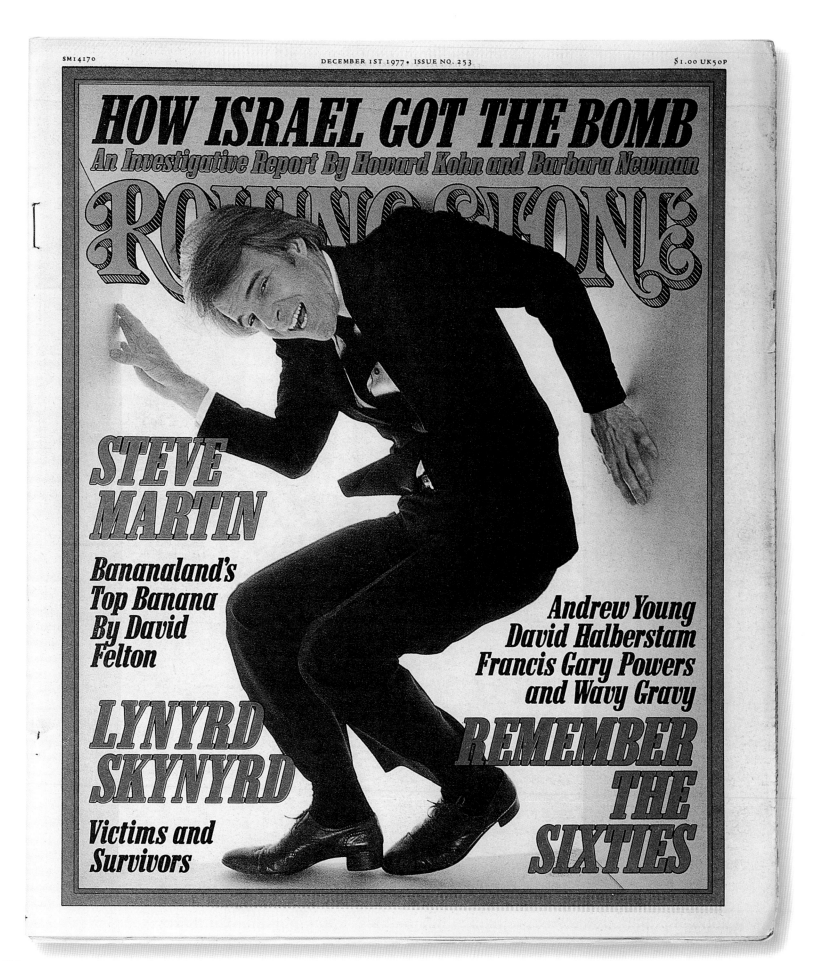

"I REMEMBER Martin Mull sent me a note, and he said, 'Congratulations on being on the cover of ROLLING STONE. Too bad you weren't on when it really meant something.'" ~ STEVE MARTIN

The Tenth Anniversary issue introduces a new logo, drawn by Jim Parkinson. It's based on "Roman and Italic typefaces that revolutionized printing in the Fifteenth Century," according to the editors. The issue's contents include a fifty-page portfolio of Annie Leibovitz's photography from 1970 to 1977. Designer Bea Feitler, previously art director of 'Harper's Bazaar' and 'Ms.,' came aboard to work with art director Roger Black putting together the photo section. Also featured were musings by the magazine's then so-called lifers, Hunter S. Thompson, Dave Marsh, Jon Landau, David Felton, Jonathan Cott and Chet Flippo. ○

CHANGE – the ability to see it and live with it – explains much of what ROLLING STONE is about. In this issue we have yet another change: a new logo. It symbolizes as much as anything what we are up to: respectful of our origins, considerate of new ideas and open to the times to come.

~ JANN S. WENNER

" 'ROLLING STONE' has – from the first – covered events and personalities that are not always a purist's idea of rock & roll. What the purists forget is that 'rock & roll' means much more than just the music. Anyone who ever took those words to heart knows that; knows that there are books and movies and people and events and attitudes that matter more to a rock & roll way of life than do many records that are labeled rock & roll. Jack Kerouac was rock & roll; Bobby Rydell was not. Tom Robbins is rock & roll; Andy Gibb is not. *Star Wars* is rock & roll; *A Star Is Born* is not. . . .

At this very minute, I can hear two other typewriters rattling away: Carl Bernstein is in the next office writing about the CIA, and next door to him John Swenson is hammering out a story on a near breakup of the Beach Boys. Both stories mean a great deal here, and that kind of mixture of subjects under the umbrella of rock & roll is exactly what ROLLING STONE is about."

~ CHET FLIPPO
ASSOCIATE EDITOR

"IN LOOKING OVER the 200-odd issues ROLLING STONE has published so far, we were struck by one common element – the photographs by Annie Leibovitz. Seeing her work together, we realized Annie was the natural anchor for this issue. No writer has appeared in ROLLING STONE as often; very few photographers have assembled such a complete record of this weird decade of rock & roll life. And virtually none has been asked to go back through it all and pick out the best and uncover the outtakes we didn't have the room, the color or the sense to print."

~ ROGER BLACK
ART DIRECTOR

" 'ROLLING STONE' is more than grinding out a magazine every two weeks, converting whole forests to self-serving pulp, exposing innocent lives, laughing at cripples and stomping on budding careers just to make a fast buck. It's people. Presently 101 people work full-time for the magazine, and all of them, practically without exception, are young, gifted, industrious, well groomed and ruggedly individualistic. Also completely nuts. Believe me, I know what I'm talking about; I've worked here for eight years. They are all nuts – maybe not dangerously nuts or dysfunctionally nuts or down-and-out, desperate-and-broken nuts, but they are definitely, certifiably and incorrigibly gonzo cuckoo bananas."

~ DAVID FELTON
ASSOCIATE EDITOR

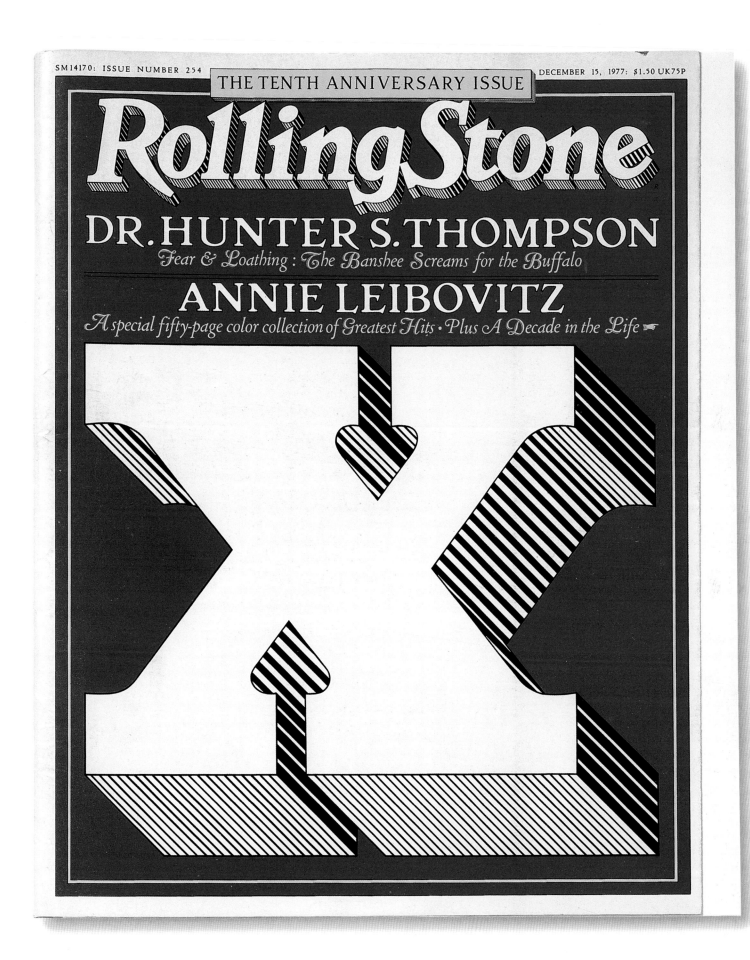

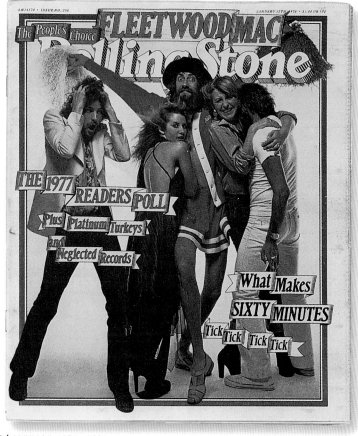

Rock & roll isn't rock & roll anymore.

You're right, there's no more rock & roll. It's an imitation, we can forget about that. Rock & roll has turned itself inside out. I never did do rock & roll, I'm just doing the same old thing I've always done.

You've never sung a rock & roll song?

No, I never have, only in spirit.

You can't really dance to one of your songs.

I couldn't.

Imagine dancing to "Rainy Day Woman #12 & 35." It's kind of alienating. Everyone thought it was about being stoned, but I always thought it was about being alone.

So did I. You could write about that for years. . . . Rock & roll ended with Phil Spector. The Beatles weren't rock & roll either. Nor the Rolling Stones. Rock & roll ended with Little Anthony and the Imperials. Pure rock & roll.

With "Goin' Out of My Head"?

The one before that. Rock & roll ended in 1959.

[EXCERPT FROM BOB DYLAN INTERVIEW BY JONATHAN COTT]

RollingStone

BOB DYLAN

THE ROLLING STONE INTERVIEW BY JONATHAN COTT

STEVEN SPIELBERG TALKS ABOUT HIS CLOSE ENCOUNTERS

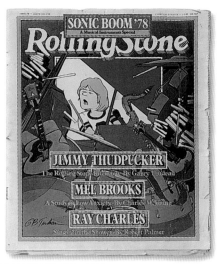

RS 258 | FEBRUARY 9TH, 1978
DOONESBURY'S
JIMMY THUDPUCKER
Illustration by GARRY TRUDEAU

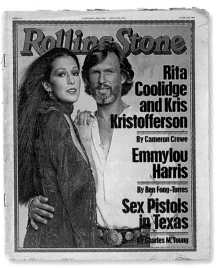

RS 259 | FEBRUARY 23RD, 1978
RITA COOLIDGE &
KRIS KRISTOFFERSON
Photograph by FRANCESCO SCAVULLO

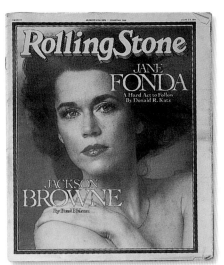

RS 260 | MARCH 9TH, 1978
JANE FONDA
Photograph by ANNIE LEIBOVITZ

RS 261 | MARCH 23RD, 1978
DONNA SUMMER
Photograph by BRIAN LEATART

RS 263 | APRIL 19TH, 1978
THE BEE GEES & PETER FRAMPTON
Illustration by BRUCE WOLFE

RS 262 | APRIL 6TH, 1978
BROOKE SHIELDS
Photograph by MAUREEN LAMBRAY

"WHEN I WAS TWELVE I was on the cover, and it was the first time I'd been on the cover, and I was *thrilled*. I felt so cool and so hip." ~ *BROOKE SHIELDS*

SM14170   MAY 4TH 1978 • ISSUE NO. 264 $1.00 UK 60P

RollingSton

FOREIGNER
JEFFERSON STARSHIP

DR. HUNTER S.
THOMPSON
FEAR AND
LOATHING
IN THE NEAR
ROOM
LAST TANGO
IN VEGAS

ALI

RS 264 | MUHAMMAD ALI | Photograph by ANNIE LEIBOVITZ | MAY 4TH, 1978

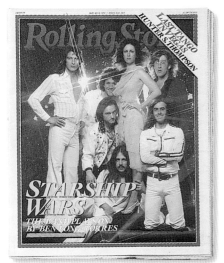

RS 265 | MAY 18TH, 1978
JEFFERSON STARSHIP
Photograph by ANNIE LEIBOVITZ

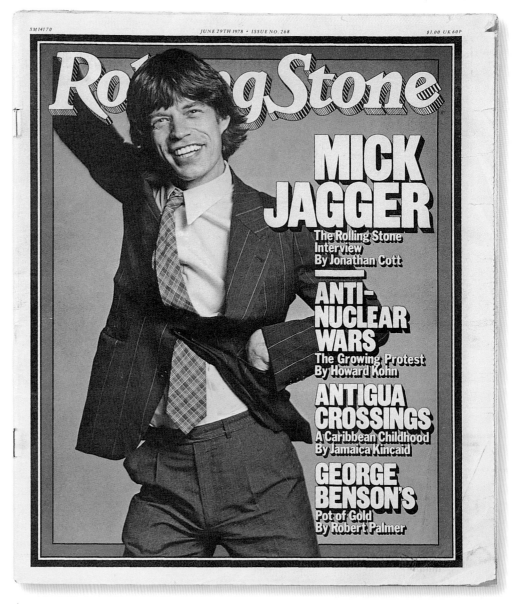

RS 268 | JUNE 29TH, 1978
MICK JAGGER
Photograph by ANNIE LEIBOVITZ

RS 266 | JUNE 1ST, 1978
CARLY SIMON
Photograph by HIRO

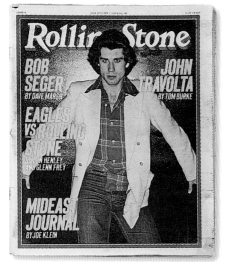

RS 267 | JUNE 15TH, 1978
JOHN TRAVOLTA
Photograph by ANNIE LEIBOVITZ

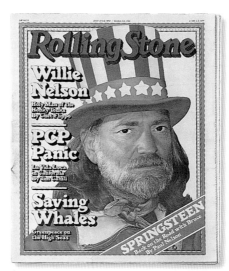

RS 269 | JULY 13TH, 1978
WILLIE NELSON
Photograph by BEVERLY PARKER, Painted by JACK DOONAN

"[THE PATTI SMITH SHOT IS] really a good story on how a lot of planning can be worthless sometimes. I had an assistant come out from California – I was just starting to work with assistants then – and I said to him, 'Listen, I want this huge wall of flame behind Patti Smith, I don't care how you do it.' He said, 'I have it all figured out.' His idea was like this kerosene-soaked net behind her. Needless to say, it lasted about five seconds, because as soon as it burned out, it fell down to the floor. So then we lit big barrels of kerosene and practically burned down the place. I think Patti did get a burn on the back of her *tutu*. The whole backside of her was red.

It's really a lot of fun taking pictures with me. And then I slap them in the mud! And then I hang them from the ceiling! And they say, 'I heard you were hard, Leibovitz. I heard it wasn't easy.' "

~ Annie Leibovitz

SM14170   JULY 27TH 1978 • ISSUE NO. 270 $1.00 UK 60P

Rolli   tone

Patti Smith

CATCHES FIRE
BY CHARLES M. YOUNG

Neil Young's
WORLD TOUR
BY PAUL NELSON

Minnesota Fats
BY ROBERT SABBAG

Olivia Newton-John
BY BEN FONG-TORRES

WALKING THROUGH THE LOBBY of the Marquis last night, just after two a.m., I ran into Bruce, who asked if I wanted to walk over to Ben Frank's for something to eat. On the way I mentioned that there must be a lot of people in line at the Roxy just up the street. Bruce gave me a look. "I don't like people waiting up all night for me," he said.

Bruce ate another prodigious meal: four eggs, toast, a grilled-cheese sandwich, large glasses of orange juice and milk. And the talk ranged widely: surfing (Bruce had lived with some of the Jersey breed for a while in the late Sixties, and he's a little frustrated with trying to give a glimmer of its complexity to a landlocked ho-dad like me), the new album and its live recording ("I don't think I'll ever go back to the overdub method," he said, mentioning that almost all of the LP was done completely live in the studio, and that "Streets of Fire" and "Something in the Night" were first takes). But mostly we talked, or rather, Bruce talked and I listened.

Springsteen can be spellbinding, partly because he is so completely ingenuous, partly because of the intensity and sincerity with which he has thought out his role as a rock star. He delivers these ideas with an air of conviction, but not a proselytizing one; some of his ideas are radical enough for Patti Smith or the punks, yet lack their sanctimonious rhetoric.

I asked him why the band plays so long – their shows are rarely less than three hours – and he said: "It's hard to explain. 'Cause every time I read stuff that I say, like in the papers, I always think I come off sounding like some kind of crazed fanatic. When I read it, it sounds like that, but it's the way I am about it. It's like you have to go the whole way because . . . that's what keeps everything *real*. It all ties in with the records and the values, the morality of the records. There's a certain morality of the show, and it's very strict." Such comments can seem not only fanatical but also self-serving. The great advantage of the sanctimony and rhetoric that infests the punks is that such flaws humanize them. Lacking such egregious characteristics, Bruce Springsteen seems too good to be true when reduced to cold type. Nice guys finish last, we are told, and here's one at the top. So what's the catch? I just don't know.

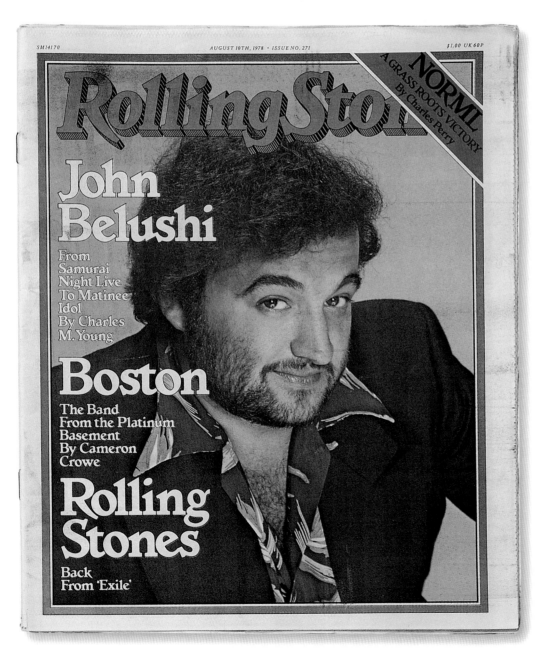

RS 271 | AUGUST 10TH, 1978
JOHN BELUSHI
Photograph by HIRO

[EXCERPT FROM RS 272 COVER STORY
BY DAVE MARSH]

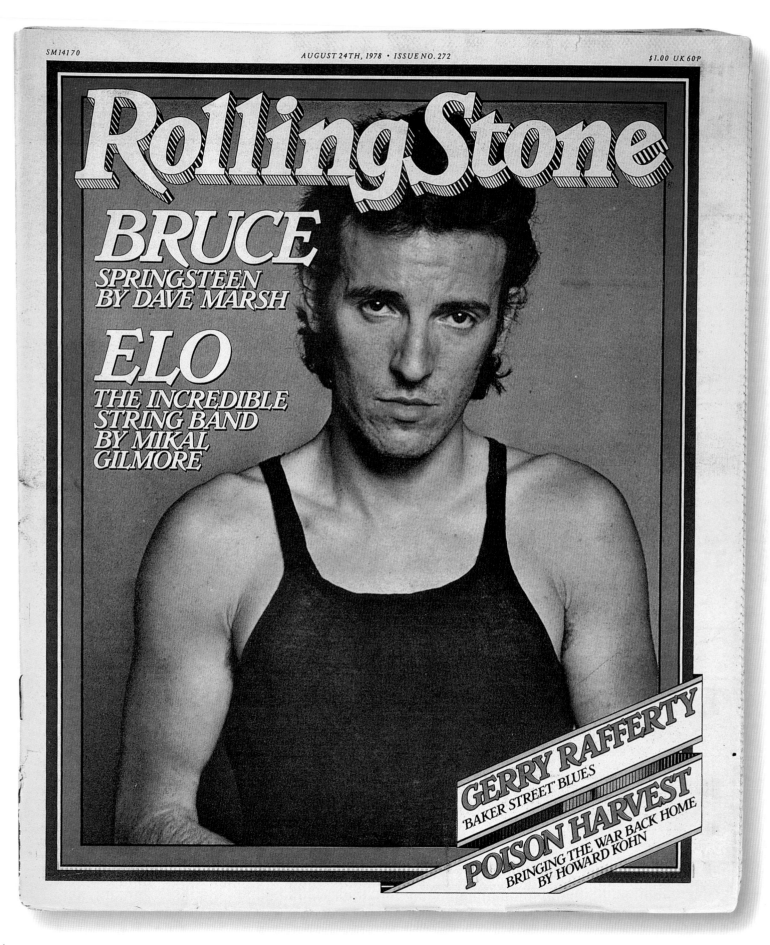

RS 286 | MARCH 8TH, 1979
TED NUGENT
Photograph by BILL KING

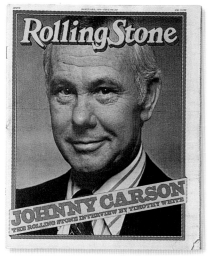

RS 287 | MARCH 22ND, 1979
JOHNNY CARSON
Photograph by ANNIE LEIBOVITZ

"THE IDEA of painting the Blues Brothers blue is too stupid. It's just too stupid. But it's something I've learned to trust: The stupider the idea is, the better it looks. Painting the Blues Brothers blue is as stupid as the Blues Brothers being the Blues Brothers. They were taking themselves so seriously about being musicians, they were forgetting that they were actors and comedians. I mean, Belushi was saying, 'Did you hear Aykroyd on the harp? Better than Paul Butterfield!' And I said, '*Whoa . . .* time to remember who you are.' That's when my job gets a little dangerous. Belushi didn't talk to me for six months. But Aykroyd always knew it was good. I knew it was good, too. It was a healthy thing to do, it was funny."

~ *ANNIE LEIBOVITZ*

RS 288 | APRIL 5TH, 1979
MICHAEL & CAMERON DOUGLAS
Photograph by ANNIE LEIBOVITZ

RS 289 | APRIL 19TH, 1979
THE VILLAGE PEOPLE
Photograph by BILL KING

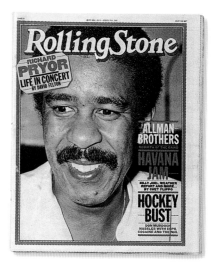

RS 290 | MAY 3RD, 1979
RICHARD PRYOR
Photograph by DAVID ALEXANDER

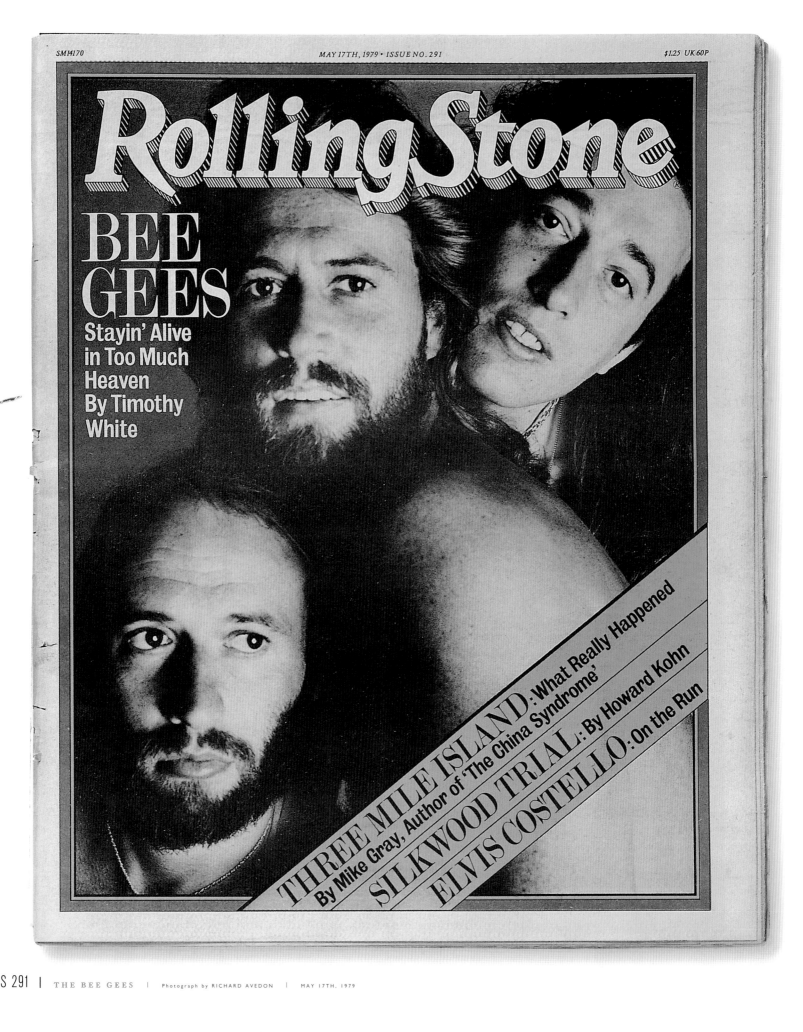

SM14170   MAY 17TH, 1979 • ISSUE NO. 291 $1.25   UK 60P

RollingStone

BEE GEES

Stayin' Alive
in Too Much
Heaven
By Timothy
White

THREE MILE ISLAND: What Really Happened
By Mike Gray, Author of 'The China Syndrome'

SILKWOOD TRIAL: By Howard Kohn

ELVIS COSTELLO: On the Run

RS 292 | MAY 31ST, 1979
JON VOIGHT
Photograph by ANNIE LEIBOVITZ

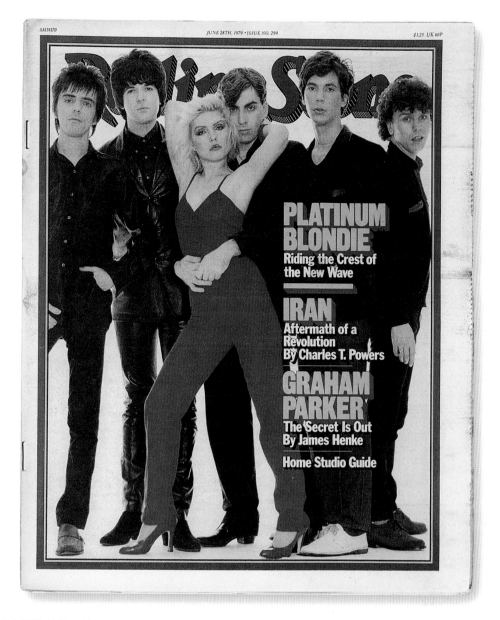

RS 294 | JUNE 28TH, 1979
BLONDIE
Photograph by ANNIE LEIBOVITZ

RS 293 | JUNE 14TH, 1979
CHEAP TRICK
Photograph by ANNIE LEIBOVITZ

RS 295 | JULY 12TH, 1979
PAUL McCARTNEY
Illustration by JULIAN ALLEN

RS 296 | JULY 26TH, 1979
JONI MITCHELL
Photograph by NORMAN SEEFF

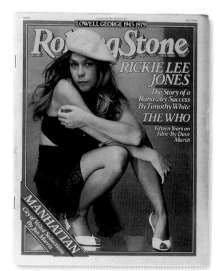

RS 297 | AUGUST 9TH, 1979
RICKIE LEE JONES
Photograph by ANNIE LEIBOVITZ

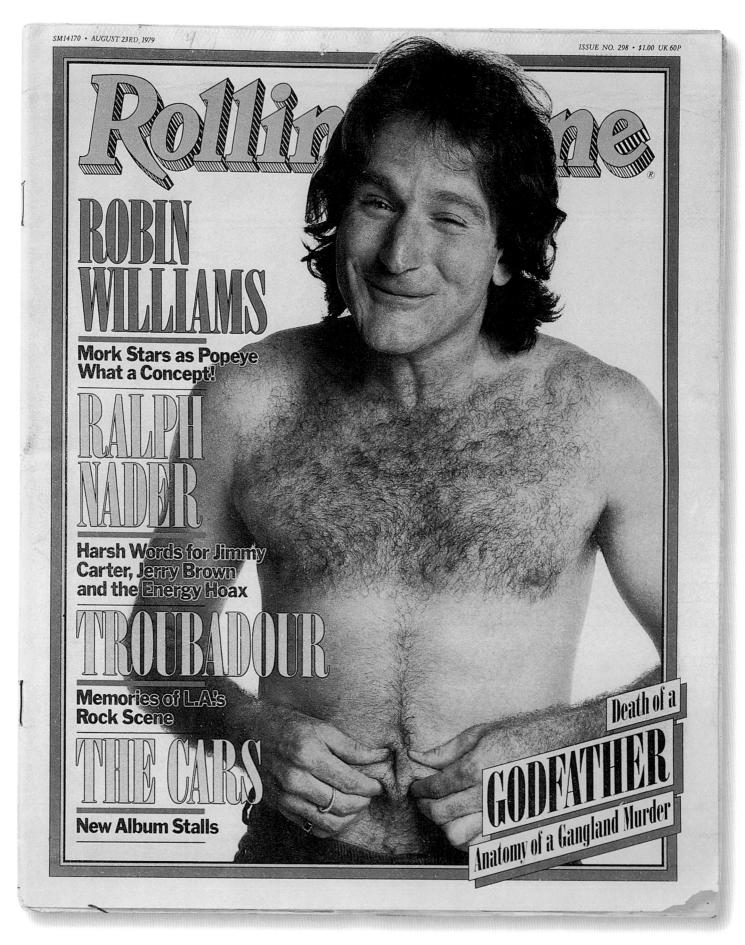

SM14170 • AUGUST 23RD, 1979

ISSUE NO. 298 • $1.00 UK 60P

Rolling Stone

ROBIN WILLIAMS

Mork Stars as Popeye What a Concept!

RALPH NADER

Harsh Words for Jimmy Carter, Jerry Brown and the Energy Hoax

TROUBADOUR

Memories of L.A.'s Rock Scene

THE CARS

New Album Stalls

Death of a GODFATHER
Anatomy of a Gangland Murder

SM14170 • SEPTEMBER 6TH, 1979

$1.25 UK 60P

Rolling Stone

MARIJUANA
Stalking Hawaii's Number One Cash Crop

JAMES TAYLOR

The Rolling Stone Interview By Peter Herbst

REGGIE JACKSON CLOSE UP

Baseball's Most Volatile Player By Roy Blount Jr.

RS 299 | JAMES TAYLOR | Photograph by ANNIE LEIBOVITZ | SEPTEMBER 6TH, 1979

RS 300 | SEPTEMBER 20TH, 1979
THE DOOBIE BROTHERS
Photograph by ANNIE LEIBOVITZ

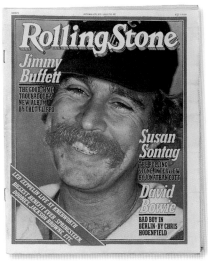

RS 301 | OCTOBER 4TH, 1979
JIMMY BUFFETT
Photograph by ANNIE LEIBOVITZ

RS 302 | OCTOBER 18TH, 1979
SISSY SPACEK
Photograph by ANNIE LEIBOVITZ

RS 303 | NOVEMBER 1ST, 1979
MARTIN SHEEN
Photograph by ANNIE LEIBOVITZ

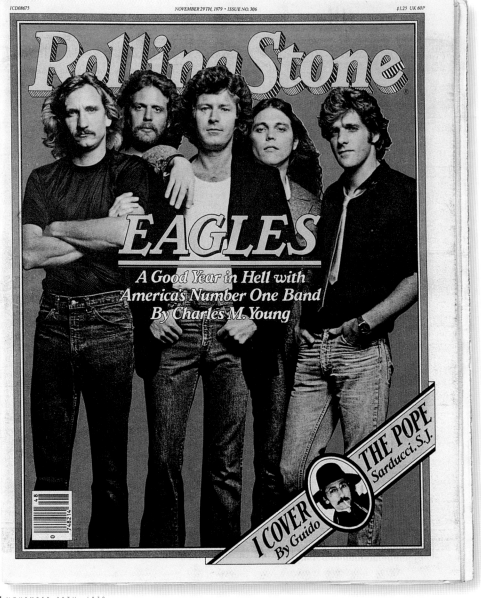

RS 304 | NOVEMBER 15TH, 1979
MUSICIANS UNITED FOR SAFE ENERGY
Photograph by ANNIE LEIBOVITZ

RS 305 | NOVEMBER 29TH, 1979
THE EAGLES
Photograph by NORMAN SEEFF

Check out RS 305. What's wrong with this picture? Look closely at the Eagles' lower extremities. Norman Seeff shot the band against a dark backdrop, so when ROLLING STONE *decided to run the picture using an orange background on the cover, one of the magazine's crack photo strippers had to cut around the band's silhouette. In doing so, he left guitarist Don Felder legless. Though sources deny there was any connection with the goof, the Eagles disbanded (for the first time) shortly thereafter. (Conspiracy theorists take note: In an infamous softball game prior to this cover, the Eagles beat* ROLLING STONE *staffers 15 – 8.)*

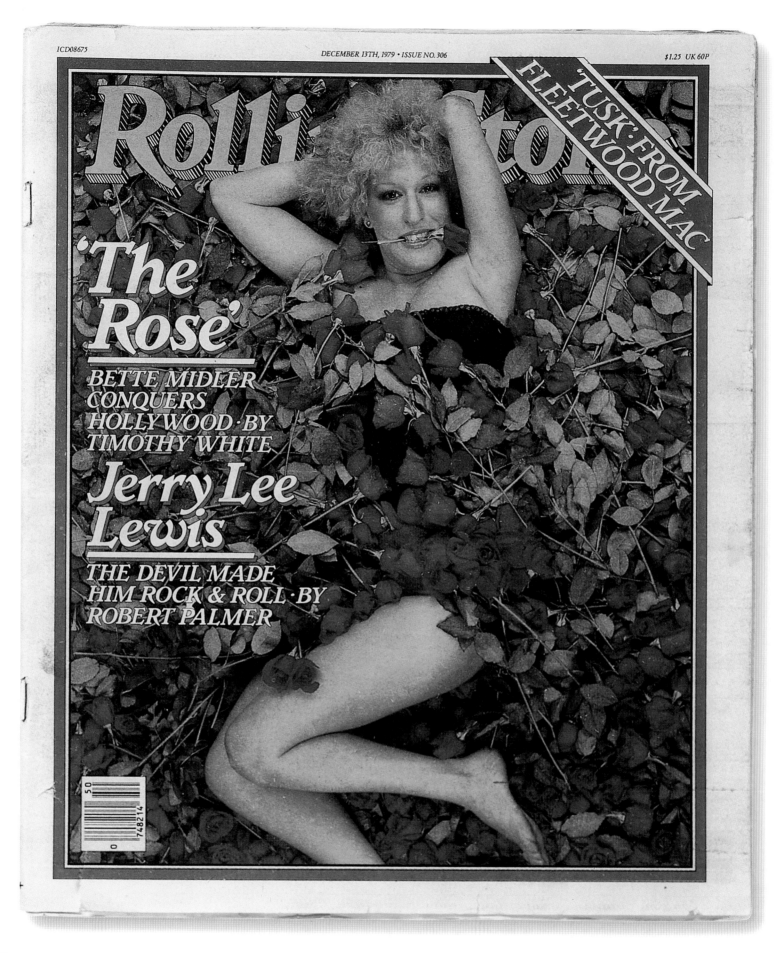

ICD08675 DECEMBER 13TH, 1979 • ISSUE NO. 306 $1.25 UK 60P

Rolling Stone

'TUSK' FROM FLEETWOOD MAC

'The Rose'

BETTE MIDLER CONQUERS HOLLYWOOD · BY TIMOTHY WHITE

Jerry Lee Lewis

THE DEVIL MADE HIM ROCK & ROLL · BY ROBERT PALMER

RS 306 | BETTE MIDLER | Photograph by ANNIE LEIBOVITZ | DECEMBER 13TH, 1979

The 1979 and '80 year-end double issues (RS 307/308 and RS 333/334) do not appear in these pages because they only reprised the year's headlines. The year-end double issues for the years 1981 through 1992 repeated each year's covers, hence their omission. For those who are counting, exactly 728 covers appear in this book. ◌

1980

"It's just a shame that in 1987 there are sixteen-year-olds who have never heard of Janis Joplin or Jimi Hendrix. Look, if Bob Dylan walked into a record company in 1987 and played them 'Subterranean Homesick Blues' and told them it was a hit record, they would show him the door. If Jimi Hendrix came along now, he wouldn't get a deal. The record companies would file him under 'Black and Confused' or 'Out of Tune.'"

~ BONO

RS 309 | JANUARY 24TH, 1980
THE WHO CONCERT TRAGEDY
PHOTOGRAPHERS UNKNOWN

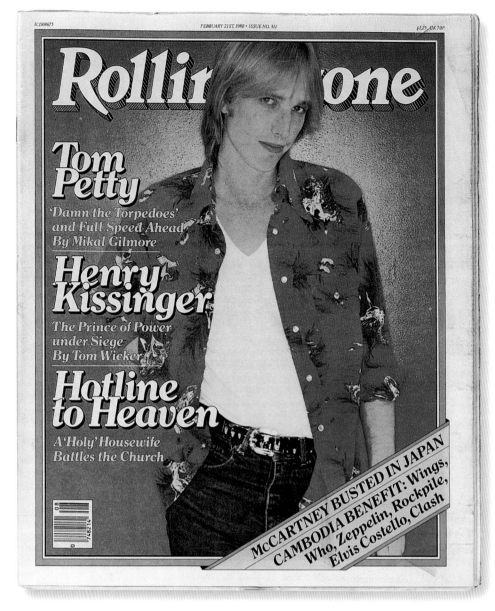

RS 311 | FEBRUARY 21ST, 1980
TOM PETTY
Photograph by ANNIE LEIBOVITZ

RS 310 | FEBRUARY 7TH, 1980
STEVIE NICKS & MICK FLEETWOOD
Photograph by RICHARD AVEDON

"**BEING ON THE COVER** of ROLLING STONE had a certain intangible thing to it – like 'You've arrived.' Those were pretty exciting days, as I remember. They wanted a red theme for the cover because it was Valentine's Day. We were told to bring red clothing, and the only red clothing I had was this red flannel shirt with bird dogs on it that I wore all the time anyway, so I just wore that. I remember Annie [Leibovitz] painting a heart on my bare chest. The shoot was really pleasant, and I liked Annie a lot. It's my favorite one of all the ones [five] I've done. Though when I saw the cover, I was in the hospital having my tonsils out, and I just kind of grunted at it."

~ TOM PETTY

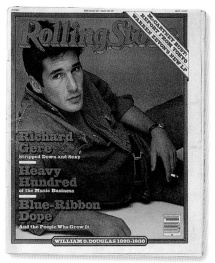

RS 312 | MARCH 6TH, 1980
RICHARD GERE
Photograph by TERRY O'NEILL

RS 313 | MARCH 20TH, 1980
BOB HOPE
Photograph by RICHARD AVEDON

RS 314 | APRIL 3RD, 1980
LINDA RONSTADT
Photograph by ANNIE LEIBOVITZ

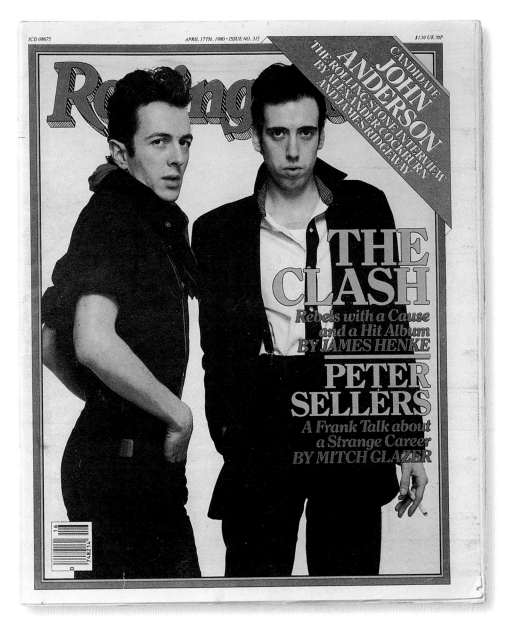

RS 315 | APRIL 17TH, 1980
JOE STRUMMER & MICK JONES
Photograph by ANNIE LEIBOVITZ

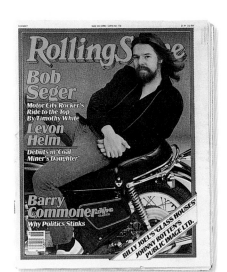

RS 316 | MAY 1ST, 1980
BOB SEGER
Photograph by ANNIE LEIBOVITZ

RS 317 | MAY 15TH, 1980
ANN & NANCY WILSON
Photograph by ANNIE LEIBOVITZ

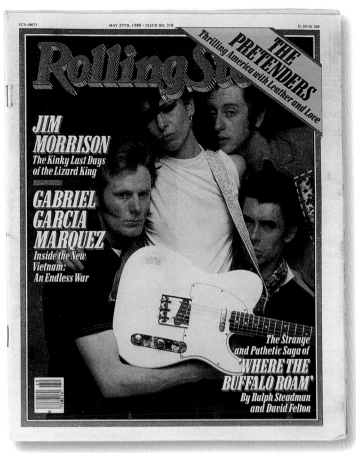

"IF I WAS STARTING out now, I probably wouldn't even want to be in a rock band because of [photo shoot] stylists, hair and makeup – all that. Back in my day, if a stylist told you what to wear [for a photo], you'd hear a resounding 'Fuck off' throughout the room. The whole idea of being in a band was that you could be exactly the way you were. And no one was going to suggest, govern or dictate to you anything. So therefore you could make ugly cool, just by sticking to it."

~ *CHRISSIE HYNDE*

*   *   *   *   *   *   *

"IN BRITAIN, at the moment, we've got 2-Tone, we've still got punk, we've got Mod bands, we've got heavy-metal bands, we've got established supergroups, we've got all kinds of *different* families of music – *each* of which takes an enormous amount of adjustment. They're intense, and very socially . . . jagged. They don't fit neatly into existing society: They challenge it. . . .

When you listen to the Sex Pistols, to "Anarchy in the U.K." and "Bodies" and tracks like that, what immediately strikes you is that *this is actually happening.* This is a bloke, with a brain on his shoulders, who is actually saying something he *sincerely* believes is happening in the world, saying it with real venom and real passion. It touches you, and it scares you – it makes you feel uncomfortable. It's like somebody saying, 'The Germans are coming! And there's no way we're gonna stop 'em!' . . .

You read the fucking words, they scare the shit out of you. The Pretenders – Chrissie Hynde's got a sweet voice, but she writes in double-speak: She's talking about getting laid by Hell's Angels on her latest record! And *raped.* The words are full of the most *brutal,* head-on feminism that has ever come out of any band, anywhere . . ."

~ *PETE TOWNSHEND*

[EXCERPT FROM RS 320 COVER STORY BY GREIL MARCUS]

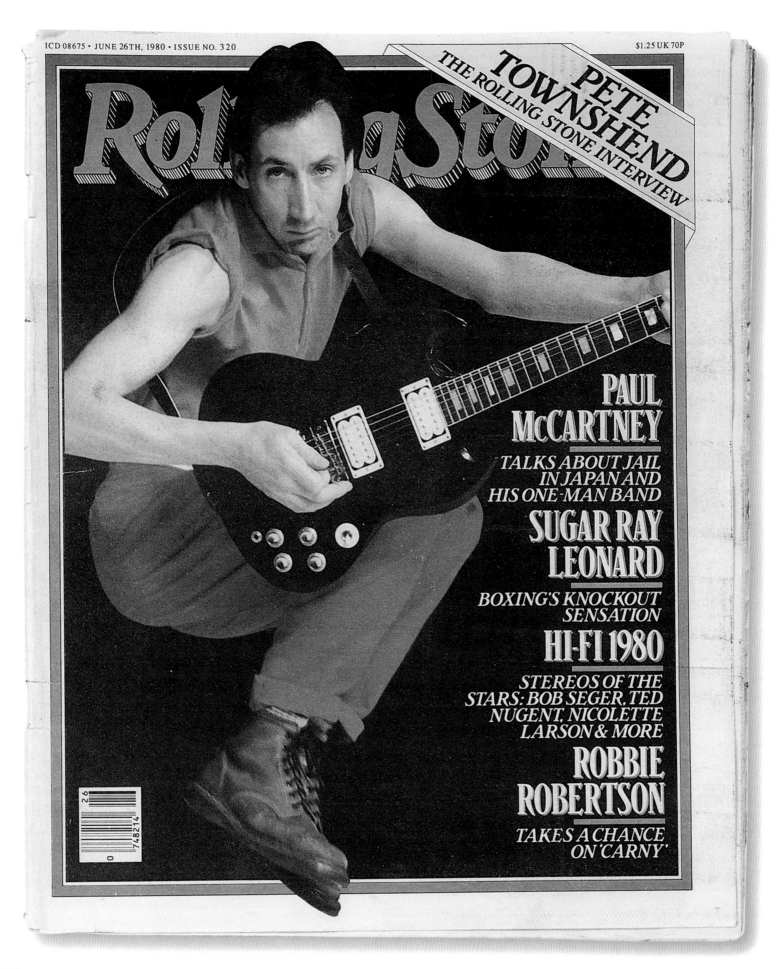

ICD 08675 • JUNE 26TH, 1980 • ISSUE NO. 320

$1.25 UK 70P

Rolling Stone

PETE TOWNSHEND
THE ROLLING STONE INTERVIEW

PAUL, McCARTNEY

TALKS ABOUT JAIL IN JAPAN AND HIS ONE-MAN BAND

SUGAR RAY LEONARD

BOXING'S KNOCKOUT SENSATION

HI-FI 1980

STEREOS OF THE STARS: BOB SEGER, TED NUGENT, NICOLETTE LARSON & MORE

ROBBIE ROBERTSON

TAKES A CHANCE ON 'CARNY'

RS 320 | PETE TOWNSHEND | Photograph by ANNIE LEIBOVITZ | JUNE 26TH, 1980

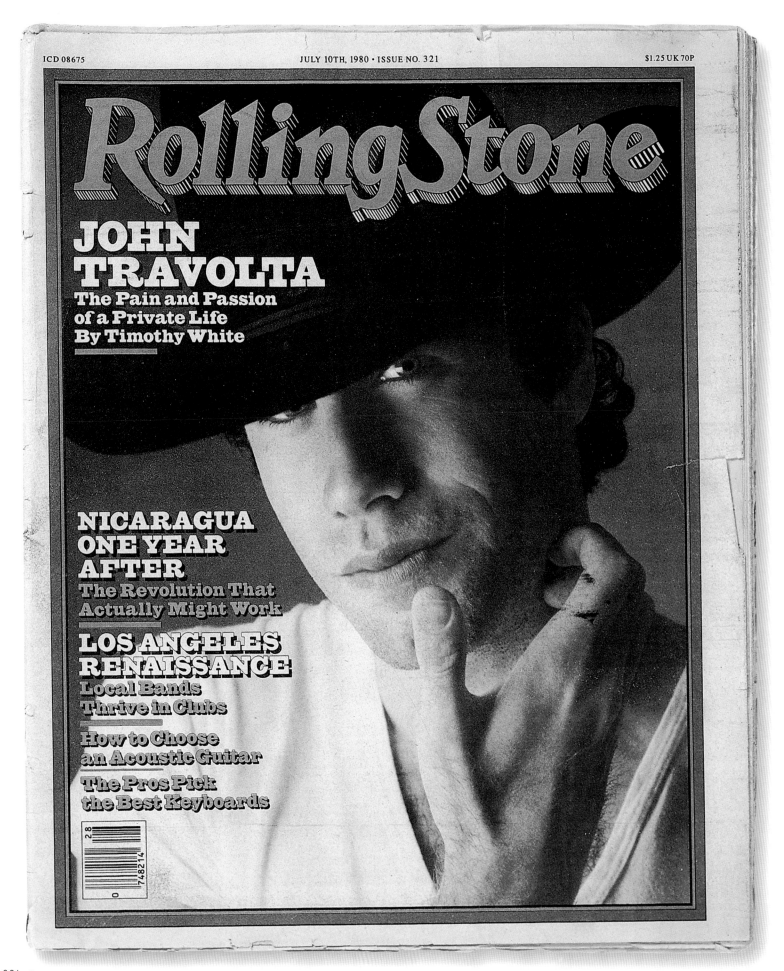

ICD 08675   JULY 10TH, 1980 · ISSUE NO. 321 $1.25 UK 70P

RollingStone

JOHN TRAVOLTA
**The Pain and Passion
of a Private Life
By Timothy White**

NICARAGUA ONE YEAR AFTER
**The Revolution That
Actually Might Work**

LOS ANGELES RENAISSANCE
**Local Bands
Thrive in Clubs**

**How to Choose
an Acoustic Guitar**

**The Pros Pick
the Best Keyboards**

RS 322 | JULY 24TH, 1980
CAST OF 'THE EMPIRE STRIKES BACK'
Photograph by ANNIE LEIBOVITZ

RS 323 | AUGUST 7TH, 1980
JACKSON BROWNE
Photograph by ANNIE LEIBOVITZ

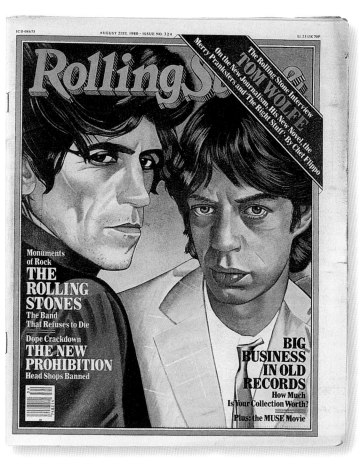

RS 324 | AUGUST 21ST, 1980
KEITH RICHARDS & MICK JAGGER
Illustration by JULIAN ALLEN

RS 325 | SEPTEMBER 4TH, 1980
BILLY JOEL
Illustration by KIM WHITESIDES

RS 326 | SEPTEMBER 18TH, 1980
RODNEY DANGERFIELD
Photograph by ANNIE LEIBOVITZ

RS 327 | OCTOBER 2ND, 1980
ROBERT REDFORD
Photograph by ANNIE LEIBOVITZ

RS 328 | OCTOBER 16TH, 1980
PAT BENATAR & NEIL GERALDO
Photograph by ANNIE LEIBOVITZ

RS 329 | OCTOBER 30TH, 1980
THE CARS
Photograph by ANNIE LEIBOVITZ

RS 330 | NOVEMBER 13TH, 1980
MARY TYLER MOORE
Photograph by ANNIE LEIBOVITZ

RS 331 | NOVEMBER 27TH, 1980
**JILL CLAYBURGH &
MICHAEL DOUGLAS**
Photograph by ANNIE LEIBOVITZ

ICD 08675   DECEMBER 11TH, 1980 • ISSUE NO. 332 $1.50 UK 70P

RollingStone

THE UNSINKABLE
DOLLY PARTON
Bursts into the Movies
By Chet Flippo

B-52'S
What Makes This Tacky Little Dance Band Tick?

PEKING GIRL
A Tender Encounter with a Victim of the Gang of Four

KENNY STABLER
Peter Gent Sacks Houston's Elusive Quarterback

THE HITMAKERS
A REPORT ON THE MOST
SENSITIVE SECRET IN THE
RECORD BUSINESS

RS 332 | DOLLY PARTON | Photograph by RICHARD AVEDON | DECEMBER 11TH, 1980

"I REMEMBER ARRIVING at the apartment that morning, December 8th, and John taking me aside and saying, 'Listen, I know they want to run me by myself on the cover, but I really want Yoko to be on the cover with me. It's really important.' They had just finished their *Double Fantasy* album, and I remember seeing the cover and being very *moved* by it, so of course when they lay down together, and John was nude curled up against her clothed, it was much more poignant. He looked much more vulnerable. I remember peeling the Polaroid and him looking at it and saying, 'This is it. This is our relationship.'

Several hours later John was murdered. I went to the Roosevelt Hospital waiting for an announcement. Early in the morning, the doctor came out – I remember that I was completely numb – I stood on a chair and I photographed the doctor giving the death announcement. I came in [to ROLLING STONE] the following day, and they were mocking up covers with John's portrait [close-ups of his face] and I said, 'Jann, I promised John that the cover would be him and Yoko.' And Jann backed me up. I said it was the last promise. Still, you can talk about this picture over and over and over again, but it's very emotional."

~ ANNIE LEIBOVITZ

ED 08675 · JANUARY 22ND, 1981 · $1.50 UK80P

RS 335 | JOHN LENNON & YOKO ONO | Photograph by ANNIE LEIBOVITZ | JANUARY 22ND, 1981

"Man shot, One West Seventy-second" was the call on the police radio just before eleven p.m. Officers Jim Moran and Bill Gamble were in the third blue-and-white that screamed to a halt outside the Dakota apartment building. The man who had been shot couldn't wait for an ambulance. They stretched him out on the backseat of their car and raced to Roosevelt Hospital, at the corner of Fifty-ninth Street and Ninth Avenue. They lifted the bloody body onto a gurney and wheeled it into the emergency room. There was nothing the doctors could do. They pronounced John Lennon dead at 11:07 p.m. . . .

Within minutes, the small, brick-walled ambulance courtyard outside the emergency room was filled with at least two hundred people who were staring dumbly at the closed double doors. . . . Some of the cabdrivers, who were depositing reporters at the rate of two or three a minute, joined the throng. One of them volunteered loudly that he had it from a good source that John Lennon had been dead on arrival. One young woman stood alone in the middle of Ninth Avenue and wept.

~ CHET FLIPPO

[EXCERPT FROM RS 335]

"IT WAS OBVIOUS that John had so many talents that he could have gone any way he wanted. But he wasn't as cynical as lots of people thought; he was just honest and straightforward, and he wouldn't stand for phoniness. He used to get the biggest kick out of some of the reviews for *A Hard Day's Night.* Writers would scrutinize the movie, find all kinds of symbolism and deep significance. John thought it was hilarious, because he knew the movie was just a comedy."

~ WALTER SHENSON
['A HARD DAY'S NIGHT' AND 'HELP!' PRODUCER]

* * * * *

"I MET THE BEATLES around 1962, when I was touring Germany; those boys were my intermission band in Hamburg and Stuttgart. They'd hurry in during intermission and play a few songs to keep things warmed up. There was no way of knowing that in a year they were gonna change the world, but they sounded good and were nice guys. Backstage afterward, we would sit and bullshit and say we loved each other's music – the typical thing that people in our musical brotherhood all do. See, we were just common people, working together.

As for John Lennon, I was spellbound and hurt and upset when he died, because he was a brilliant musician, and I respected what the man stood for. John Lennon was one of our own, and losing him just makes me mad as shit. We've got to have some damned gun-control laws, and psychiatrists should examine the people who buy them. Hell, anything that can kill people should be controlled; it's easier to get a gun in this country than a driver's license."

~ RAY CHARLES

"We have lost a genius of the spirit."

~ Norman Mailer

S FAR AS I CAN TELL from the daily papers, his last word was "Yeah." In the police car that took him to the emergency room, someone asked him if he was John Lennon, and he said "Yeah." There are compilations of the last words of the great and the famous, and some of them are real rousers. Yet John Lennon's simple syllable allows me to lean closer to the true and absolute reality of life running out, death hurtling forward, because with John Lennon, we somehow knew everything he meant, everything he implied: the sudden thrusts of meaning, the cast of his eye, the silences.

His death is everywhere. Like his life and his art, it is a unifying force. The astonishing – and for me, unduplicated – characteristic of his art was that it brought together people who may have had no other single thing in common. It was the only true mass phenomenon that's ever touched me. Through the Beatles – and, I think, primarily through John – I was able to share with millions my thoughts and their thoughts – *our thoughts* – about growing old, falling in love, seizing happiness, transcendence. A genius is a connector of theretofore disparate elements. A genius can take an orange and a chunk of coal and create a unity. A genius like John Lennon can create a community of hearts and minds from ten million separate appetites. Part of the grief we feel about his murder is our longing to once more belong to something larger than ourselves, to feel our heart beat in absolute synchrony with hearts everywhere.

He had a magnificent life. He fell deeply in love and knew enough about the heart and its lazy habits to never allow his essential connections to go stale. Like other great artists, he was a teacher. He taught us something about integrity. And risk. He taught us about speaking up against injustice. And he is an integral part of my most extravagant, far-flung dreams about the potential power of art. It is no inspiring feat to capture the attention of millions – *Dallas* can do that. But to capture the *imagination* of millions is an accomplishment on a wholly different scale. It is mythic. . . . He proved that you can follow your vision, explore your talents, speak your mind – take any leap you dare. In a cautious age, John Lennon was uninterested in existing on any but his own terms. He sang and wrote what he believed, and he trusted us to listen. And he was right: We listened.

~ Scott Spencer

[EXCERPT FROM RS 335]

THE BEATLES and their fans played out an image of utopia, of a good life, and the image was that one could join a group and by doing so not lose one's identity as an individual but find it: find one's own voice. . . . At the heart of this cheeky, joyful, shining utopia was romanticism: the best account of pop hopes and dreams anyone had ever heard. But that utopia was grounded – by John Lennon – in wit, worry, contingency, doubt and struggle. John Lennon was part of the pleasure principle of the Beatles; no one who has heard him sing "Eight Days a Week" could miss that. But he was also the reality principle of the Beatles, and that is why so many became obsessed with him. If the Beatles were a common adventure, John Lennon was its point man and its center. It was John Lennon who was never satisfied with pop rewards, who kept questions open and alive while the Beatles continued – What is the group for? What can it do? When must it be abandoned? – and it was John Lennon who, once the Beatles ended, sustained the struggle over an image of utopia. . . .

~ Greil Marcus

[EXCERPT FROM RS 335]

* * * * *

MORE THAN any other rock musician (with the possible exception of Bob Dylan), John Lennon personalized the political and politicized the personal, often making the two stances interchangeable but sometimes ripping out the seams altogether. Whereas Dylan expressed his personal and political iconoclasm mainly by expanding and exploding the narrative line (thus forcing the melody to accommodate a torrent of language and imagery), Lennon assaulted pop music from a dozen different directions. He not only attacked the war – *any* war – but questioned and confronted the very methods and structures he'd utilized in his attack, thereby pushing rock & roll up against the wall to test limits and demand answers. John Lennon believed passionately that popular music could and should do more than merely entertain, and by acting out this conviction, he changed the face of rock & roll forever. By taking such huge risks, he sometimes failed or seemed silly. Yet, in retrospect, even his failures take on the glow of nobility: The fact that he *cared* so much shines through his occasional shortcomings.

~ Stephen Holden

[EXCERPT FROM RS 335]

ICD 08675 • ISSUE NO. 336 • FEBRUARY 5TH, 1981 • $1.50 UK 80P

Walter Cronkite on Himself ▪ Mean Fiction by Jayne Anne Phillips ▪ Libyan Assassins in America

RollingSto

BRUCE SPRINGSTEEN
and the Secret of the World

RS 336 | BRUCE SPRINGSTEEN | Photograph by ANNIE LEIBOVITZ | FEBRUARY 5TH, 1981

In discussing ROLLING STONE with Jann Wenner, Mick Jagger implies that the logo lost its character when it lost its balls. Hence the introduction of a redesigned logo by typographer Jim Parkinson combining elements of the previous logos. In addition, glossy paper and trimmed pages replace rough-edged newsprint, and the cover's dimensions decrease to 10 by 12 inches, the size it has remained ever since. ○

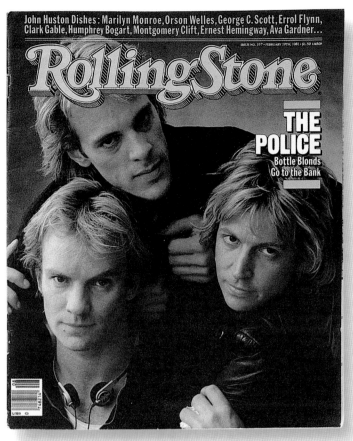

RS 337 | FEBRUARY 19TH, 1981
THE POLICE
Photograph by KLAUS LUCKA

RS 338 | MARCH 5TH, 1981
GOLDIE HAWN
Photograph by DENIS PIEL

RS 339 | MARCH 19TH, 1981
WARREN ZEVON
Photograph by ANNIE LEIBOVITZ

RS 340 | APRIL 2ND, 1981
ROMAN POLANSKI
Illustration by JULIAN ALLEN

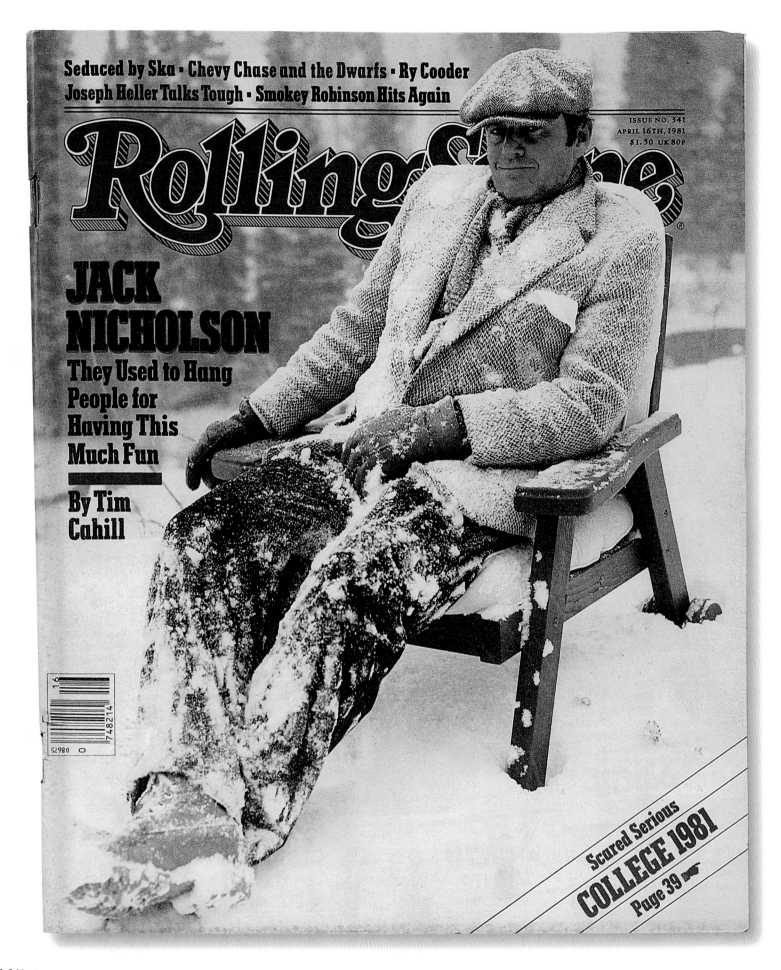

Seduced by Ska · Chevy Chase and the Dwarfs · Ry Cooder
Joseph Heller Talks Tough · Smokey Robinson Hits Again

Rolling Stone

ISSUE NO. 341
APRIL 16TH, 1981
$1.50   UK 80P

JACK NICHOLSON

They Used to Hang People for Having This Much Fun

By Tim Cahill

Scared Serious
COLLEGE 1981
Page 39

RS 341 | JACK NICHOLSON | Photograph by ALBERT WATSON | APRIL 16TH, 1981

Albert Watson traveled to Jack Nicholson's house in Aspen, Colorado, for this cover shot. When snow started falling hard, the actor asked Watson to leave him alone outdoors for fifteen minutes. Nicholson, by the way, had just completed work on 'The Shining,' in which his character freezes to death. Perhaps still in character, Nicholson waited until he had slightly more than a dusting before getting his photo taken. ○

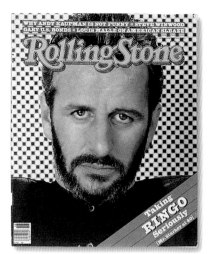

RS 342 | APRIL 30TH, 1981
RINGO STARR
Photograph by MICHAEL CHILDERS

RS 344 | MAY 28TH, 1981
SUSAN SARANDON
Photograph by ALBERT WATSON

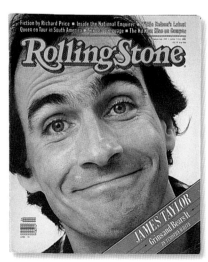

RS 345 | JUNE 11TH, 1981
JAMES TAYLOR
Photograph by AARON RAPOPORT

MIDNIGHT, Saturday night. After I came clean with the cop and told him I was a reporter working on a story, he volunteered to put me in touch with a black-market gun dealer. The meeting place was the gunrunner's car in a motel parking lot. He patted me down for a hidden mike and then we drove around aimlessly, until he was satisfied there was no tail. He spoke with a Brooklyn accent, but his guns were from Florida – RG guns, the brand John Hinckley used.

The triggers and barrels and cylinders are imported from Germany and assembled in Miami, where labor is cheap. The RG Industries factory is a small whitewashed structure that looks as if it has been thrown up, ready to be abandoned at a moment's notice. Approximately 350,000 guns are assembled there each year.

"I don't buy right out of the factory. I buy wholesale," the gunrunner said. "I got a connect." He showed me a large metal-frame suitcase. Ziplock plastic bags were arranged by size among three dividers, and inside each bag was an RG Special. He conducts his business from motel rooms. Three or four times a week he changes locations – and jurisdictions – in the suburbs around Washington. You have to find him. A lot of people do. "You betcha," he said. "Some of my best customers are cabbies."

What if Congress were to pass a federal law like the one in D.C.? "Suits me. Business would go sky-high. I'd have to open franchises." How big is the black market today? A grin. No answer. Is the mob involved? "Not with me, no way. But look, you go ahead and get gun control passed and the mob's gonna be all over this business like flies over candy." He says he's a pessimist. Guns are part of America. Go ahead, shut down RG Industries, lock up the gunrunners, legislate and confiscate all you want, and there will still be guns. Zip guns made from car aerials. Starter pistols with the barrels hollowed out and the gas ports covered with Silly Putty and needles for ammo. Shotguns fashioned from pipes, rubber bands, blocks of wood, firing nails. On the black market, the quality of merchandise varies, but prices tend to level out. The RG guns are bottom-of-the-line – sometimes defective – Saturday-night specials. But you can buy a Smith & Wesson as well. About $100 is added to the price of all guns, to pay the dealer's expenses and allow him a profit margin. Statistically, in gun crimes, quality merchandise is used as often as junk. As the National Rifle Association will tell you, all guns are equal before the Constitution.

[EXCERPT FROM RS 343 COVER STORY BY HOWARD KOHN]

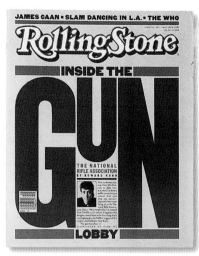

RS 343 | MAY 14TH, 1981
GUN CONTROL & JOHN LENNON
Photograph by ANNIE LEIBOVITZ

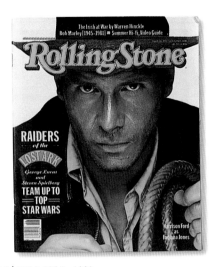

RS 346 | JUNE 25TH, 1981
HARRISON FORD
Photograph by BILL KING

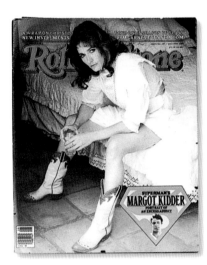

RS 347 | JULY 9TH, 1981
MARGOT KIDDER
Photograph by DENIS PIEL

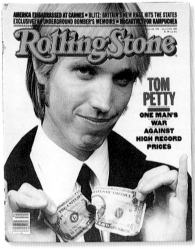

RS 348 | JULY 23RD, 1981
TOM PETTY
Photograph by AARON RAPOPORT

RS 349 | AUGUST 6TH, 1981
RICKIE LEE JONES
Photograph by ANNIE LEIBOVITZ

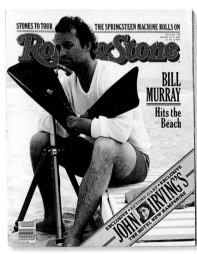

RS 350 | AUGUST 20TH, 1981
BILL MURRAY
Photograph by ANDREA BLANCH

RS 351 | SEPTEMBER 3RD, 1981
STEVIE NICKS
Photograph by ANNIE LEIBOVITZ

ROLLING STONE'S most famous (or infamous) cover line ran with a 1968 photograph of Jim Morrison taken by his lover/confidante, longtime '16' magazine editor Gloria Stavers. During her stint (from 1957 to 1975) at the preeminent teen 'zine, Stavers – who would die two years after this issue, in 1983, of lung cancer – practically invented provocative cover lines. She was also an early champion of ROLLING STONE, writing a feature in '16' about the new rock rag not long after it began publication and later giving Jann Wenner advice about rock photography.

As for ROLLING STONE'S cover line, a handful of staffers have taken credit for writing it, and, simply put, it works. As the cover story detailed, a full ten years after Morrison's death, Doors records were selling better than ever, hordes of kids were making the pilgrimage to his grave in Paris's Père-Lachaise cemetery and the lead singer's poetry was being revered. ○

*   *   *   *   *

"**I WAS FIGHTING** the record industry to keep prices down to $8.98. So ROLLING STONE wanted me in a suit and tie [for RS 348] to reflect some kind of corporate angle. It really looked silly to me – like my head had been cut off and pasted onto another body. I was not really all that comfortable with it. But Mick Jagger told me not long afterwards that that cover had helped them. The Stones really wanted to keep the price down on their upcoming record, and they were at a meeting about it, and someone brought that cover in, and it helped to resolve the whole argument. It really did hold prices down for quite a while after that. I was sort of proud of that – it's a case of using your position to speak to the masses and send your opinion out."

~ TOM PETTY

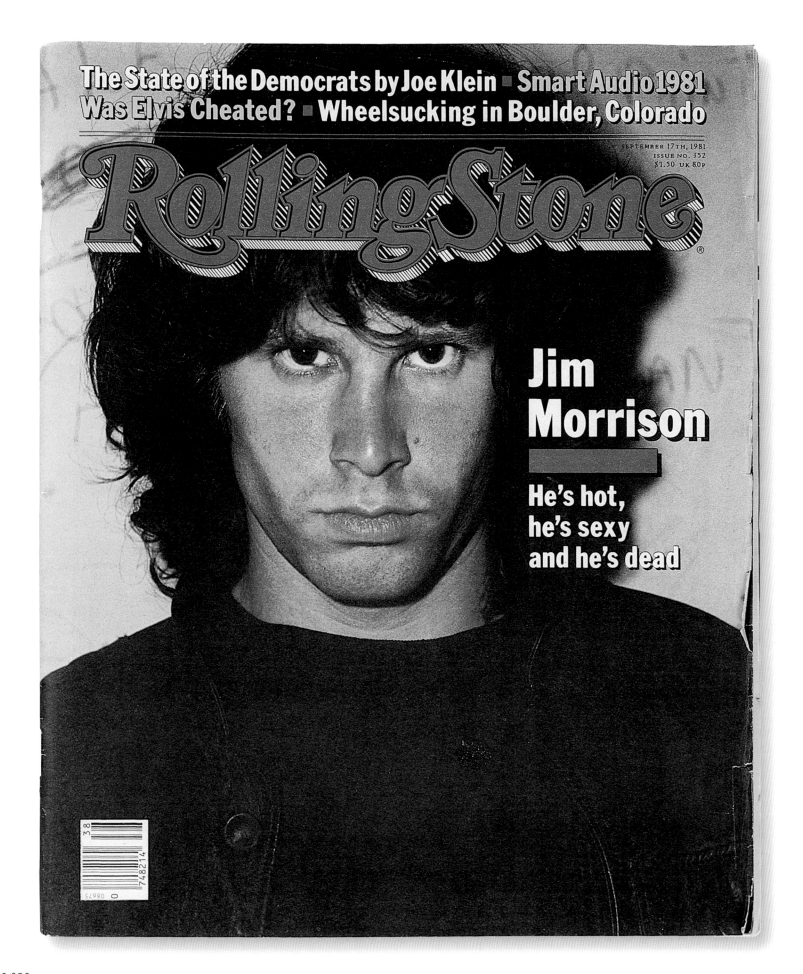

The State of the Democrats by Joe Klein ■ Smart Audio 1981
Was Elvis Cheated? ■ Wheelsucking in Boulder, Colorado

RollingStone

SEPTEMBER 17TH, 1981
ISSUE NO. 352
$1.50 UK 80p

Jim
Morrison

He's hot,
he's sexy
and he's dead

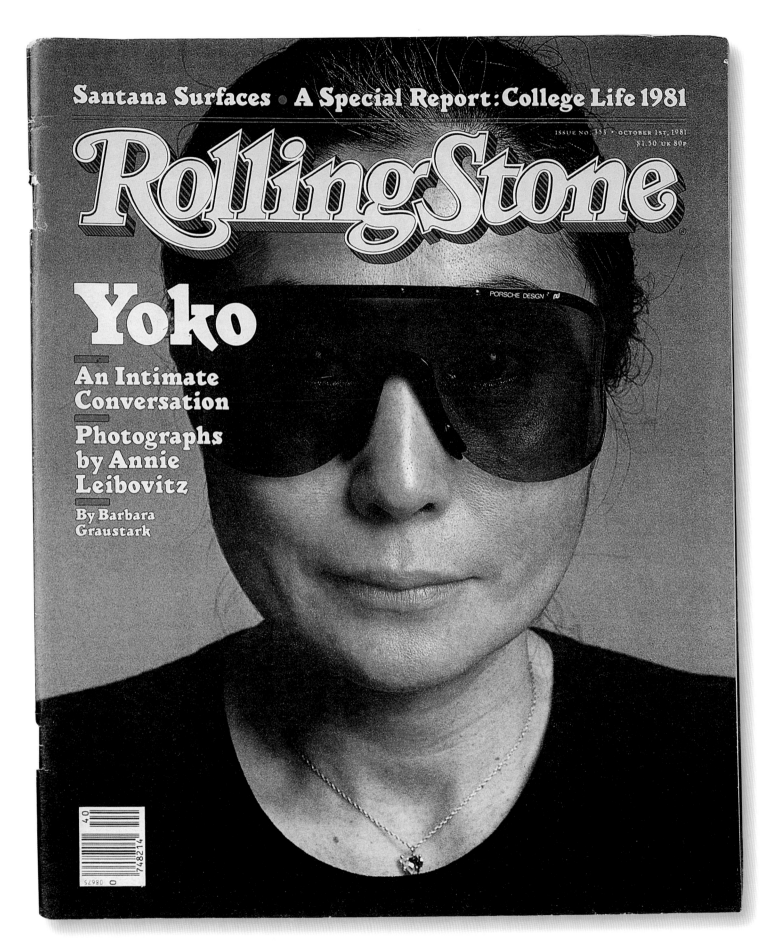

Santana Surfaces • A Special Report: College Life 1981

ISSUE NO. 353 • OCTOBER 1ST, 1981
$1.50 UK 80p

RollingStone

Yoko

An Intimate Conversation

Photographs by Annie Leibovitz

By Barbara Graustark

PORSCHE DESIGN

"[WHEN THIS PHOTO WAS TAKEN] I was walking in a daze. But I think it helped that it was Annie [who took the picture] rather than a stranger."

~ *YOKO ONO*

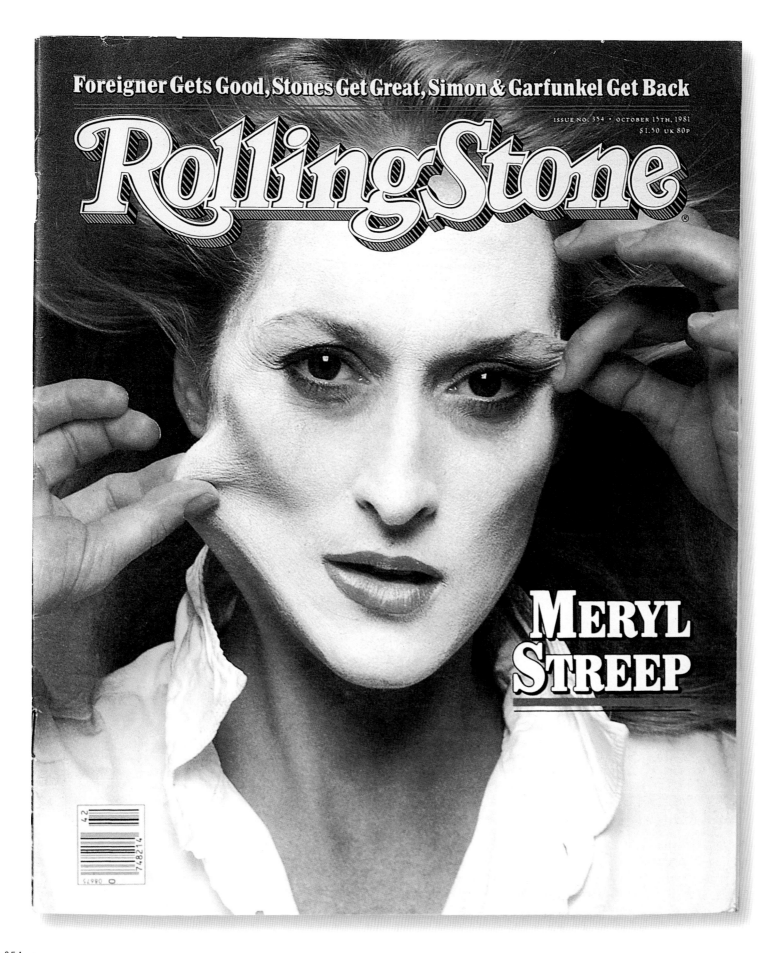

Foreigner Gets Good, Stones Get Great, Simon & Garfunkel Get Back

ISSUE NO. 354 • OCTOBER 15TH, 1981
$1.50 UK 80P

RollingStone

MERYL
STREEP

RS 354 | MERYL STREEP | Photograph by ANNIE LEIBOVITZ | OCTOBER 15TH, 1981

"PUT YOURSELF in this position. You're passing the newsstand at Fifty-seventh Street and Sixth Avenue, and there's your face on the cover of a magazine. And one week later, you're on the subway, and there's that cover, with your face, on the floor. Somebody's probably pissed on it." ~ *MERYL STREEP*

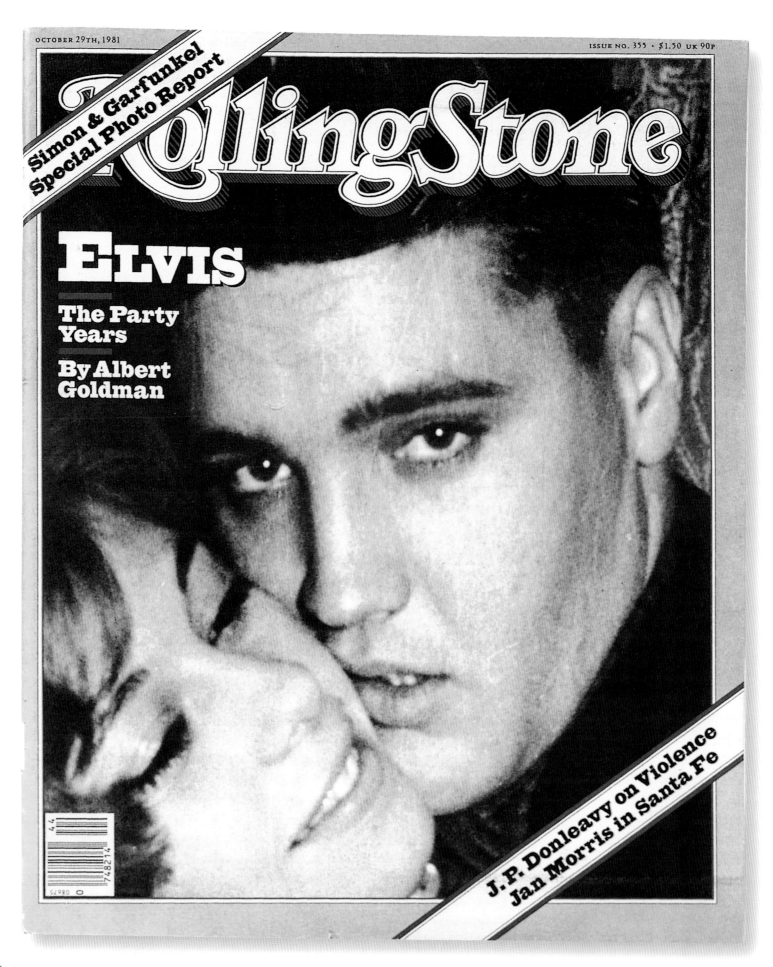

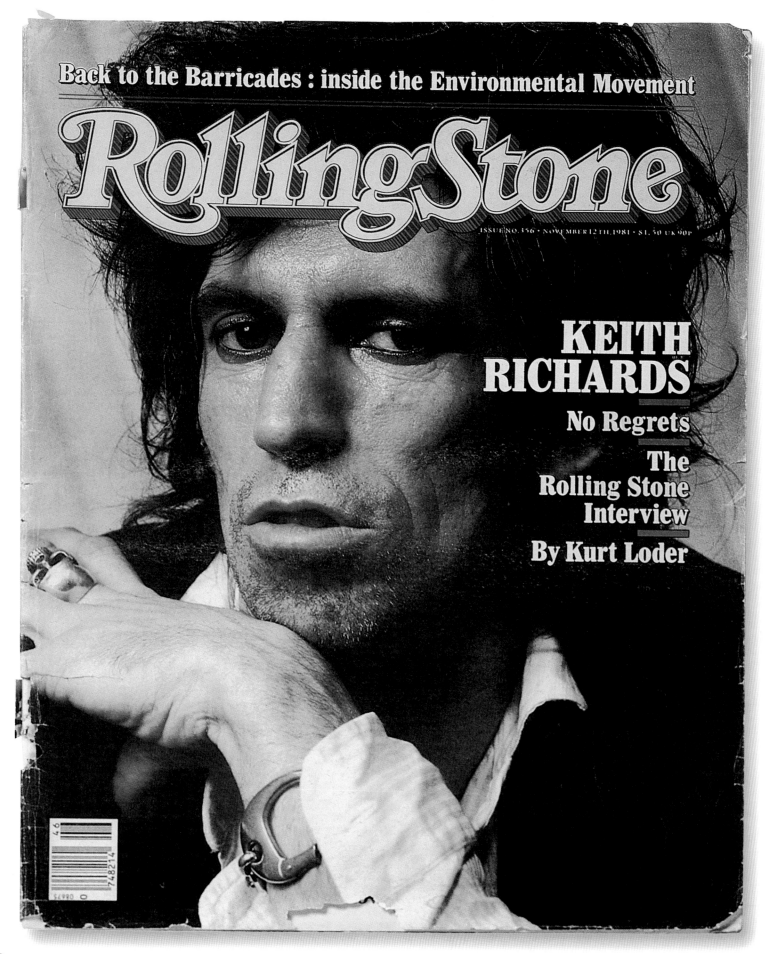

Back to the Barricades : inside the Environmental Movement

RollingStone

ISSUE NO. 356 · NOVEMBER 12TH, 1981 · $1.50 UK 90P

KEITH RICHARDS

No Regrets

The Rolling Stone Interview

By Kurt Loder

RS 356 | KEITH RICHARDS | Photograph by ANNIE LEIBOVITZ | NOVEMBER 12TH, 1981

"I GO THROUGH two packs of cigarettes on photo sessions. Left on my own, I smoke half a pack a day. These photographers are killing me."
~ *KEITH RICHARDS*

RS 357 | NOVEMBER 26TH, 1981
WILLIAM HURT
Photograph by ANNIE LEIBOVITZ

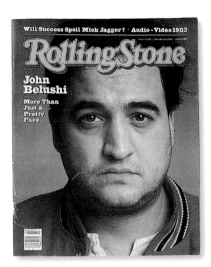

RS 361 | JANUARY 21ST, 1982
JOHN BELUSHI
Photograph by ANNIE LEIBOVITZ

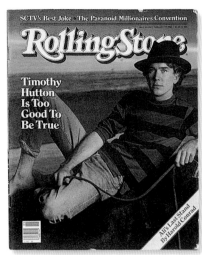

RS 362 | FEBRUARY 4TH, 1982
TIMOTHY HUTTON
Photograph by ANNIE LEIBOVITZ

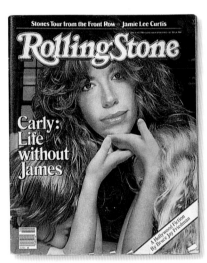

RS 358 | DECEMBER 10TH, 1981
CARLY SIMON
Photograph by JIM VARRIALE

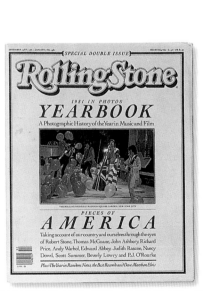

RS 359/360 | DECEMBER 24TH, 1981 · JANUARY 7TH, 1982
THE ROLLING STONES
Photograph by LYNN GOLDSMITH

RS 363 | FEBRUARY 18TH, 1982
STEVE MARTIN
Photograph by ANNIE LEIBOVITZ

RS 364 | MARCH 4TH, 1982
PETER WOLF
Photograph by ANNIE LEIBOVITZ

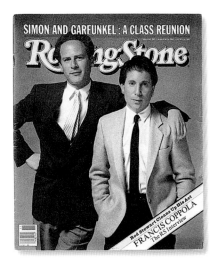

RS 365 | MARCH 18TH, 1982
ART GARFUNKEL & PAUL SIMON
Photograph by ANNIE LEIBOVITZ

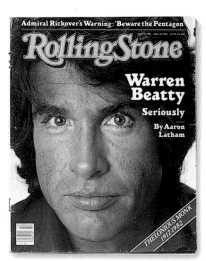

RS 366 | APRIL 1ST, 1982
WARREN BEATTY
Photograph by JACK MITCHELL

"**STEVE MARTIN**, actually, he says to me, 'Annie, I've pushed myself in my movies and in my career; everything's gone further except for the photographs of myself.' And he was really interested in trying to take a new picture. He had just bought that Franz Kline, it was the kind of thing only museums can afford, and it seemed so strange to have it in his home. And he was just in love with it. He said, 'I see myself in that picture.'

When I went out there I wanted to do him in tails, but then I realized he was already beyond the tails. This was a way of throwing away the tails so he could move forward – he could have been stuck in that *Pennies From Heaven* genre for some time. Originally we were going to paint him black, put him in the painting, but then I came up with the idea of painting the tux like the painting."

~ *ANNIE LEIBOVITZ*

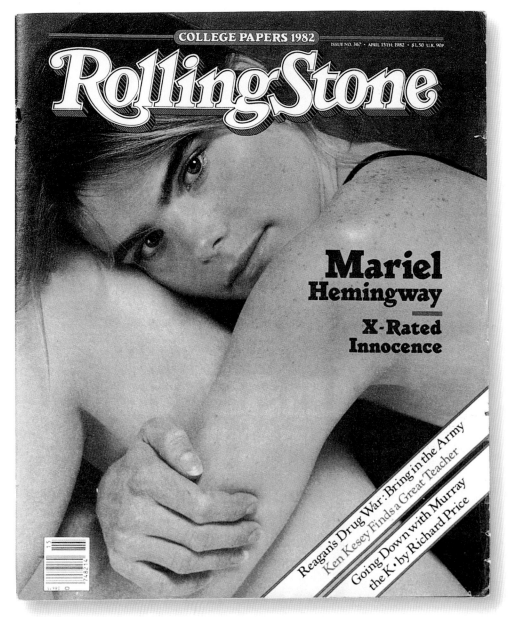

RS 367 | APRIL 15TH, 1982
MARIEL HEMINGWAY
Photograph by ANNIE LEIBOVITZ

ISSUE NO. 368 • APRIL 29TH, 1982 $1.50 U.K. 90P

RollingStone

John Belushi

By Dan Aykroyd, Jim Belushi, Mitchell Glazer
Brian Doyle-Murray, Michael O'Donoghue
Jack Nicholson, Hunter S. Thompson
Laraine Newman, Don Novello
and friends...

JOHN BELUSHI 1949 – 1982

"**WHEN I WAS ON THE ROAD** with John in *Lemmings*, we used to room together occasionally. I had a habit of putting my girlfriend's picture up on my bureau. John walked in one night, looked at the photo and said, 'Oh, you've got one of her too, eh? I've got the version with the donkey in the picture.'"

~ *CHEVY CHASE*

* * * * *

"'**NATIONAL LAMPOON'S ANIMAL HOUSE**' was a lowball project in Hollywood when Sean Daniels asked me to develop it. I read the script and loved it, but the studio said no movie unless I got this guy named Belushi to play Bluto Blutarski. I flew to New York and arranged a meeting with John at the Drake Hotel. He came up to my room, ordered ten shrimp cocktails, twenty beers and ten Perriers. I told him that Bluto would be on screen less time than any of the other characters and that he'd have the least dialogue. In the end, the film was to be designed for Bluto's entrances and exits.

John threw out ideas. I said no to all of them, thinking at the moment that I was losing my star and my movie.

'No?' he said.

'No,' I said.

'Good,' he said. 'I was just testing you. I'll do the film.' He got up and left, and then, of course, all the food and drink arrived."

~*JOHN LANDIS*

* * * * *

"**I NOT ONLY WORKED WITH JOHN** on the Blues Brothers film, I also worked with him on *Saturday Night Live*. He was the kind of guy who would volunteer to sit with me and help me prepare my lines, since I obviously could not rely on cue cards. He was a sweet, gentle, thoughtful man who did everything he could think of to make me feel comfortable while we were putting the show, and later the film, together.

John was a loyal fan of rhythm & blues, and I know for a fact that the Blues Brothers movie and soundtrack got a hell of a lot of people back into R&B. They especially helped people like Aretha Franklin and me reach the young kids who might not have even known we existed. During recent European and Asian tours, I met any number of young people who got hip to the music through the Blues Brothers film and records, and I'm telling you that as far as commercial interest in R&B is concerned, John helped get the ball rolling again. Man, we owe him."

~ *RAY CHARLES*

* * * * *

"**EVEN THOUGH HE WAS A BIT OF A MONSTER**, he was *our* monster, as well as a damned good person you could count on for help in the dark times. There was a ten-day period one recent summer when I sought refuge with him. We fooled around in his speedboat, dug clams and steamed them, and he lifted me out of the pit with his considerable powers as a host. The most drugs we did was a little pot, and he seemed as peaceful as I'd ever seen him.

The last time he visited me, he caught my neighbor a bit offguard by 'borrowing' his truck for a spell. But, hell, he brought it back in pretty good condition. As far as I'm concerned, John is welcome at my house anytime, dead or alive. For me, John's epitaph is: THIS MAN WAS THE REAL THING, HE NEVER NEEDED PROPS."

~ *HUNTER S. THOMPSON*

* * * * *

"**A FEW WEEKS BEFORE HE DIED**, John grabbed me at a party in New York, threw me into the bathroom, barricaded the door and said, 'Listen, I want you to tell George Lucas that Danny and I want to be space monsters in the next *Star Wars* sequel! And after that, Penny, Danny, you and I will do a new production of *Guys and Dolls*. We're not leaving this bathroom till you agree.'

I agreed. They would have been ideal as funky space monsters, and John would have made a good Nathan Detroit in *Guys and Dolls*. Most of all, I liked those little unexpected get-togethers with John. He once sat with me for three hours in a Beverly Hills beauty salon while I had my hair done, and he was like the world's largest puppy, charming the whole place."

~ *CARRIE FISHER*

RS 369 | MAY 13TH, 1982
SISSY SPACEK
Photograph by ANNIE LEIBOVITZ

RS 370 | MAY 27TH, 1982
NASTASSIA KINSKI
Photograph by RICHARD AVEDON

RS 371 | JUNE 10TH, 1982
DAVID LETTERMAN
Photograph by HERB RITTS

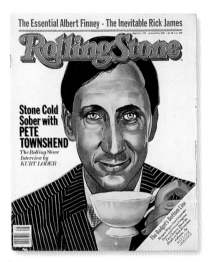

RS 372 | JUNE 24TH, 1982
PETE TOWNSHEND
Illustration by JULIAN ALLEN

RS 373 | JULY 8TH, 1982
SYLVESTER STALLONE
Photograph by ANNIE LEIBOVITZ

RS 374 | JULY 22ND, 1982
E.T.
Photograph by AARON RAPOPORT

RS 376 | AUGUST 19TH, 1982
JEFF BRIDGES
Photograph by ANNIE LEIBOVITZ

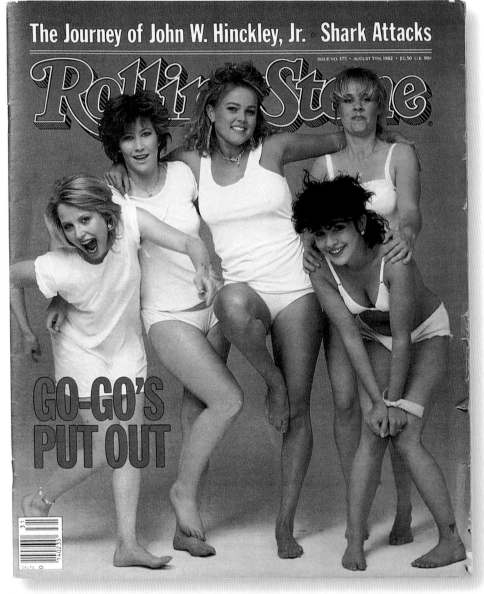

RS 375 | AUGUST 5TH, 1982
THE GO-GO'S
Photograph by ANNIE LEIBOVITZ

Jann Wenner hires art director Derek Ungless (RS 373), whose background was in European magazine design, to give ROLLING STONE *a cleaner, more spare look.*

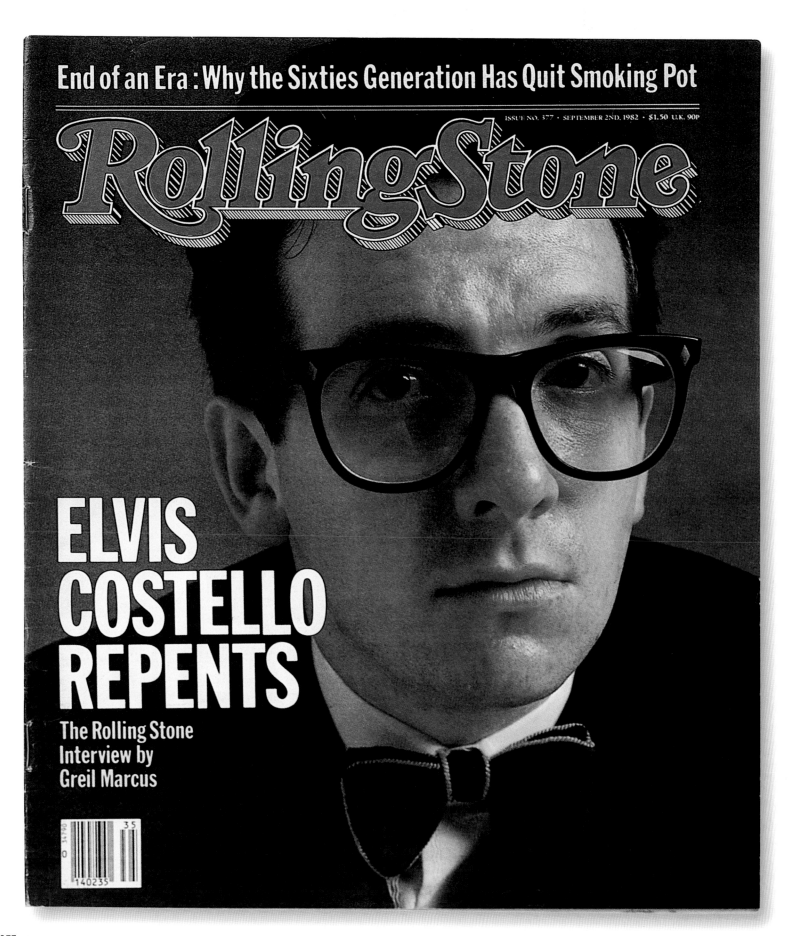

End of an Era : Why the Sixties Generation Has Quit Smoking Pot

ISSUE NO. 377 · SEPTEMBER 2ND, 1982 · $1.50 U.K. 90P

RollingStone

ELVIS COSTELLO REPENTS

The Rolling Stone
Interview by
Greil Marcus

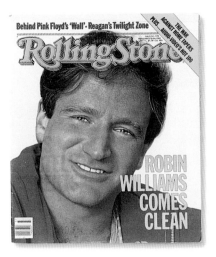

RS 378 | SEPTEMBER 16TH, 1982
ROBIN WILLIAMS
Photograph by BONNIE SCHIFFMAN

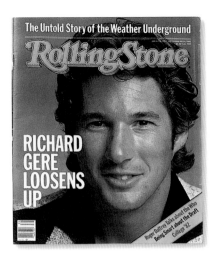

RS 379 | SEPTEMBER 30TH, 1982
RICHARD GERE
Photograph by HERB RITTS

RS 380 | OCTOBER 14TH, 1982
JOHN LENNON & YOKO ONO
Photograph by ALLAN TANNENBAUM

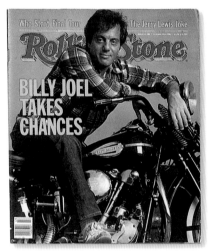

RS 381 | OCTOBER 28TH, 1982
BILLY JOEL
Photograph by ANNIE LEIBOVITZ

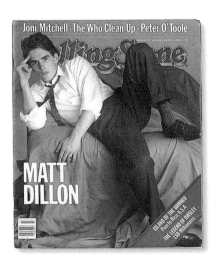

RS 383 | NOVEMBER 25TH, 1982
MATT DILLON
Photograph by ANNIE LEIBOVITZ

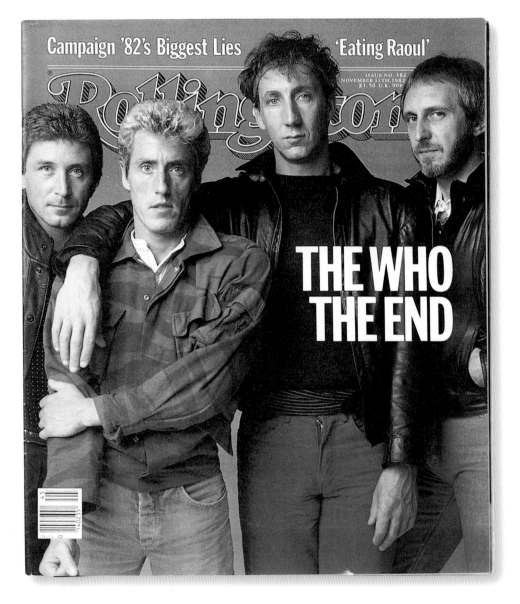

RS 382 | NOVEMBER 11TH, 1982
THE WHO
Photograph by ANNIE LEIBOVITZ

John Cougar · Gary Gilmore by Mikal Gilmore · Radio Racism

The Divine
Ms. Midler
**BETTE
NOIRE**

RS 384 | DECEMBER 9TH, 1982
BETTE MIDLER
Photograph by GREG GORMAN

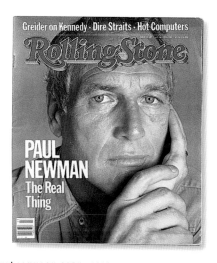

Greider on Kennedy · Dire Straits · Hot Computers

**PAUL
NEWMAN**
The Real
Thing

RS 387 | JANUARY 20TH, 1983
PAUL NEWMAN
Photograph by JIM VARRIALE

California's Handgun Vote · Ray Mancini: a Death in the Ring

ISSUE NO. 389
FEBRUARY 17TH, 1983
$1.50 U.K. £1

**MICHAEL
JACKSON**
Life as
a Man

RS 389 | FEBRUARY 17TH, 1983
MICHAEL JACKSON
Photograph by BONNIE SCHIFFMAN

America's New Plague: Contagious Sexual Cancer · Bob Seger

**DUSTIN
DEAREST**

RS 388 | FEBRUARY 3RD, 1983
DUSTIN HOFFMAN
Photograph by RICHARD AVEDON

"NOT WHAT YOU EXPECTED, HUH?" From behind a mask of bony fingers, Michael Jackson giggles. Having settled his visitor on the middle floor of his own three-level condo, Michael explains that the residence is temporary, while his Encino, California, home is razed and rebuilt. He concedes that this is an unlikely spot for a young prince of pop.

It is also surprising to see that Michael has decided to face this interview alone. He says he has not done anything like this for over two years. And even when he did, it was always with a cordon of managers, other Jackson brothers, and, in one case, his younger sister Janet parroting a reporter's questions before Michael would answer them. The small body of existing literature paints him as excruciatingly shy. He ducks, he hides, he talks to his shoe tops. Or he just doesn't show up. He is known to conduct his private life with almost obsessive caution, "just like a hemophiliac who can't afford to be scratched in any way." The analogy is his.

[EXCERPT FROM RS 389 COVER STORY BY GERRY HIRSHEY]

RS 390 | MARCH 3RD, 1983
THE STRAY CATS
Photograph by RICHARD AVEDON

RS 391 | MARCH 17TH, 1983
JESSICA LANGE
Photograph by JIM VARRIALE

RS 392 | MARCH 31ST, 1983
DUDLEY MOORE
Photograph by BONNIE SCHIFFMAN

RS 393 | APRIL 14TH, 1983
JOAN BAEZ
Photograph by DAVID MONTGOMERY

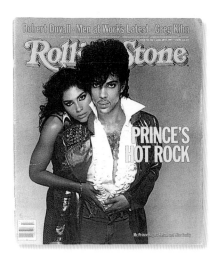

RS 394 | APRIL 28TH, 1983
PRINCE & VANITY
Photograph by RICHARD AVEDON

RS 395 | MAY 12TH, 1983
DAVID BOWIE
Photograph by DAVID BAILEY

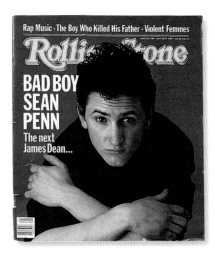

RS 396 | MAY 26TH, 1983
SEAN PENN
Photograph by MARY ELLEN MARK

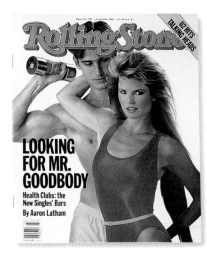

RS 397 | JUNE 9TH, 1983
CHRISTIE BRINKLEY &
MICHAEL IVES
Photograph by E.J. CAMP

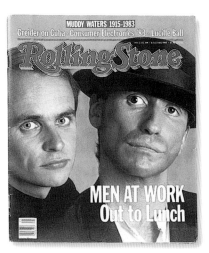

RS 398 | JUNE 23RD, 1983
MEN AT WORK
Photograph by AARON RAPOPORT

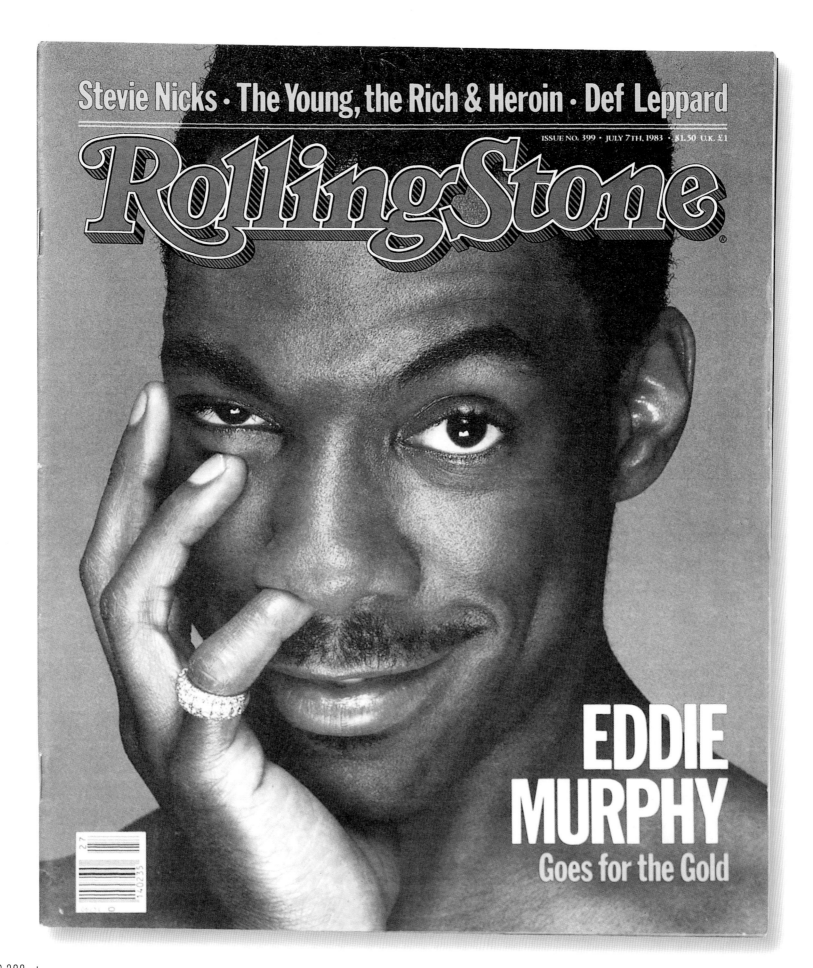

Stevie Nicks • The Young, the Rich & Heroin • Def Leppard

ISSUE NO. 399 • JULY 7TH, 1983 • $1.50 U.K. £1

RollingStone

EDDIE MURPHY
Goes for the Gold

RS 400/401 | JULY 21ST – AUGUST 4TH, 1983
CAST OF 'RETURN OF THE JEDI'
Photograph by AARON RAPOPORT

RS 402 | AUGUST 18TH, 1983
JOHN TRAVOLTA
Photograph by RICHARD AVEDON

RS 403 | SEPTEMBER 1ST, 1983
STING
Photograph by LYNN GOLDSMITH

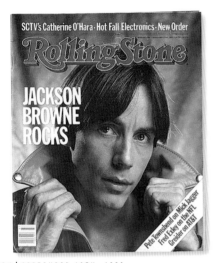

RS 404 | SEPTEMBER 15TH, 1983
JACKSON BROWNE
Photograph by AARON RAPOPORT

RS 405 | SEPTEMBER 29TH, 1983
ANNIE LENNOX
Photograph by E.J. CAMP

RS 406 | OCTOBER 13TH, 1983
CHEVY CHASE
Photograph by BONNIE SCHIFFMAN

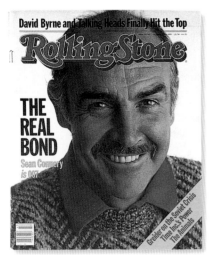

RS 407 | OCTOBER 27TH, 1983
SEAN CONNERY
Photograph by DAVID MONTGOMERY

RS 408 | NOVEMBER 10TH, 1983
BOY GEORGE
Photograph by DAVID MONTGOMERY

RS 410 | DECEMBER 8TH, 1983
MICHAEL JACKSON &
PAUL McCARTNEY
Illustration by VIVIENNE FLESHER

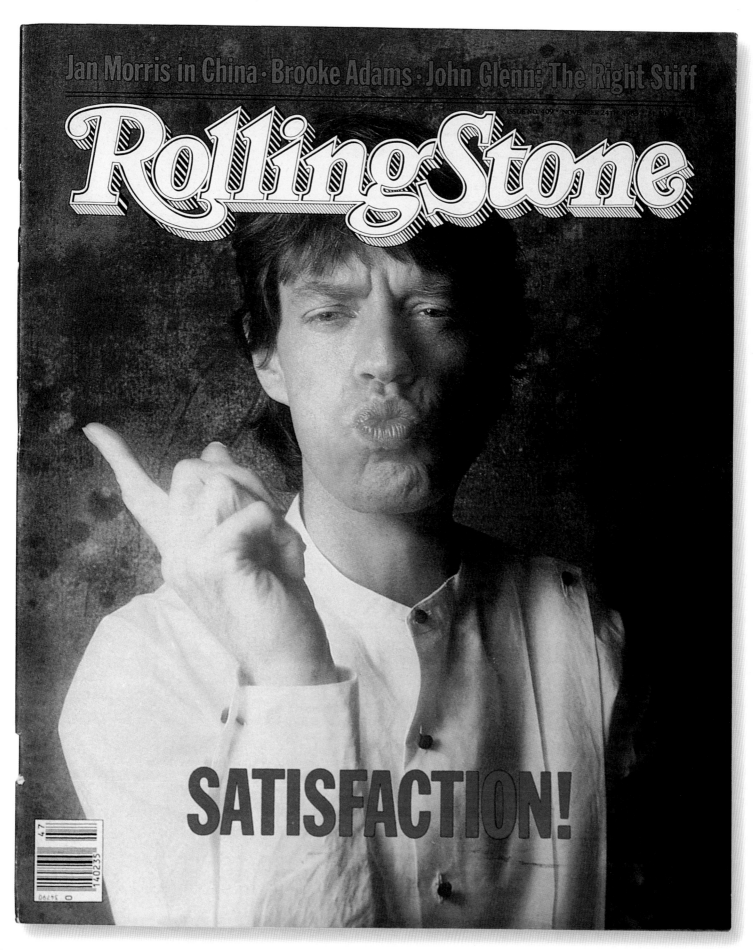

Jan Morris in China · Brooke Adams · John Glenn: The Right Stiff

RollingStone

ISSUE NO. 409 · NOVEMBER 24TH, 1983

SATISFACTION!

RS 409 | MICK JAGGER | Photograph by WILLIAM COUPON | NOVEMBER 24TH, 1983

"**MICK IS** and always has been, a boy. A boy that I'd be. Now, if I was male and you said who would you want to be like, I guess I could say I'd want to dance better than Mick. But I like how he does it. He's naughty, he's got a great boy inside of that man's body." ~ *TINA TURNER*

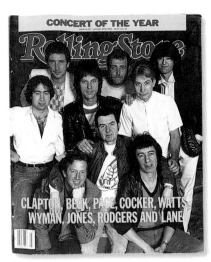

RS 413 | JANUARY 19TH, 1984
ARMS CONCERT PARTICIPANTS
Photograph by BONNIE SCHIFFMAN

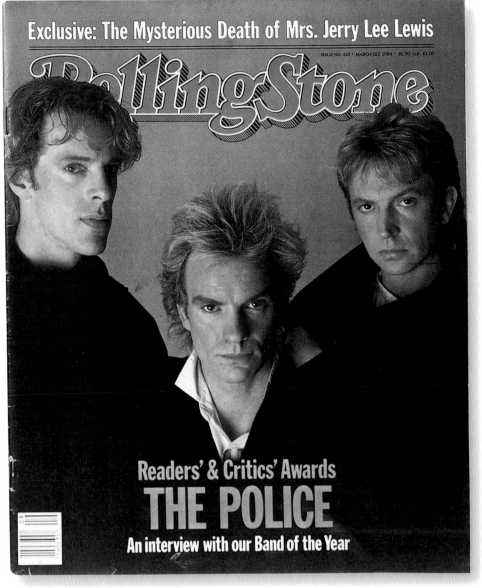

RS 416 | MARCH 1ST, 1984
THE POLICE
Photograph by DAVID BAILEY

RS 414 | FEBRUARY 2ND, 1984
DURAN DURAN
Photograph by DAVID MONTGOMERY

RS 415 | FEBRUARY 16TH, 1984
THE BEATLES
Photograph by JOHN LAUNOIS

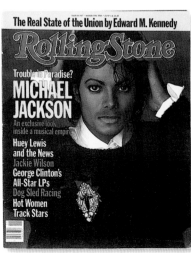

RS 417 | MARCH 15TH, 1984
MICHAEL JACKSON
Photograph by MATTHEW ROLSTON

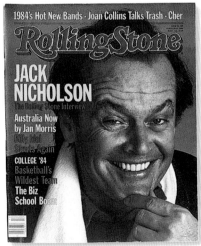

RS 418 | MARCH 29TH, 1984
JACK NICHOLSON
Photograph by RICHARD AVEDON

HE WAS, above all, a preacher. He came to preach to his people, to all people. He did so once, calling his sermon *What's Going On*. I believe he was called to preach again, to write and sing songs about the Jesus he loved so sincerely. But now we'll never know. A great artist – of the magnitude of Michelangelo and the sweetness of Mozart – is dead, and all we can do is praise the power that brought him forth.

His Oedipal struggle, his battles with the elements are finally laid to rest. He has written his own Greek tragedy – the story of a boy who became a man who became a god, only to be devoured, like Dionysus, by some demonic, self-destructive bent. The dark cloud that had long hung over his head has exploded. In his softly sloped eyes, in his exquisitely high-pitched speaking voice, even in his lighthearted, quick-witted banter, one heard the troubled vibe, the aching blue note. Marvin Gaye sang with a tear in his voice. He had the blues. His depressions were as deep as the Grand Canyon, his heartaches painful and prolonged. His romantic aura brings to mind Keats, a poet "half in love with easeful Death."

Like Mahalia Jackson's, his cry soars far beyond this world, reaching its crescendo in the arms of God. It is there where Marvin Gaye rests, peaceful at last. Whenever the voice of an angel is set free, there is cause for celebration. With Marvin, there is much to celebrate. He left behind a golden legacy. The gift of his genius and the truth of his preaching are now matters of historical record. He has not died, nor will he ever die. The message of his music is rooted in love, and love lives forever.

[EXCERPT FROM MARVIN GAYE
TRIBUTE BY DAVID RITZ]

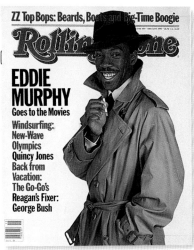

RS 419 | APRIL 12TH, 1984
EDDIE MURPHY
Photograph by RICHARD AVEDON

RS 420 | APRIL 26TH, 1984
DARYL HANNAH
Photograph by E.J. CAMP

RS 421 | MAY 10TH, 1984
MARVIN GAYE
Photograph by NEAL PRESTON

RS 422 | MAY 24TH, 1984
CYNDI LAUPER
Photograph by RICHARD AVEDON

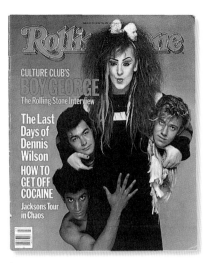

RS 423 | JUNE 7TH, 1984
CULTURE CLUB
Photograph by RICHARD AVEDON

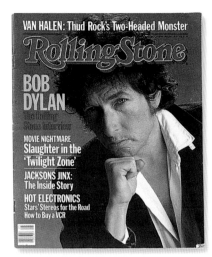

RS 424 | JUNE 21ST, 1984
BOB DYLAN
Photograph by KEN REGAN

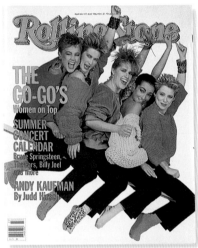

RS 425 | JULY 5TH, 1984
THE GO-GO'S
Photograph by ALBERT WATSON

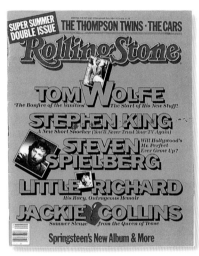

RS 426/427 | JULY 19TH – AUGUST 2ND, 1984
TOM WOLFE, STEVEN SPIELBERG,
LITTLE RICHARD
VARIOUS PHOTOGRAPHERS

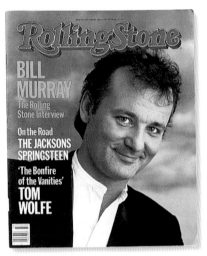

RS 428 | AUGUST 16TH, 1984
BILL MURRAY
Photograph by BARBARA WALZ

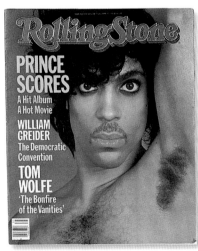

RS 429 | AUGUST 30TH, 1984
PRINCE
Photograph by RICHARD AVEDON

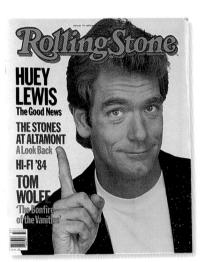

RS 430 | SEPTEMBER 13TH, 1984
HUEY LEWIS
Photograph by AARON RAPOPORT

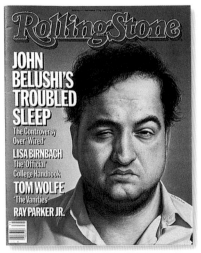

RS 431 | SEPTEMBER 27TH, 1984
JOHN BELUSHI
Illustration by GOTTFRIED HELNWEIN

ISSUE NO. 432 • OCTOBER 11TH, 1984 • $1.95 U.K. £1.20

Rolling Stone

TINA TURNER
She's Got Legs!

FRANKIE GOES TO HOLLYWOOD
England's Music Sensation

TOM WOLFE
'The Vanities'

STYLE
Rebel without a Cause, 1984

IT'S LIKELY that her videos were the breakthrough, as Madonna perfectly merged her dance training with her knowledge of the randier things in life. How did she manage to put across such seething sexuality where so many others have tried and failed? "I think that has to do with them not being in touch with that aspect of their personality," according to Madonna. "They say, 'Well, I have to do a video now, and a pop star has to come on sexually, so how do I do that?' instead of being in touch with that part of their self to begin with. I've been in touch with that aspect of my personality since I was five."

[EXCERPT FROM RS 435 COVER STORY
BY CHRISTOPHER CONNELLY]

* * * * *

HERE'S THE CHECK.

"I'll let you pay," says Billy Idol, "but it better be a good article, you cunt."

"Right," I say.

"Otherwise, stick it up your ass. Don't tell me you'll pay for it."

"Okay," I say, laughing.

We are in a back booth at Emilio's in New York City's Greenwich Village. We are on a date set up by ROLLING STONE. Billy Idol has had two bottles of wine. It is one in the morning.

"Anyway, ROLLING STONE sucks," says Billy, affably. "If ROLLING STONE was clever, they would have bought their own TV channel. And put me on it. I *know* they're rich enough."

He's in a high mood.

"That's why, 'Don't fuck with me, motherfuckers!'" He bangs

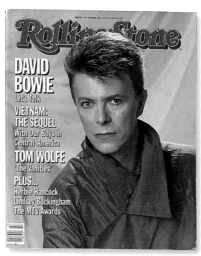

RS 433 | OCTOBER 25TH, 1984
DAVID BOWIE
Photograph by GREG GORMAN

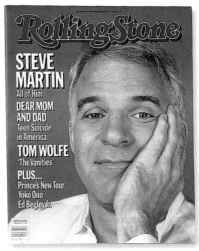

RS 434 | NOVEMBER 8TH, 1984
STEVE MARTIN
Photograph by BONNIE SCHIFFMAN

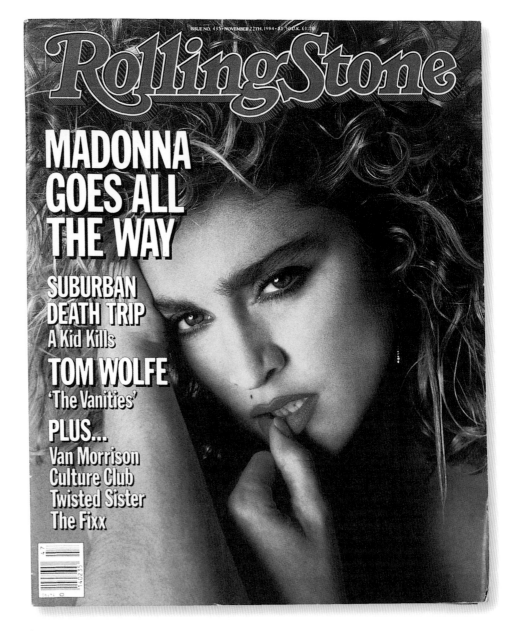

RS 435 | NOVEMBER 22ND, 1984
MADONNA
Photograph by STEVEN MEISEL

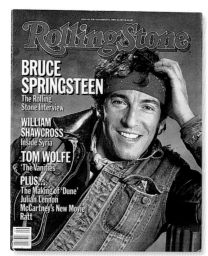

RS 436 | DECEMBER 6TH, 1984
BRUCE SPRINGSTEEN
Photograph by AARON RAPOPORT

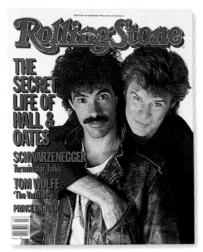

RS 439 | JANUARY 17TH, 1985
DARYL HALL & JOHN OATES
Photograph by BERT STERN

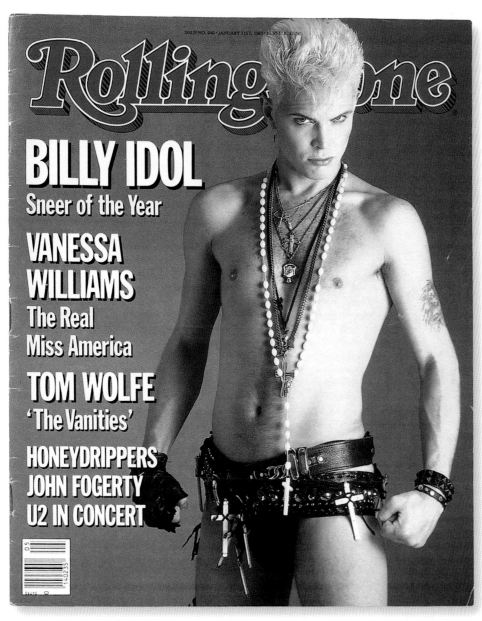

RS 440 | JANUARY 31ST, 1985
BILLY IDOL
Photograph by E.J. CAMP

on the table. " 'Cause I'm going to be rich enough soon, I'll be at your economic level, and then fuck *you,* ROLLING STONE."

"Right," I say, paralyzed with delight.

"I want to be on the *back* of that motherfucker!" says Billy. "Don't put me on the front!" He pushes his dark glasses up on his nose. "I think it *sucks* being on the front of ROLLING STONE!" He bends toward the tape recorder. "I love you *all,* you motherfuckers. But you should have fucking had a bit more respect when I came up in 1977, '78 to see you in your Fifth Avenue offices! But I don't care. Now maybe you understand that I *am* worth being on the front cover of your magazine, for the *right* reasons, mother- fuckers! Don't put me on if you don't like me! Fucking *don't* put me on it!"

"Well, you're probably going to be on it," I say.

He drops his lower lip and looks for the cigarettes.

"Well, I better be real on there," he says, slapping his coat for the lighter. "We don't want no Cyndi Lauper this year."

"You'll be real," I say.

"I didn't like the picture they put of me in the year-end issue."

He lights up.

"You didn't?"

"No, I thought it sucked." He takes the cigarette out of his mouth and leans toward the recorder again. "You put the wrong picture in, and you know you did . . . ooooaaaah [*chuckling*] I know. I know. Don't fuck with me. All right. Let's go."

[EXCERPT FROM RS 440 COVER STORY
BY E. JEAN CARROLL]

RS 441 | FEBRUARY 14TH, 1985
MICK JAGGER
Photograph by STEVEN MEISEL

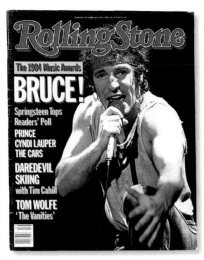

RS 442 | FEBRUARY 28TH, 1985
BRUCE SPRINGSTEEN
Photograph by NEAL PRESTON

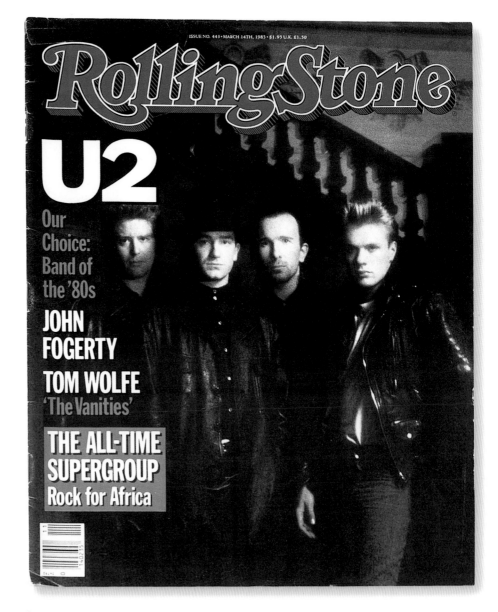

RS 443 | MARCH 14TH, 1985
U2
Photograph by REBECCA BLAKE

IN AMERICA, their names are not household words, and their faces are unfamiliar even to some of their fans. They have yet to notch a Top Ten album or single. Only now are they beginning to tour arena-sized venues. But for a growing number of rock & roll fans, U2 – vocalist Paul "Bono" Hewson, twenty-four; guitarist Dave "the Edge" Evans, twenty-two; bassist Adam Clayton, twenty-four; and drummer Larry Mullen Jr., twenty-two – has become the band that matters most, maybe even the only band that matters. It's no coincidence that U2 sells more T-shirts and merchandise than groups that sell twice as many records, or that four of

U2's five albums are currently on *Billboard*'s Top 200. The group has become one of the handful of artists in rock & roll history (the Who, the Grateful Dead, Bruce Springsteen) that people are eager to identify themselves with. And they've done it not just with their music but with a larger message as well – by singing "Pride (In the Name of Love)" while most other groups sing about pride in the act of love.

The band's appeal doesn't seem to be sexual; no member of U2 appears to have seen the inside of a health club or a New Wave haberdashery, and only Mullen could pass for a Cute Guy. U2's strength, it seems, goes deeper. Like most rock & roll bands, U2 articulates, at top volume, the alienation that young people can feel from their country, their hometown, their family, their sexuality. Like some of the best rock & roll bands, U2 also shows how that alienation might be overcome. But unlike anyone else in rock & roll, U2 also addresses the most ignored – and most volatile – area of inquiry: alienation from religion.

"Sadomasochism is not taboo in rock & roll," notes Bono. "Spirituality is." Indeed, when religion in America seems sadly synonymous with the electronic evangelism of Jimmy Swaggart and Jerry Falwell, U2 dares to proclaim its belief in Christianity – at top volume – while grappling with the ramifications of its faith. Each member is careful to avoid discussing the specifics of his beliefs (the perfectly amiable Mullen, in fact, customarily declines to give interviews), and the band's musical message is hardly a proselytizing one. But even to raise the issue, to suggest that a person who loves rock & roll can unashamedly find peace with God as well, is a powerful statement. This is a band that onstage and offstage seems guided by a philosophy not included in such yuppie maxims as "feeling good" and "go for it": not how might we live our lives (what we can get away with) but how ought we to live our lives.

Lofty goals, but while the promise of U2's records has always been great, it is a promise that remains largely unfulfilled. In the past year and a half, U2 has found itself faced with several critical decisions: artistic, financial, personal, even patriotic. Each choice represented a test of whether the band could continue to articulate its message and fulfill its promise without drowning in contradictions. And while the outcome isn't settled yet, U2 seems to have come through its crises in good shape – due in large part, perhaps, to the band members' willingness to acknowledge their own weaknesses.

"It interests me that I'm portrayed as some sort of strong man," says Bono with genuine perplexity. "I don't see myself in that way. I know my weaknesses. When I see the albums, I don't see them as anthemic. I think that's what's uplifting, that's what connects with people. I think people relate to U2 because they've seen us fall on our face so many times."

[EXCERPT FROM RS 443 COVER STORY
BY CHRISTOPHER CONNELLY]

RS 444 | MARCH 28TH, 1985
DON JOHNSON &
PHILLIP MICHAEL THOMAS
Photograph by DEBORAH FEINGOLD

RS 445 | APRIL 11TH, 1985
DAVID LEE ROTH
Photograph by BRADFORD BRANSON

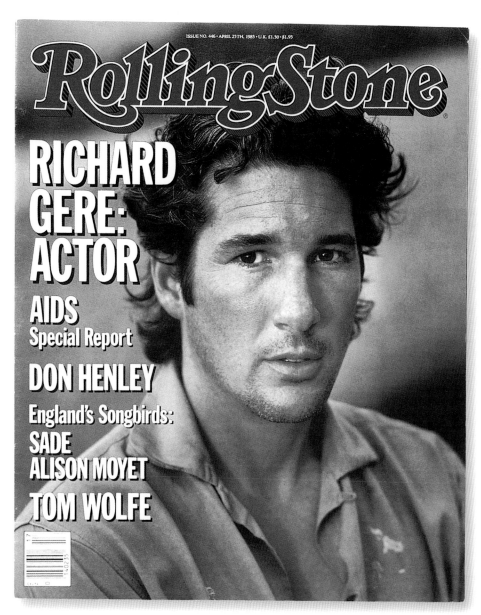

RS 446 | APRIL 25TH, 1985
RICHARD GERE
Photograph by HERB RITTS

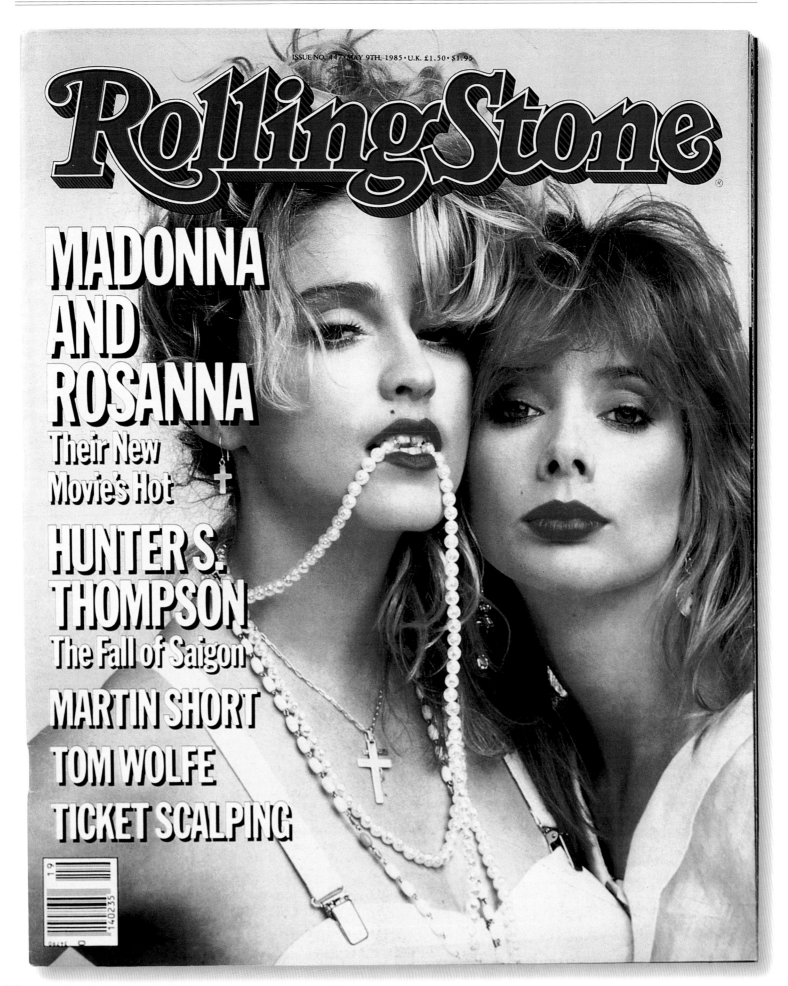

ISSUE NO. 447 · MAY 9TH, 1985 · U.K. £1.50 · $1.95

RollingStone

MADONNA AND ROSANNA
Their New Movie's Hot

HUNTER S. THOMPSON
The Fall of Saigon

MARTIN SHORT

TOM WOLFE

TICKET SCALPING

RS 447 | MADONNA & ROSANNA ARQUETTE | Photograph by HERB RITTS | MAY 9TH, 1985

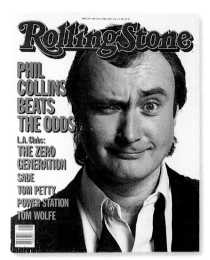

RS 448 | MAY 23RD, 1985
PHIL COLLINS
Photograph by AARON RAPOPORT

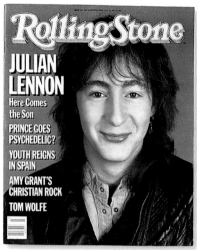

RS 449 | JUNE 6TH, 1985
JULIAN LENNON
Photograph by RICHARD AVEDON

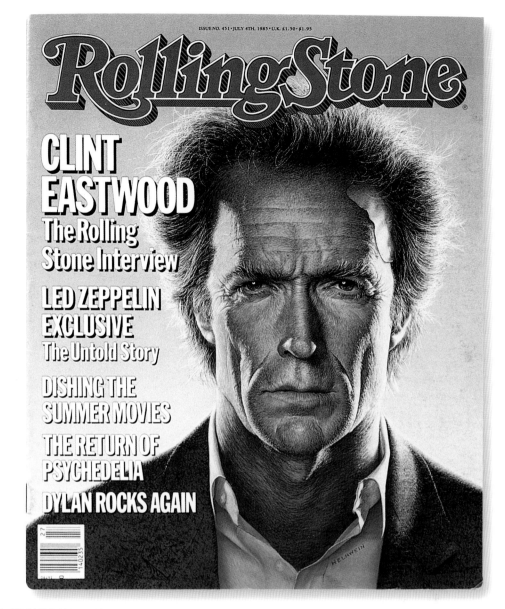

RS 451 | JULY 4TH, 1985
CLINT EASTWOOD
Illustration by GOTTFRIED HELNWEIN

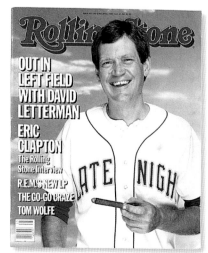

RS 450 | JUNE 20TH, 1985
DAVID LETTERMAN
Photograph by DEBORAH FEINGOLD

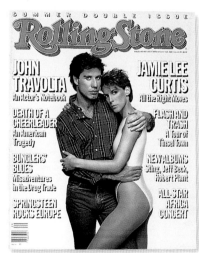

RS 452/453 | JULY 18TH – AUGUST 1ST, 1985
JOHN TRAVOLTA &
JAMIE LEE CURTIS
Photograph by PATRICK DEMARCHELIER

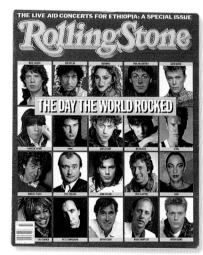

RS 454 | AUGUST 15TH, 1985
LIVE AID PARTICIPANTS
VARIOUS PHOTOGRAPHERS

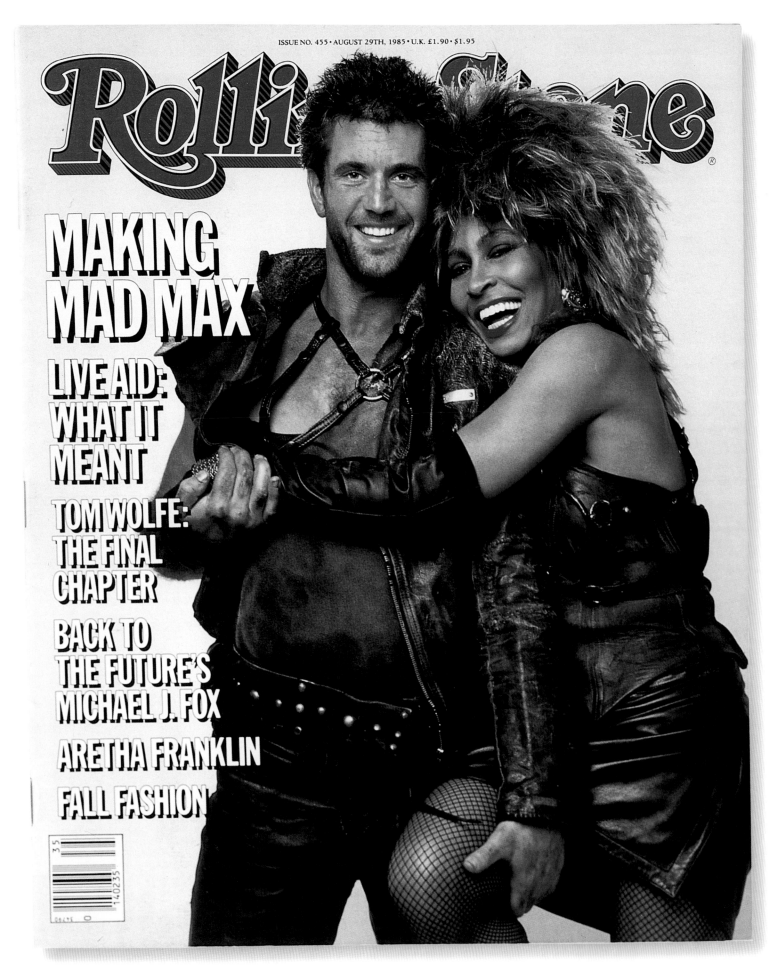

ISSUE NO. 455 • AUGUST 29TH, 1985 • U.K. £1.90 • $1.95

Rolling Stone

MAKING MAD MAX

LIVE AID: WHAT IT MEANT

TOM WOLFE: THE FINAL CHAPTER

BACK TO THE FUTURE'S MICHAEL J. FOX

ARETHA FRANKLIN

FALL FASHION

RS 456 | SEPTEMBER 12TH, 1985
PRINCE
"RASPBERRY BERET" VIDEO STILL

RS 457 | SEPTEMBER 26TH, 1985
STING
Photograph by ERIC BOMAN

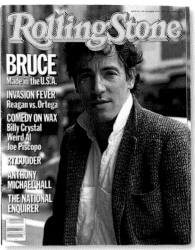

RS 458 | OCTOBER 10TH, 1985
BRUCE SPRINGSTEEN
Photograph by NEAL PRESTON

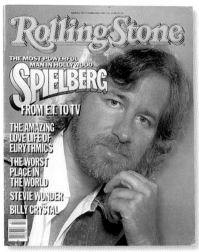

RS 459 | OCTOBER 24TH, 1985
STEVEN SPIELBERG
Photograph by MOSHE BRAKHA

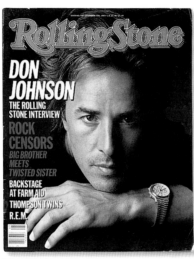

RS 460 | NOVEMBER 7TH, 1985
DON JOHNSON
Photograph by HERB RITTS

RS 461 | NOVEMBER 21ST, 1985
MARK KNOPFLER
Photograph by DEBORAH FEINGOLD

RS 462 | DECEMBER 5TH, 1985
BOB GELDOF
Photograph by DAVIES & STARR

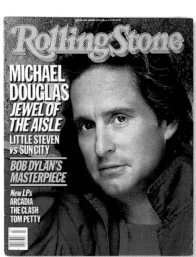

RS 465 | JANUARY 16TH, 1986
MICHAEL DOUGLAS
Photograph by E.J. CAMP

RS 466 | JANUARY 30TH, 1986
JOHN COUGAR MELLENCAMP
Photograph by HERB RITTS

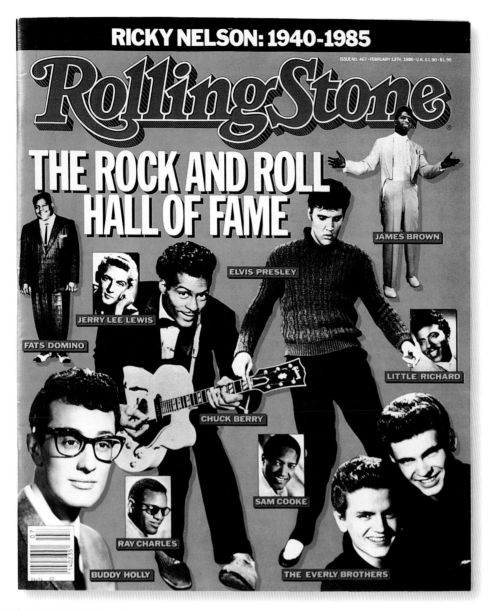

RS 470 | MARCH 27TH, 1986
BRUCE WILLIS
Photograph by BONNIE SCHIFFMAN

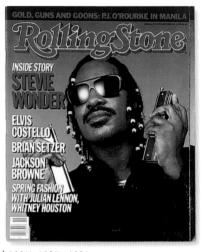

RS 471 | APRIL 10TH, 1986
STEVIE WONDER
Photograph by MARK HANAUER

RS 467 | FEBRUARY 13TH, 1986
ROCK AND ROLL HALL OF FAME INDUCTEES
VARIOUS PHOTOGRAPHERS

RS 468 | FEBRUARY 27TH, 1986
BRUCE SPRINGSTEEN
Photograph by AARON RAPOPORT

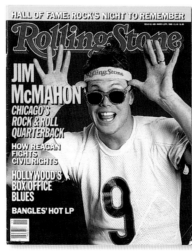

RS 469 | MARCH 13TH, 1986
JIM McMAHON
Photograph by KEN REGAN

RS 472 | APRIL 24TH, 1986
PRINCE WITH WENDY & LISA
Photograph by JEFF KATZ

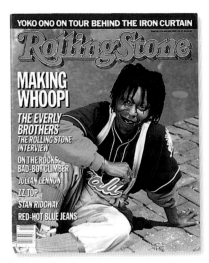

RS 473 | MAY 8TH, 1986
WHOOPI GOLDBERG
Photograph by BONNIE SCHIFFMAN

RS 474 | MAY 22ND, 1986
MICHAEL J. FOX
Photograph by CHRIS CALLIS

RS 475 | JUNE 5TH, 1986
MADONNA
Photograph by MATTHEW ROLSTON

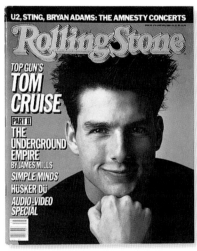

RS 476 | JUNE 19TH, 1986
TOM CRUISE
Photograph by HERB RITTS

RS 477 | JULY 3RD, 1986
VAN HALEN
Photograph by DEBORAH FEINGOLD

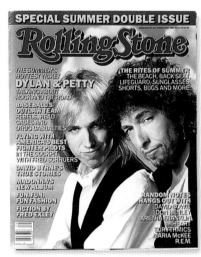

RS 478/479 | JULY 17TH – JULY 31ST, 1986
TOM PETTY & BOB DYLAN
Photograph by AARON RAPOPORT

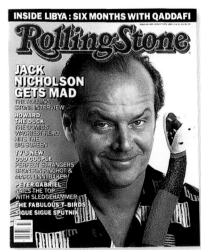

RS 480 | AUGUST 14TH, 1986
JACK NICHOLSON
Photograph by HERB RITTS

RS 481 | AUGUST 28TH, 1986
BOY GEORGE
Photograph by NORMAN WATSON

Though Bob Dylan has been one of ROLLING STONE'S *most frequent cover subjects (13 times), he's also been one of the most elusive. On one occasion, he refused to allow RS's photographer to shoot him; instead, he enlisted a buddy, Morgan Renard, to photograph him in the backstage men's room at Madison Square Garden (RS 278). For RS 478/479, Dylan only showed up at the last-minute for the shoot with Tom Petty. The session started without him, and the next thing Petty knew, "Bob arrived, came straight across the room and just stepped into the frame with me. I don't think he really said anything to anyone. After they'd shot two pictures, Bob leaned over to me and said, 'I gotta go,' and then left. I remember trying to get it across to Aaron [Rapoport] that he was actually gone."* ROLLING STONE *wasn't happy with the two shots, so after a rehearsal one night, Petty recalls, "We went back and did the shot they actually used. That time we were both there."* ○

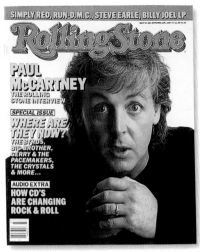

RS 482 | SEPTEMBER 11TH, 1986
PAUL McCARTNEY
Photograph by HARRY DeZITTER

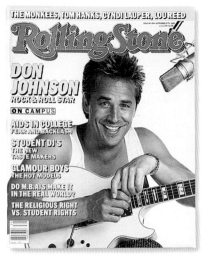

RS 483 | SEPTEMBER 25TH, 1986
DON JOHNSON
Photograph by E.J. CAMP

RS 484 | OCTOBER 9TH, 1986
CYBILL SHEPHERD
Photograph by MATTHEW ROLSTON

RS 485 | OCTOBER 23RD, 1986
TINA TURNER
Photograph by MATTHEW ROLSTON

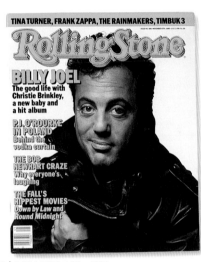

RS 486 | NOVEMBER 6TH, 1986
BILLY JOEL
Photograph by ALBERT WATSON

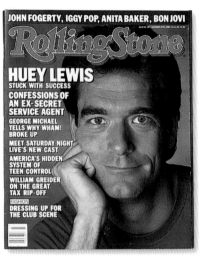

RS 487 | NOVEMBER 20TH, 1986
HUEY LEWIS
Photograph by TIM BOOLE

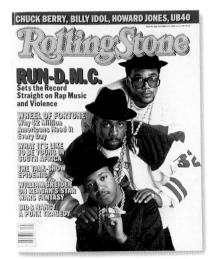

RS 488 | DECEMBER 4TH, 1986
RUN-D.M.C.
Photograph by MOSHE BRAKHA

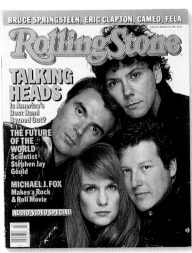

RS 491 | JANUARY 15TH, 1987
TALKING HEADS
Photograph by RICHARD CORMAN

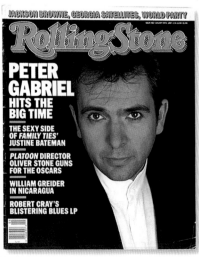

RS 492 | JANUARY 29TH, 1987
PETER GABRIEL
Photograph by ROBERT MAPPLETHORPE

BRUCE HORNSBY, CYNDI LAUPER, BEASTIE BOYS

ISSUE 493 · FEBRUARY 12TH, 1987
U.K. £1.90 · $1.95

Rolling Stone

TV STAR PEE·WEE HERMAN
SATURDAY-MORNING FEVER

MEET THE NEW MEMBERS OF THE ROCK AND ROLL HALL OF FAME

BO DIDDLEY THE ROLLING STONE INTERVIEW

THE CONTROVERSY OVER ABC'S AMERIKA

WILLIAM GREIDER IN HONDURAS

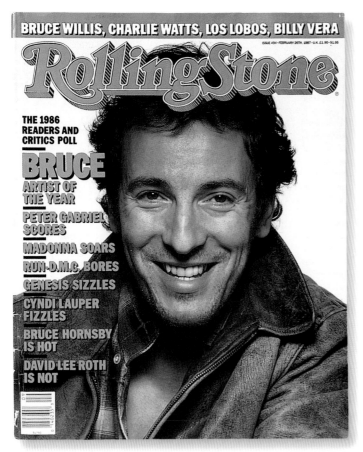

RS 494 | FEBRUARY 26TH, 1987
BRUCE SPRINGSTEEN
Photograph by ALBERT WATSON

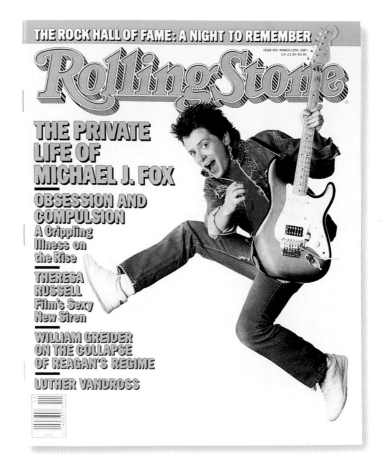

RS 495 | MARCH 12TH, 1987
MICHAEL J. FOX
Photograph by DEBORAH FEINGOLD

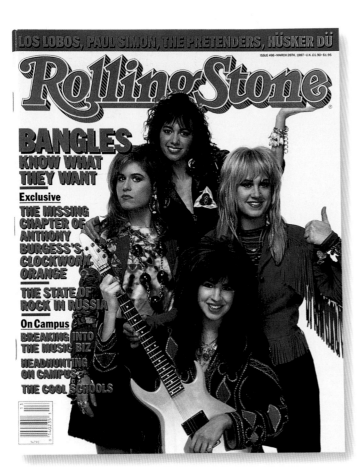

RS 496 | MARCH 26TH, 1987
THE BANGLES
Photograph by BONNIE SCHIFFMAN

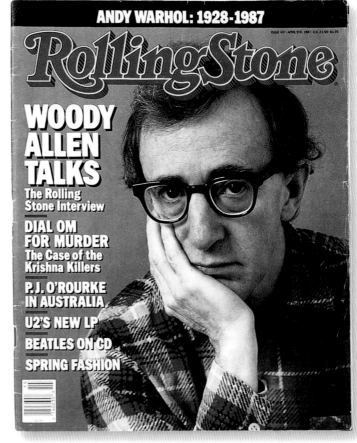

RS 497 | APRIL 9TH, 1987
WOODY ALLEN
Photograph by BRIAN HAMILL

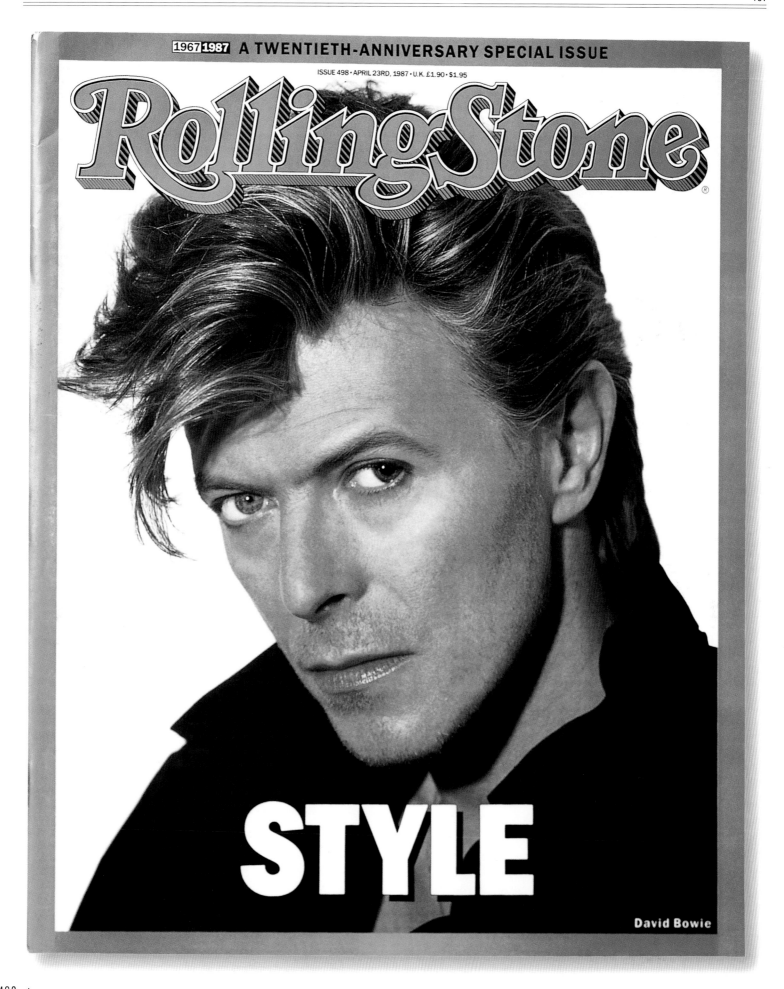

RS 498 | TWENTIETH ANNIVERSARY: STYLE – DAVID BOWIE | Photograph by HERB RITTS | APRIL 23RD, 1987

"THE BEST THING is to have absolutely no idea what you're doing. I much prefer the planned accident to the 'Well, if you turn your head this way, deah, your cheekbone stands out' approach. I've got to have a photograph that's sort of extraordinary looking rather than beautiful." ~ *DAVID BOWIE*

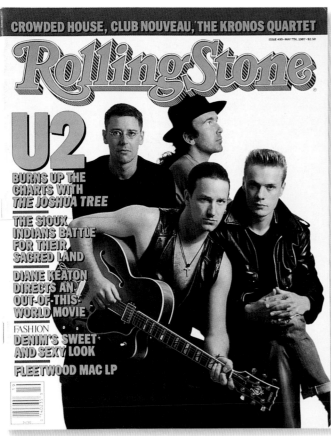

RS 499 | MAY 7TH, 1987
U2
Photograph by ANTON CORBIJN

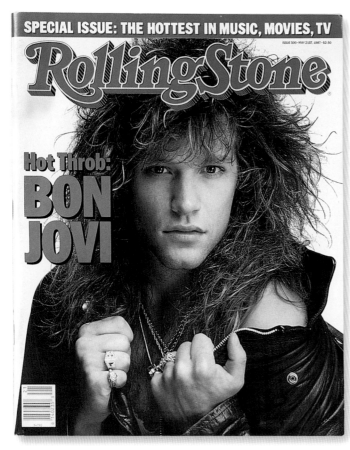

RS 500 | MAY 21ST, 1987
JON BON JOVI
Photograph by E.J. CAMP

For a Twentieth Anniversary special issue, ROLLING STONE selected these as the most exciting, musically outstanding and historically significant concerts and tours of the magazine's first two decades. ○

Cream
The Royal Albert Hall, London
November 26th, 1968

Elvis Presley
"Elvis" NBC TV
December 3rd, 1968

Led Zeppelin
U.S. Tour
December 1968–January 1969

The Beatles
Apple Records building roof, London
January 30th, 1969

The Rolling Stones
U.S. Tour
November–December 1969

John Lennon and the Plastic Ono Band
Varsity Stadium, Toronto
September 13th, 1969

Jimi Hendrix and the Band of Gypsys
The Fillmore East, New York City
December 31st, 1969, and January 1st, 1970

The Who
The Metropolitan Opera House, New York City
June 7th, 1970

Elton John
The Troubadour, Los Angeles
August 25th–30th, 1970

The Allman Brothers Band
The Fillmore East, New York City
March 11th–13th, 1971

David Bowie and the Spiders From Mars
U.S. Tour
September–December 1972

Bob Dylan and the Band
U.S. Tour
January–February 1974

Bruce Springsteen and the E Street Band
The Bottom Line, New York City
August 13th–17th, 1975

Bob Marley and the Wailers
The Roxy, Los Angeles
May 26th, 1976

The Sex Pistols
Winterland, San Francisco
January 14th, 1978

Neil Young and Crazy Horse
U.S. Tour
September–October 1978

The Police
U.S. Tour
October–November 1978

Pink Floyd
The Wall Tour
February–August 1980

The Jacksons
U.S. Tour
July–December 1981

Prince
U.S. Tour
November 1982–March 1983

"**I REMEMBER** very well they told me that they couldn't put five guys on the cover. That was exactly how they sold it to us: 'You can't put five guys on the cover.' And then we saw Paul Simon and twelve guys on the cover [RS 503]. And we went, 'uh-huh!'" ~ *JON BON JOVI*

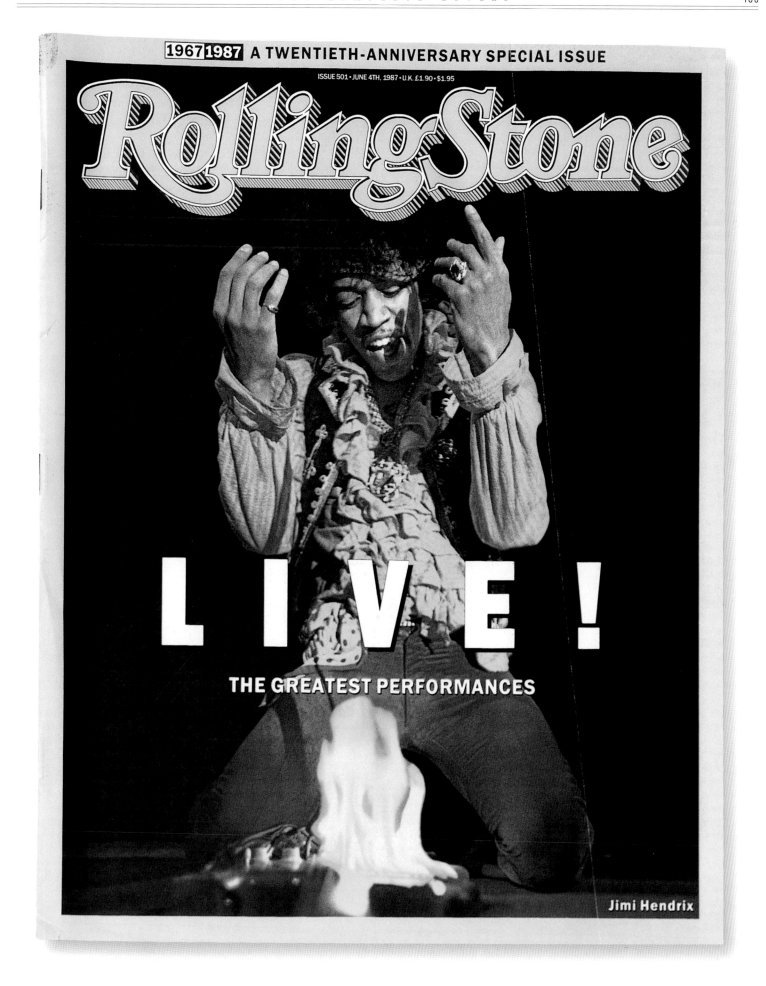

1967 1987 A TWENTIETH-ANNIVERSARY SPECIAL ISSUE

ISSUE 501 • JUNE 4TH, 1987 • U.K. £1.90 • $1.95

RollingStone

LIVE!
THE GREATEST PERFORMANCES

Jimi Hendrix

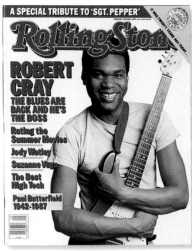

RS 502 | JUNE 18TH, 1987
ROBERT CRAY
Photograph by DEBORAH FEINGOLD

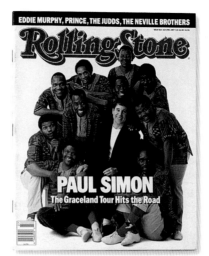

RS 503 | JULY 2ND, 1987
PAUL SIMON &
LADYSMITH BLACK MAMBAZO
Photograph by MARK SELIGER

RS 504/505 | JULY 16TH – JULY 30TH, 1987
THE GRATEFUL DEAD
Photograph by MICHAEL O'NEILL

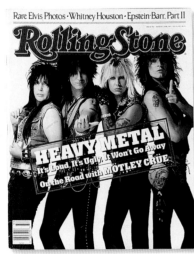

RS 506 | AUGUST 13TH, 1987
MÖTLEY CRÜE
Photograph by E.J. CAMP

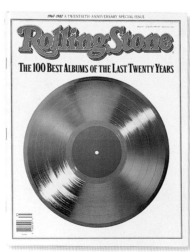

RS 507 | AUGUST 27TH, 1987
THE 100 BEST ALBUMS
OF THE LAST 20 YEARS
Photograph by CONSTANCE HANSEN

For RS 507, the editors of ROLLING STONE *selected the best 100 albums from 1967-1987. These are the Top 25.*

1. **Sgt. Pepper's Lonely Hearts Club Band**
   The Beatles

2. **Never Mind the Bollocks, Here's the Sex Pistols**
   The Sex Pistols

3. **Exile on Main Street**
   The Rolling Stones

4. **Plastic Ono Band**
   John Lennon

5. **Are You Experienced?**
   The Jimi Hendrix Experience

6. **The Rise and Fall of Ziggy Stardust and the Spiders From Mars**
   David Bowie

7. **Astral Weeks**
   Van Morrison

8. **Born to Run**
   Bruce Springsteen

9. **The Beatles [The White Album]**
   The Beatles

10. **What's Going On**
    Marvin Gaye

11. **This Year's Model**
    Elvis Costello

12. **Blood on the Tracks**
    Bob Dylan

13. **The Basement Tapes**
    Bob Dylan and the Band

14. **London Calling**
    The Clash

15. **Beggars Banquet**
    The Rolling Stones

16. **Horses**
    Patti Smith

17. **Abbey Road**
    The Beatles

18. **Let It Bleed**
    The Rolling Stones

19. **The Band**
    The Band

20. **Dirty Mind**
    Prince

21. **The Velvet Underground**
    The Velvet Underground and Nico

22. **Who's Next**
    The Who

23. **Layla**
    Derek and the Dominos

24. **Shoot Out the Lights**
    Richard and Linda Thompson

25. **The Doors**
    The Doors

The work of ROLLING STONE'S *current chief photographer Mark Seliger appears on the cover for the first time on RS 503; he'll shoot 72 more covers (and counting).*

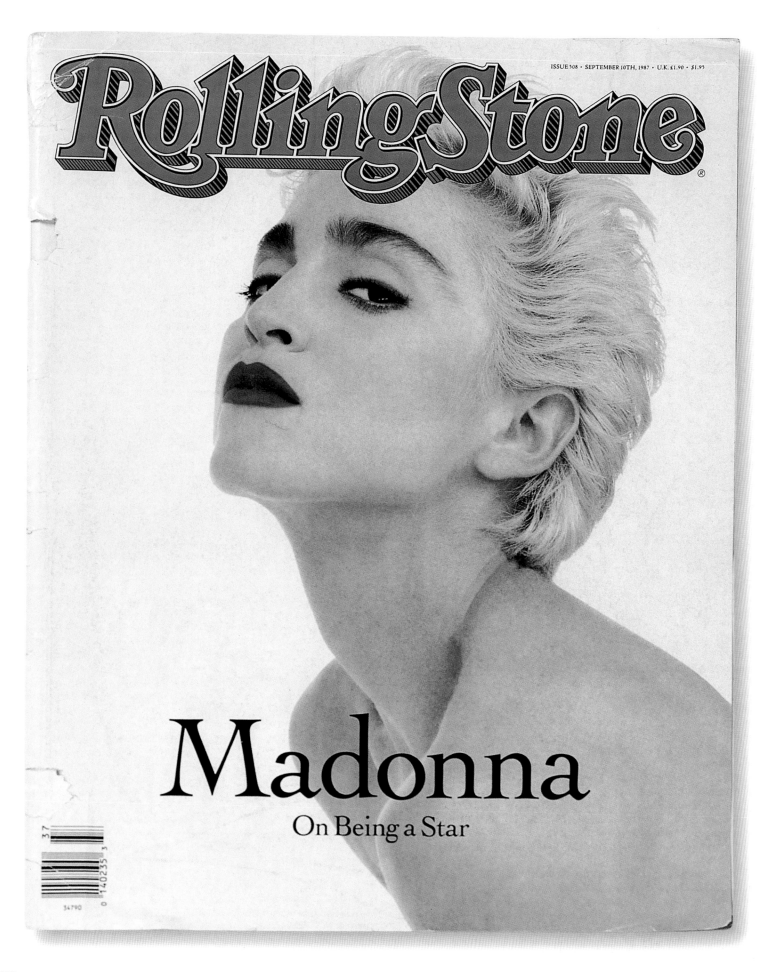

ISSUE 508 · SEPTEMBER 10TH, 1987 · U.K. £1.90 · $1.95

Madonna
On Being a Star

RS 508 | MADONNA | Photograph by HERB RITTS | SEPTEMBER 10TH, 1987

A LETTER FROM THE EDITOR

ROLLING STONE turns twenty years old with this issue. What was started with $7,000 in a loft above a printer in San Francisco is now one of America's leading publications, with offices in six cities and a paid circulation of more than one million.

That ROLLING STONE survived and prospered is due in part to the talent and devotion of the people who have worked on it; to the vitality and growth of the music and culture from which it came and which it covers; and to its own deeply held beliefs and values. This twentieth anniversary is, in a sense, an affirmation of what ROLLING STONE writes about and what it stands for.

We read and hear a lot about the Sixties these days. We are told that they were the most exciting of times, years of great passion and commitment. We are also told that those passions and ideals were full of sound and fury, signifying nothing, that no beliefs or tangible benefits came from that period, and that everyone grew up to be a stockbroker. A lot of people would like to have us believe that what we stood for and what we believed in was childish, shallow and powerless stuff.

In our series of twentieth-anniversary issues, we have attempted to assess those times. In this final anniversary issue we have asked people whose work has stood out and whose voices have often been heard in the pages of ROLLING STONE to talk about their experiences during the past two decades, their understanding of what has survived and what they see ahead.

ROLLING STONE, at age twenty, holds these things dear: high standards in its own craft – writing, reporting, photography, editing, design, publishing; rock & roll music and the popular arts it touches; a commitment to stimulating and nourishing musicians and artists; and having a voice of reason that will be heard in the politics and policies of this country.

We will continue to try our best. We ain't perfect. But we're good, and we're getting better.

~ JANN S. WENNER
[OCTOBER 1987]

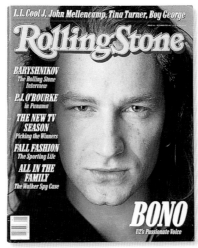

RS 510 | OCTOBER 8TH, 1987
BONO
Photograph by MATTHEW ROLSTON

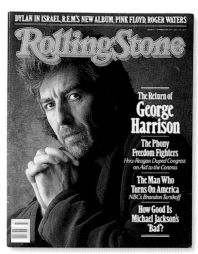

RS 511 | OCTOBER 22ND, 1987
GEORGE HARRISON
Photograph by WILLIAM COUPON

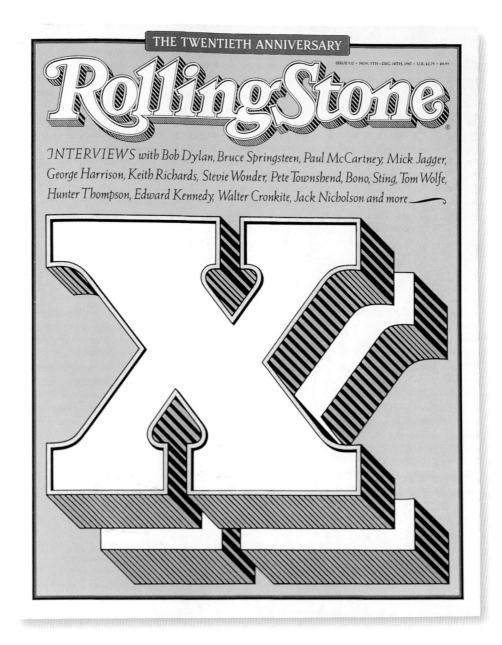

RS 512 | NOVEMBER 5TH – DECEMBER 10TH, 1987
TWENTIETH ANNIVERSARY
Typography by JIM PARKINSON

RS 512 becomes the second best-selling issue in ROLLING STONE's history (and the only all-type cover to make it into the magazine's Top 100 best-sellers). It was the seventh issue designed by ROLLING STONE's current art director, Fred Woodward.

RS 513 | NOVEMBER 19TH, 1987
PINK FLOYD
Illustration by MELISSA GRIMES

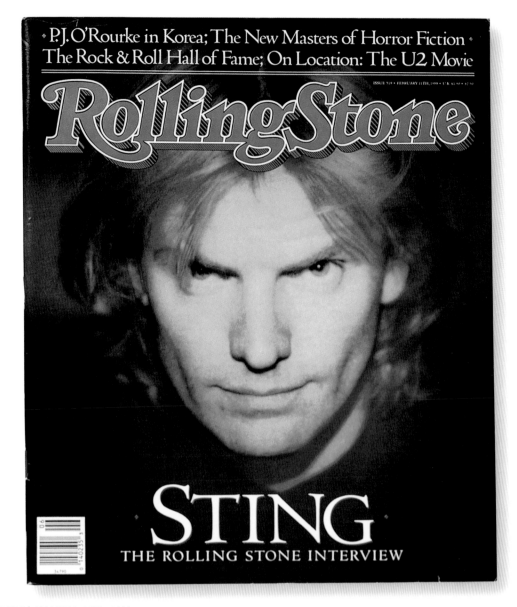

RS 519 | FEBRUARY 11TH, 1988
STING
Photograph by MATT MAHURIN

RS 514 | DECEMBER 3RD, 1987
R.E.M.
Photograph by BRIAN SMALE

RS 517 | JANUARY 14TH, 1988
MICHAEL DOUGLAS
Photograph by ALBERT WATSON

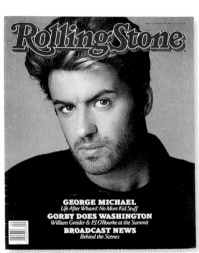

RS 518 | JANUARY 28TH, 1988
GEORGE MICHAEL
Photograph by MATTHEW ROLSTON

Do you remember the last time you were on the cover of Rolling Stone, *in 1982?*

Wasn't the basic premise that I'd cleaned up my act?

The headline was "Robin Williams Comes Clean." Was that honestly the end of the self-abusive chapter in your life?

There was no going back. I realized that the reason I did cocaine was so I wouldn't have to talk to anybody. Cocaine made me so paranoid: If I was doing this interview on cocaine, I would be looking out the window, thinking that somebody might be crawling up fourteen floors to bust me or kick down the door. Then I wouldn't have to talk. Some people have the metabolism where cocaine stimulates them, but I would literally almost get sleepy. For me, it was like a sedative, a way of pulling back from people and from a world that I was afraid of.

[EXCERPT FROM ROBIN WILLIAMS
INTERVIEW BY BILL ZEHME]

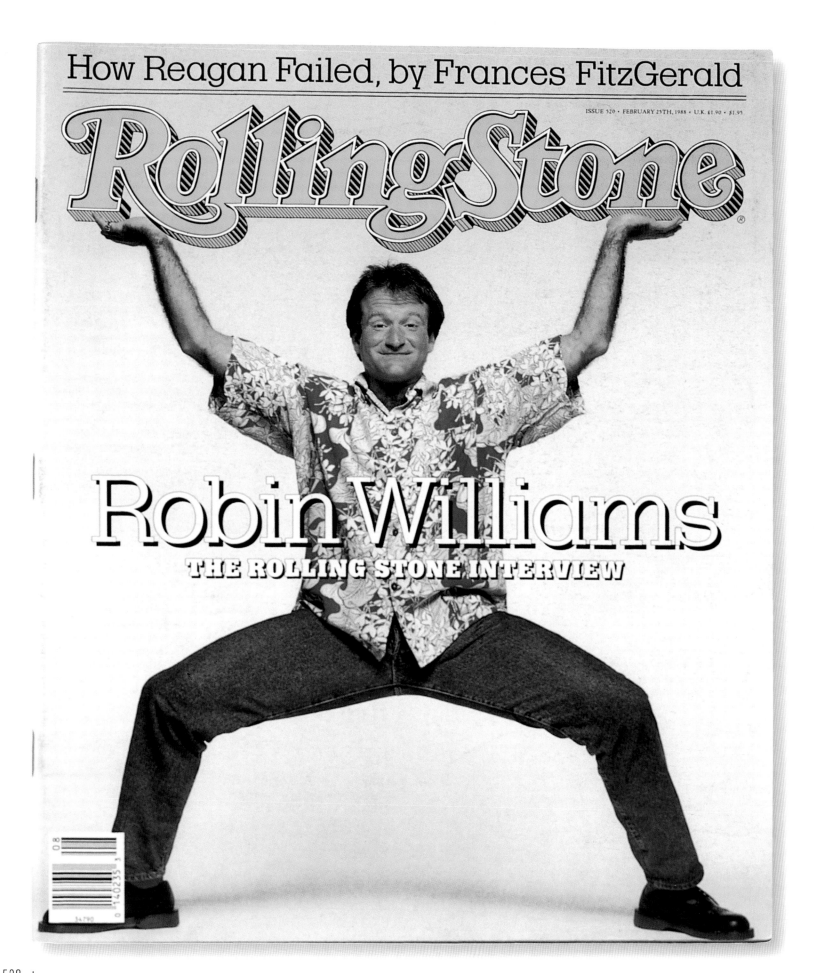

How Reagan Failed, by Frances FitzGerald

ISSUE 520 • FEBRUARY 25TH, 1988 • U.K. £1.90 • $1.95

RollingStone

Robin Williams
THE ROLLING STONE INTERVIEW

RS 521 | MARCH 10TH, 1988
U2
Photograph by MATTHEW ROLSTON

RS 522 | MARCH 24TH, 1988
ROBERT PLANT
Photograph by DAVID MONTGOMERY

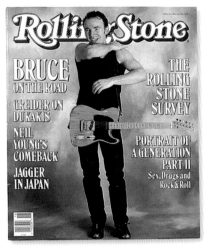

RS 525 | MAY 5TH, 1988
BRUCE SPRINGSTEEN
Photograph by NEAL PRESTON

RS 523 | APRIL 7TH, 1988
MARTIN LUTHER KING JR.
Illustration by PAUL DAVIS

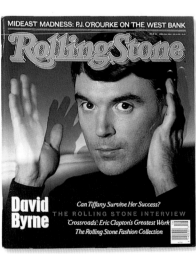

RS 524 | APRIL 21ST, 1988
DAVID BYRNE
Photograph by HIRO

RS 526 | MAY 19TH, 1988
LISA BONET
Photograph by MATTHEW ROLSTON

ROLLING STONE's seventh best-selling cover: Lisa Bonet. At twenty, she was looking for a new image. She'd just completed a stint on the wholesome 'Cosby Show' and was pregnant with her first child by then-husband Lenny Kravitz. At the photo session, her publicist insisted that there be no nude shots. But once Matthew Rolston started shooting, her clothes started dropping faster than the camera could click. Later, when Bonet learned that ROLLING STONE didn't choose the totally nude shot for the cover (it appeared inside), she came to the magazine's offices to lobby – unsuccessfully – for it. The white blouse, obviously, did not hurt sales. ○

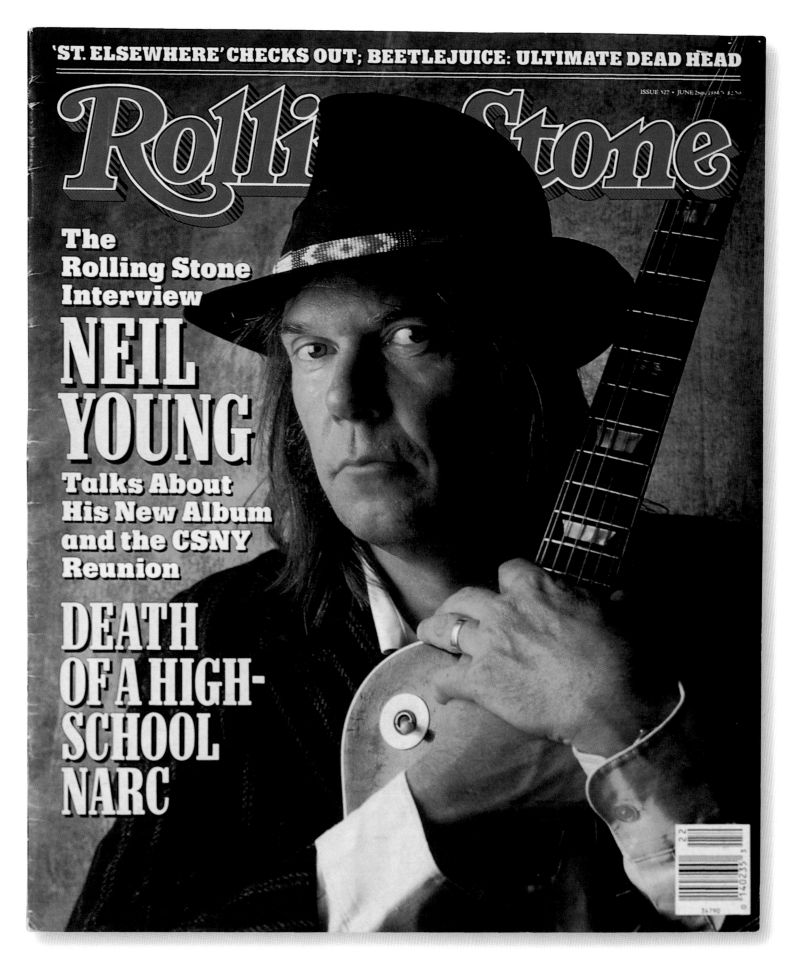

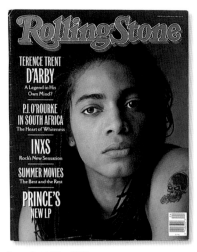

RS 528 | JUNE 16TH, 1988
TERENCE TRENT D'ARBY
Photograph by MATTHEW ROLSTON

RS 529 | JUNE 30TH, 1988
TOM HANKS
Photograph by HERB RITTS

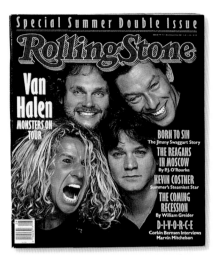

RS 530/531 | JULY 14TH – JULY 28TH, 1988
VAN HALEN
Photograph by TIMOTHY WHITE

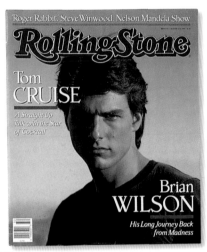

RS 532 | AUGUST 11TH, 1988
TOM CRUISE
Photograph by HERB RITTS

RS 533 | AUGUST 25TH, 1988
ERIC CLAPTON
Photograph by DAVID BAILEY

RS 534 | SEPTEMBER 8TH, 1988
THE 100 BEST SINGLES OF THE LAST TWENTY-FIVE YEARS
Illustration by STEVE PIETZSCH

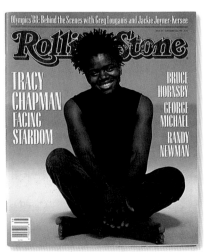

RS 535 | SEPTEMBER 22ND, 1988
TRACY CHAPMAN
Photograph by HERB RITTS

RS 536 | OCTOBER 6TH, 1988
KEITH RICHARDS
Photograph by ALBERT WATSON

RS 537 | OCTOBER 20TH, 1988
JOHN LENNON
Illustration by BARBARA NESSIM

RS 538 | NOVEMBER 3RD, 1988
JOHNNY CARSON &
DAVID LETTERMAN
Photograph by BONNIE SCHIFFMAN

FOR TWENTY-SIX YEARS, Johnny Carson has prodded the content of American life, but Letterman aims at the form of television itself. Carson, a precise, surgical comedian, guided the nation through six presidencies and was, in fact, the president of comedy, governing cleanly, dispensing patronage, steering the dialogue, his staff supporting him as it would a head of state.

Then Letterman entered the talk-show mainstream by reinventing the genre called found comedy, which casts a cold video eye on the conventions of the landscape – dumb ads, bad TV, stores that advertise things they don't have. It was the high point of consumer comedy: Letterman got on the telephone and sent out cameras to try and gauge the disparity between what television had told us and what really existed. For six years and eight months, he has been shooting arrows at television, at the culture, and they never seem to fall back to earth, like the pencils that still hang from the acoustically dotted ceiling of his office. "I mean," he often says on the show, "what's the *deal* here?"

Letterman seemed Carson's heir apparent, and knowing it would do him no good to compete with Johnny's monologues, he tried the very worst jokes, pleasing the audiences with *that* statement about the rest of television. And at first he was bad at, almost embarrassed by, interviewing people. But he slowly became better at making his suspicion of convention work for him. His staff often points out his interview with boxing promoter Don King as the breakthrough: "Come on, Don," he said. "What's the deal with the hair?"

[EXCERPT FROM RS 538 COVER STORY BY PETER W. KAPLAN]

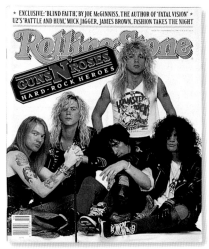

RS 539 | NOVEMBER 17TH, 1988
GUNS N' ROSES
Photograph by TIMOTHY WHITE

RS 540 | DECEMBER 1ST, 1988
STEVE WINWOOD
Photograph by HERB RITTS

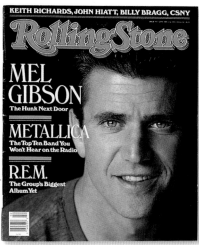

RS 543 | JANUARY 12TH, 1989
MEL GIBSON
Photograph by HERB RITTS

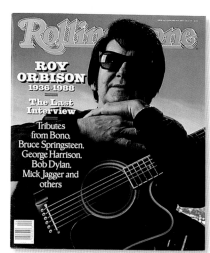

RS 544 | JANUARY 26TH, 1989
ROY ORBISON
Photograph by ANN SUMMA

RS 545 | FEBRUARY 9TH, 1989
JON BON JOVI
Photograph by TIMOTHY WHITE

RS 546 | FEBRUARY 23RD, 1989
SAM KINISON
Photograph by MARK SELIGER

1988 READERS AND CRITICS POLL

U2
BAND OF THE YEAR

BONO
VOICE OF THE YEAR

LOYALTIES
THE NEW BOOK
BY CARL BERNSTEIN

P.J.
O'ROURKE ON GEORGE

BUSH

RS 547 | BONO | Photograph by ANTON CORBIJN | MARCH 9TH, 1989

RS 548 | MARCH 23RD, 1989
MADONNA
Photograph by HERB RITTS

RS 549 | APRIL 16TH, 1989
JAMES BROWN
Illustration by GOTTFRIED HELNWEIN

RS 552 | MAY 18TH, 1989
UMA THURMAN
Photograph by MATTHEW ROLSTON

Frequent cover boy Bono ties with Keith Richards for seventh place with ten covers. RS 547 is his first of four solo showings. U2 has appeared on the cover five times, and Bono was one of twenty for the Live Aid concert cover. Madonna, the woman to appear most often beneath the ROLLING STONE logo, has appeared alone six times (RS 548 is her fourth) and three times with others. With six covers, R.E.M. is one of the only bands with multiple appearances to have always appeared as a group. ○

RS 550 | APRIL 20TH, 1989
R.E.M.
Photograph by TIMOTHY WHITE

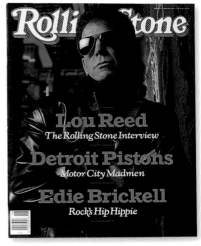

RS 551 | MAY 4TH, 1989
LOU REED
Photograph by MARK SELIGER

RS 553 | JUNE 1ST, 1989
CAST OF 'GHOSTBUSTERS II'
Photograph by TIMOTHY WHITE

RS 554 | JUNE 15TH, 1989
PAUL McCARTNEY
Photograph by HERB RITTS

RS 555 | JUNE 29TH, 1989
MICHAEL KEATON
Photograph by BONNIE SCHIFFMAN

RS 556/557 | JULY 13TH – JULY 27TH, 1989
THE WHO
Photograph by DAVIES & STARR

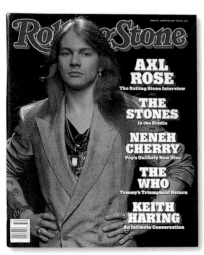

RS 558 | AUGUST 10TH, 1989
AXL ROSE
Photograph by ROBERT JOHN

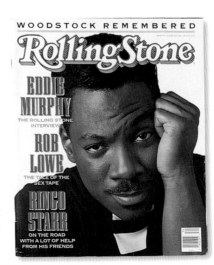

RS 559 | AUGUST 24TH, 1989
EDDIE MURPHY
Photograph by BONNIE SCHIFFMAN

HIS FRIENDS CALL HIM Money. He looks like money, like $40 million, if perchance one speculates. He looks crisp, controlled. He is twenty-eight yet not terribly youthful; he fancies himself much older, more world-weary. He stares straight ahead and seems to notice no one, but he sees all and hears even more. Unless he's erupting into his deft repertoire of character voices, his presence is shy, inscrutable. Usually he is sullen, almost somber – but this creates a quiet aura of power.

You've probably heard this before, but you don't smile much for someone with such a famous smile.

People come up to me and ask me to smile all the time. The thing I hear most is "Yo, smile! Why aren't you smiling? *Smile.* Smile for me!" And it gets irritating. Sometimes in restaurants, I'll see people across the room pressing their fingers into the corners of their mouths, showing me how to smile. I kid you not. When I'm driving down the street, people pull up to me and ask why I'm not smiling. Never mind that if I was driving around with a big smile, then people would think I was a lunatic.

Maybe you're just shy.

That, and I've got a mouth full of fillings. I'm a sugar freak – that's my one indulgence, so I get a lot of cavities, and I have to go to the dentist more often than most.

So the million-dollar smile is fake?

The million-dollar smile is hollow, actually. At any moment, the teeth could all fall out. It's the sad truth: The million-dollar smile is rotten. So I'll fucking smile when I want!

[EXCERPT FROM EDDIE MURPHY
INTERVIEW BY BILL ZEHME]

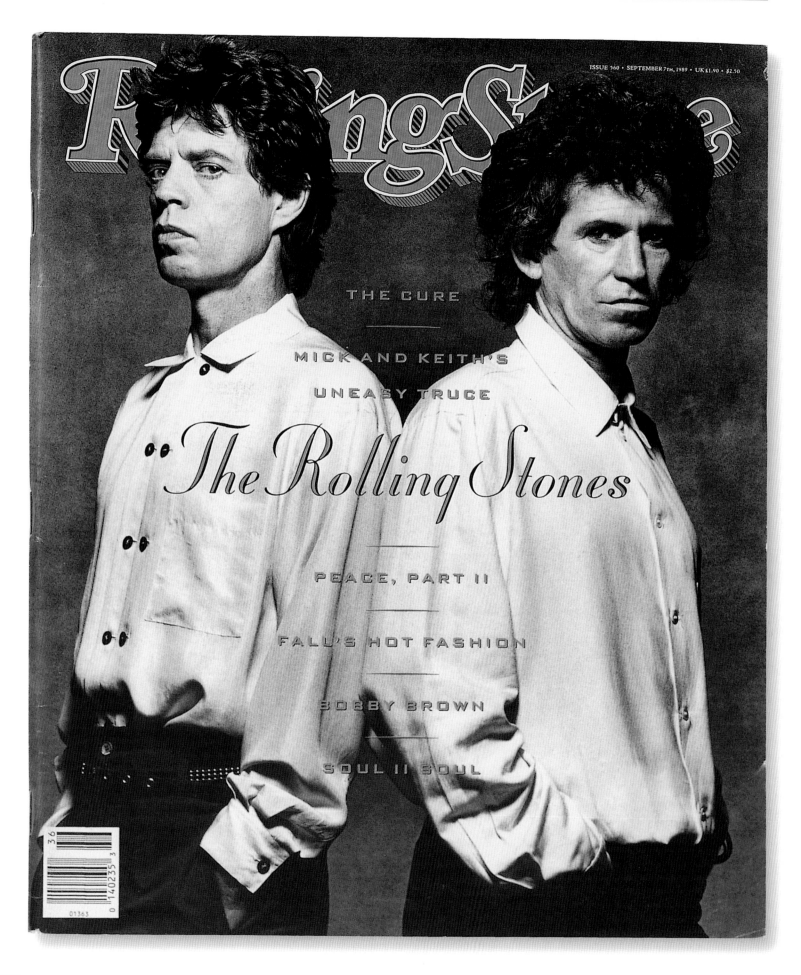

RS 560 | MICK JAGGER & KEITH RICHARDS | Photograph by ALBERT WATSON | SEPTEMBER 7TH, 1989

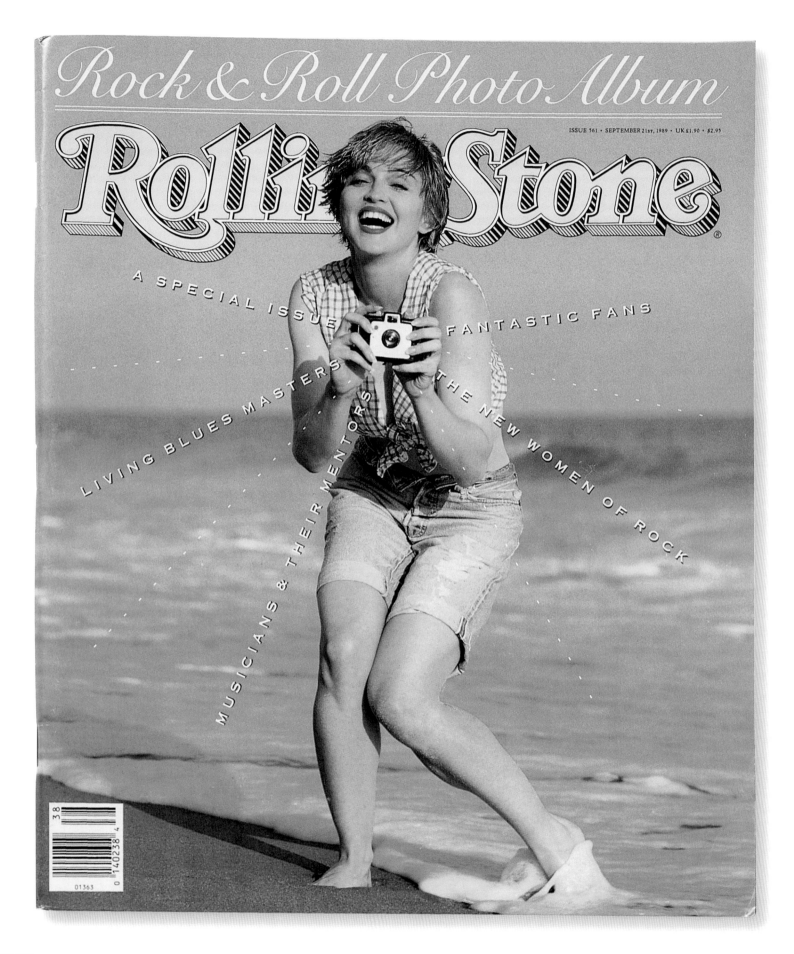

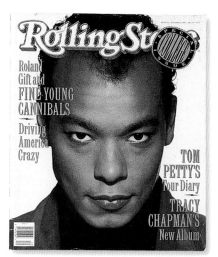

RS 562 | OCTOBER 5TH, 1989
ROLAND GIFT
Photograph by ANDREW MacPHERSON

RS 563 | OCTOBER 19TH, 1989
ANDIE MacDOWELL
Photograph by MATTHEW ROLSTON

RS 564 | NOVEMBER 2ND, 1989
JAY LENO & ARSENIO HALL
Photograph by BONNIE SCHIFFMAN

RS 565 | NOVEMBER 16TH, 1989
THE 100 GREATEST ALBUMS
OF THE EIGHTIES
Illustration by TERRY ALLEN

AS ROCK STARS come to exercise increasing control over their images, photographers face the challenge of finding ways to exercise their own powerful art, finding ways to say something unique and penetrating about people who are often extremely wary – or manipulatively savvy – about how they are represented. Photographers must also search for surprising aspects of the world of music to bring to light.

In this Rock & Roll Photo Album, ROLLING STONE's photographers do both with wit and flair. Herb Ritts captures a frolicsome Madonna turning the tables on her fans – and doctoring still another spin of the carefully crafted image that has helped make her one of the most recognizable stars in the world.

[EXCERPT FROM RS 561 ESSAY
BY ANTHONY DeCURTIS]

RS 566 | NOVEMBER 30TH, 1989
JERRY GARCIA
Photograph by WILLIAM COUPON

1990

" For a few years in Seattle, it was the Summer of Love, and it was so great. To be able to just jump out on top of the crowd with my guitar and be held up and pushed to the back of the room and then brought back with no harm done to me – it was a celebration of something that no one could put their finger on. But once it got into the mainstream, it was over. "

~ KURT COBAIN

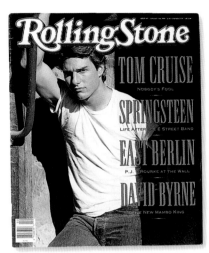

RS 569 | JANUARY 11TH, 1990
TOM CRUISE
Photograph by HERB RITTS

RS 570 | JANUARY 25TH, 1990
BILLY JOEL
Photograph by TIMOTHY WHITE

RS 571 | FEBRUARY 8TH, 1990
PAUL McCARTNEY
Photograph by TIMOTHY WHITE

RS 572 | FEBRUARY 22ND, 1990
JANET JACKSON
Photograph by MATTHEW ROLSTON

RS 573 | MARCH 8TH, 1990
KEITH RICHARDS & MICK JAGGER
Photograph by NEAL PRESTON

RS 574 | MARCH 22ND, 1990
THE B-52'S
Photograph by MARK SELIGER

FOR SOME OF US, it began late at night: huddled under bedroom covers with our ears glued to a radio pulling in black voices charged with intense emotion and propelled by a wildly kinetic rhythm through the after-midnight static. Growing up in the white-bread America of the Fifties, we had never heard anything like it, but we reacted, or remember reacting, instantaneously and were converted. We were believers before we knew what it was that had so spectacularly ripped the dull, familiar fabric of our lives. We asked our friends, maybe an older brother or sister. We found out that they called it rock & roll. It was so much more vital and alive than

any music we had ever heard before that it needed a new category: Rock & roll was much more than new music for us. It was an obsession, and a way of life.

For some of us, it began a little later, with our first glimpse of Elvis on the family television set. But for those of us growing up in the Fifties, it didn't seem to matter how or where we first heard the music. Our reactions were remarkably uniform. Here, we knew, was a sonic cataclysm come bursting (apparently) out of nowhere, with the power to change our lives forever. Because it was obviously, inarguably *our* music. If we had any initial doubt about that, our parents' horrified – or at best dismissive – reactions banished those doubts. Growing up in a world we were only beginning to understand, we had finally found something for us; for us together, for us alone.

[EXCERPT FROM ESSAY ON THE FIFTIES BY ROBERT PALMER]

RS 575 | APRIL 5TH, 1990
AEROSMITH
Photograph by MARK SELIGER

RS 577 | MAY 3RD, 1990
BONNIE RAITT
Photograph by E.J. CAMP

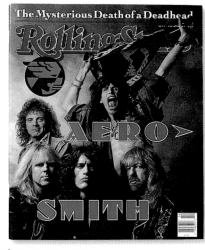

RS 576 | APRIL 19TH, 1990
THE FIFTIES
Illustration by TERRY ALLEN & DENNIS ORTIZ-LOPEZ

RS 578 | MAY 17TH, 1990
CLAUDIA SCHIFFER
Photograph by HERB RITTS

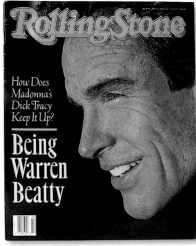

RS 579 | MAY 31ST, 1990
WARREN BEATTY
Photograph by HERB RITTS

HE IS A GHOST. He is human ectoplasm. He is here, and then he is gone, and then you aren't sure he was ever here to begin with. He has had sex with everyone, or at least tried. He has had sex with someone you know or someone who knows someone you know or someone you wish you knew, or at least tried. He is famous for sex, he is famous for having sex with the famous, he is famous. He makes mostly good films when he makes films, which is mostly not often. He has had sex with most of his leading ladies. He befriends all women and many politicians and whispers advice to them on the telephone in the dead of night. Or else he does not speak at all to anyone ever, except to those who know him best, if anyone can really know him. He is an adamant enigma, elusive for the sake of elusiveness, which makes him desirable, although for what, no one completely understands. He is much smarter than you think but perhaps not as smart as he thinks, if only because he thinks too much about being smart. He admits to none of this. He admits to nothing much. He denies little. And so his legend grows.

He has talked. And talked. For days, I have listened to him talk. I have listened to him listen to himself talk. I have probed and pelted and listened some more. For days. He speaks slowly, fearfully, cautiously, editing every syllable, slicing off personal color and spontaneous wit, steering away from opinion, introspection, humanness. He is mostly evasive. His pauses are elephantine. Broadway musicals could be mounted during his pauses. He *works* at this. Ultimately, he renders himself blank. In *Dick Tracy,* he battles a mysterious foe called the Blank. In life, he is the Blank doing battle with himself. It is a fascinating showdown, exhilarating to behold.

To interview Warren Beatty is to want to kill him.

Do you aspire to marriage?

I have never bristled at the notion.

Would you have limitations as a husband?

No. I haven't been in a bubble. I've had very close relationships with people that have lasted longer than my friends' marriages that existed at the same time.

What's the most important thing to know about women?

[*Pauses twenty-one seconds*] That they're not very different from men.

What do you mean?

That's eight pages.

Eight classic pages. What do you mean?

[*Pauses fourteen seconds*] Well, I'm lucky that I grew up in an atmosphere in which I was taught to treat women as respectfully as I would treat men. I don't differentiate. Sometimes people don't treat themselves very seriously, but that might happen more often when this business of sexual attraction rears its head and we all get a little giddy.

Are you a better friend to women than you are to men?

I hope not. I'm probably guilty of giving more women the benefit of the doubt than men. And I think there are probably more women that give me the benefit of the doubt than men do. But I'm not even sure of that.

Describe what love feels like to you.

Do unto others.

Romantic love.

Define romantic love.

When you're in love.

Well, as soon as you use the word *romantic,* then the word *fiction* begins to peep around the corner, or the word *bullshit* begins to lurk in the shadow. But if you say *sexual love,* which I think is not bullshit and not fictitious, that's something else. But I think there's a certain amount of do unto others even in that.

How do you know you're in love? What incites your love?

I don't know if you ever figure that out. If you're smart, you don't figure it out. Of course, you always try to figure it out. But if you're smart, you know you can't. I take great pride in my stupidity in this area. I have no clear way of being able to define at what point [*twenty-one seconds*] passion for loyalty has overcome me.

Has your heart been broken?

Sure.

How many times?

[*Laughs richly, then seventeen-second pause*] I'm sure I've reached my quota. But then you'd have to define *break* and *heart.*

How do you mend yours? Give advice.

To the lovelorn? There is no away. Nobody goes away. Except the Big Away, and there's nothing you can do about it. If you really love someone [*seventeen seconds*] and they're healthy and happy . . . you ought to be able to live with that.

Can you always be that philosophical?

[*Twenty-four seconds*] Pretty close.

[EXCERPT FROM WARREN BEATTY
INTERVIEW BY BILL ZEHME]

ISSUE 580 • JUNE 14TH, 1990 • $2.50 • CAN $2.95 • UK £2.00

Nothing Compares to

SINÉAD O'CONNOR

RS 580 | SINÉAD O'CONNOR | Photograph by ANDREW MacPHERSON | JUNE 14TH, 1990

RS 581 | JUNE 28TH, 1990
BART SIMPSON
Illustration by MATT GROENING

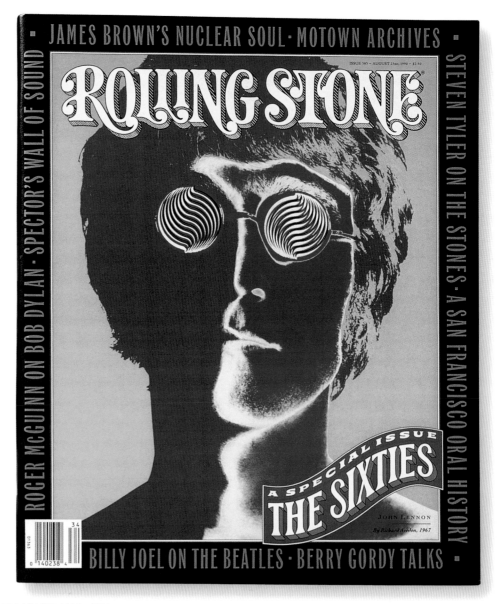

RS 585 | AUGUST 23RD, 1990
THE SIXTIES – JOHN LENNON
Photograph by RICHARD AVEDON

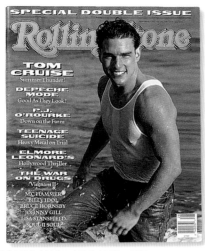

RS 582/583 | JULY 12TH – JULY 26TH, 1990
TOM CRUISE
Photograph by HERB RITTS

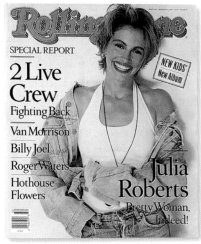

RS 584 | AUGUST 9TH, 1990
JULIA ROBERTS
Photograph by HERB RITTS

RS 586 | SEPTEMBER 6TH, 1990
M.C. HAMMER
Photograph by FRANK W. OCKENFELS 3

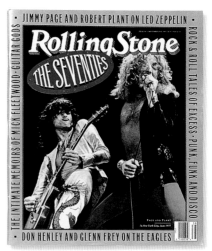

RS 587 | SEPTEMBER 20TH, 1990
THE SEVENTIES –
JIMMY PAGE & ROBERT PLANT
Photograph by BOB GRUEN

To date, Bart Simpson holds the record as ROLLING STONE's *youngest cover subject (RS 581) – not counting the babies or children pictured with cover subjects Doug Sahm (RS 23), Joe Dallesandro (RS 80),*
Jackson Browne (RS 161), Michael Douglas (RS 288) or Rodney Dangerfield (RS 326).

FOR A LONG and unforgettable season, rock was a voice of unity and liberty. In the 1950s, rock & roll meant disruption: It was the clamor of young people, kicking hard against the Eisenhower era's ethos of vapid repression. By the onset of the 1960s, that spirit had been largely tamed or simply impeded by numerous misfortunes, including the film and army careers of Elvis Presley, the death of Buddy Holly, the blacklisting of Jerry Lee Lewis and Chuck Berry and the persecution of DJ Alan Freed, who had been stigmatized by payola charges by Tin Pan Alley interests and politicians angered with his championing of R&B and rock & roll. In 1960, the music of Frankie Avalon, Paul Anka, Connie Francis and Mitch Miller (an avowed enemy of rock & roll) ruled the airwaves and the record charts, giving some observers the notion that decency and order had returned to the popular mainstream. But within a few years, rock would regain its disruptive power with a joyful vengeance until, by the decade's end, it would be seen as a genuine force of cultural and political consequence. For a long and unforgettable season, it was a truism – or threat, depending on your point of view – that rock & roll could (and *should*) make a difference: that it was eloquent and inspiring and principled enough to change the world – maybe even to save it.

[EXCERPT FROM THE SIXTIES ESSAY BY MIKAL GILMORE]

RS 588 | OCTOBER 4TH, 1990
THE WOMEN OF 'TWIN PEAKS'
Photograph by MATTHEW ROLSTON

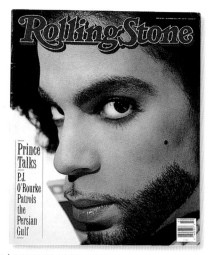

RS 589 | OCTOBER 18TH, 1990
PRINCE
Photograph by JEFF KATZ

RS 590 | NOVEMBER 1ST, 1990
LIVING COLOUR
Photograph by MARK SELIGER

"THE IDEA of America as a family is naive, maybe sentimental or simplistic, but it's a good idea." ~ *Bruce Springsteen*

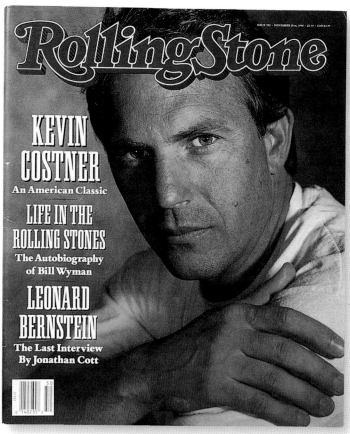

RS 592 | NOVEMBER 29TH, 1990
KEVIN COSTNER
Photograph by GWENDOLEN CATES

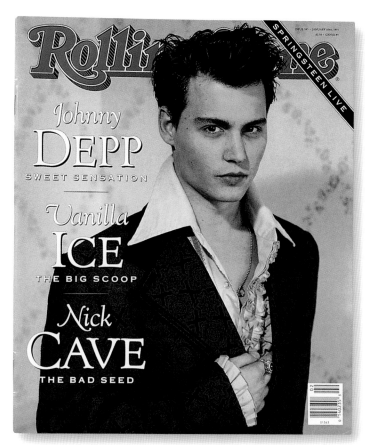

RS 595 | JANUARY 10TH, 1991
JOHNNY DEPP
Photograph by HERB RITTS

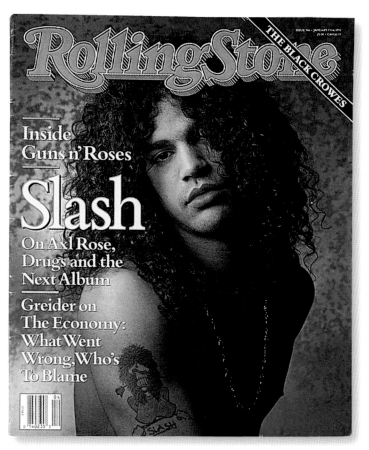

RS 596 | JANUARY 24TH, 1991
SLASH
Photograph by MARK SELIGER

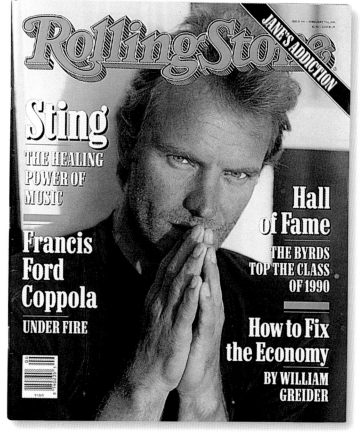

RS 597 | FEBRUARY 7TH, 1991
STING
Photograph by HERB RITTS

READERS SOUND OFF: ANNUAL MUSIC AWARDS

RollingStone

O'ROURKE IN THE GULF

ISSUE 599 • MARCH 7TH, 1991 • $2.50 • CAN $2.95

Artist
of the Year
Sinéad
O'CONNOR

The
Rolling Stone
Interview

RS 600 | MARCH 21ST, 1991
JODIE FOSTER
Photograph by MATTHEW ROLSTON

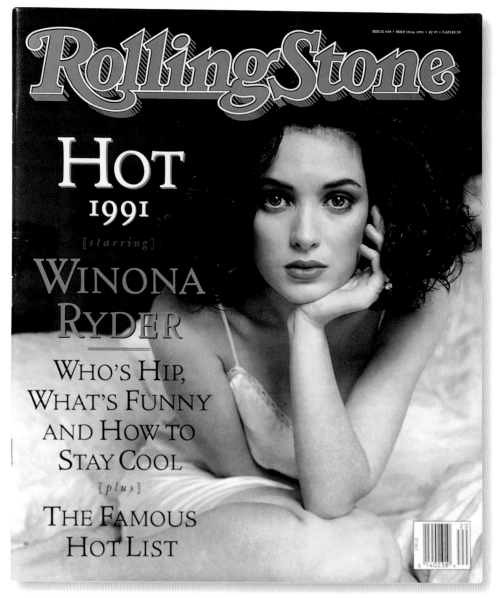

RS 604 | MAY 16TH, 1991
WINONA RYDER
Photograph by HERB RITTS

RS 601 | APRIL 4TH, 1991
JIM MORRISON
Photograph by JOEL BRODSKY

RS 602 | APRIL 18TH, 1991
NEW FACES 1991
VARIOUS PHOTOGRAPHERS

RS 603 | MAY 2ND, 1991
WILSON PHILLIPS
Photograph by ANDREW ECCLES

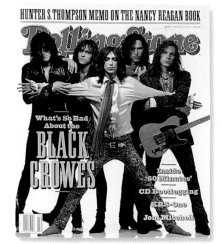

RS 605 | MAY 30TH, 1991
THE BLACK CROWES
Photograph by MARK SELIGER

"THIS WAS a great chance to re-create an era that I feel I would have really flourished in, [when] nothing I would have done would have been censored."
~ *MADONNA*

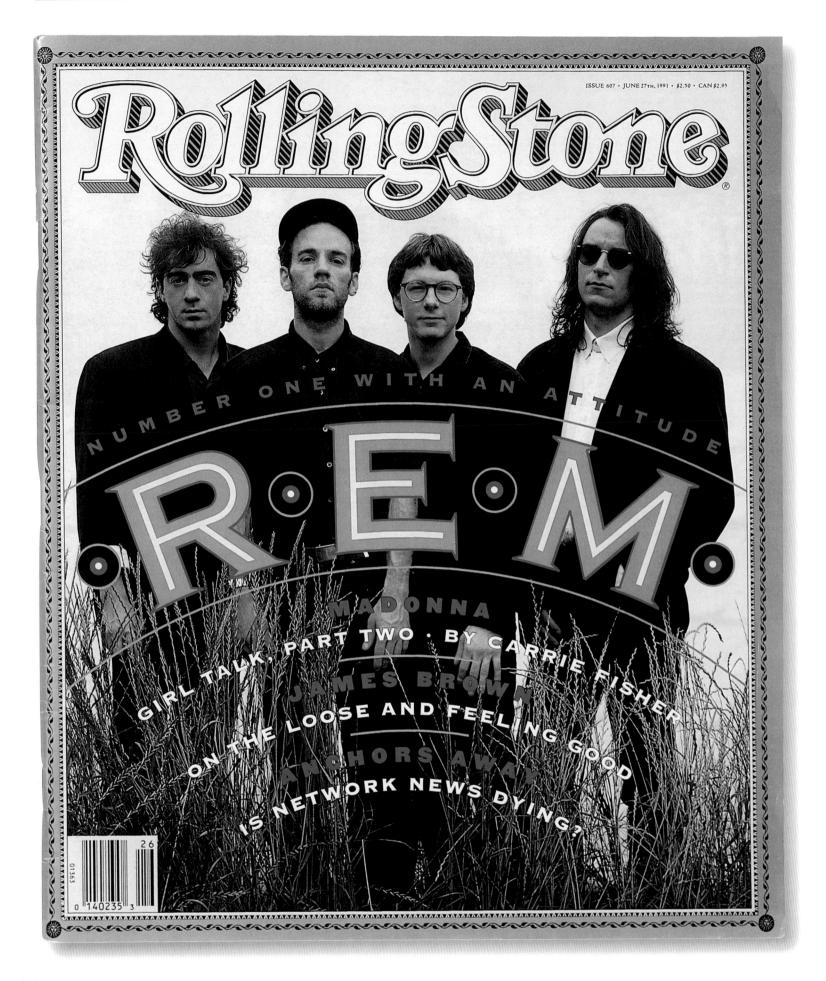

ISSUE 607 • JUNE 27TH, 1991 • $2.50 • CAN $2.95

RollingStone

NUMBER ONE WITH AN ATTITUDE

·R·E·M·

MADONNA

GIRL TALK, PART TWO · BY CARRIE FISHER

JAMES BROWN
ON THE LOOSE AND FEELING GOOD

ANCHORS AWAY
IS NETWORK NEWS DYING?

THIS IS A DAY like I thought being a pop star would be like when I was a kid. You get in the limo, you go across town to do a photo session, you buy a shirt and then wear it right away and get photographed for the cover of ROLLING STONE. You get in another limo with a couple of journalists who hang on your every word, and then go speak to Southeast Asia."

~ PETER BUCK

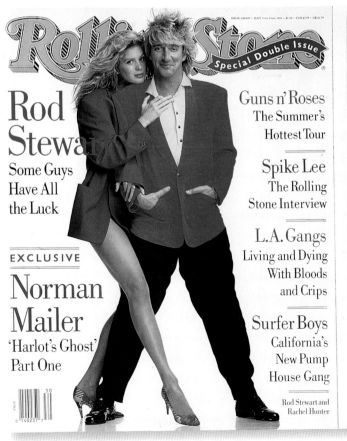

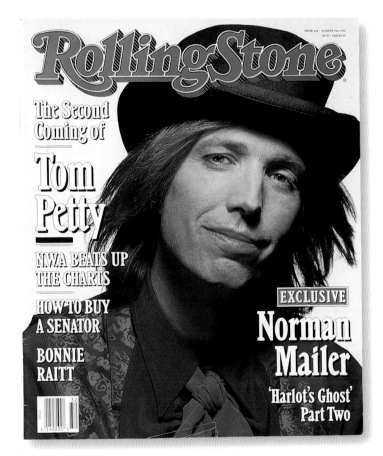

RS 608/609 | JULY 11TH–JULY 25TH, 1991
ROD STEWART & RACHEL HUNTER
Photograph by ANDREW ECCLES

RS 610 | AUGUST 8TH, 1991
TOM PETTY
Photograph by MARK SELIGER

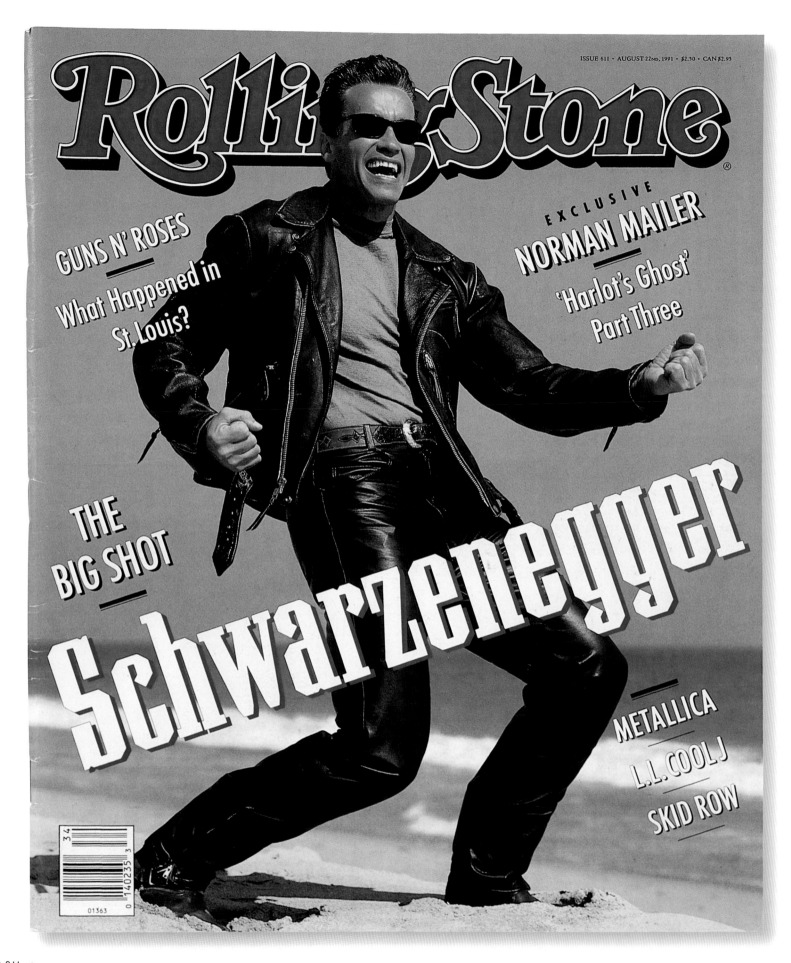

ISSUE 611 · AUGUST 22ND, 1991 · $2.50 · CAN $2.95

GUNS N' ROSES

What Happened in St. Louis?

EXCLUSIVE
NORMAN MAILER

'Harlot's Ghost' Part Three

THE BIG SHOT

Schwarzenegger

METALLICA

L.L. COOL J

SKID ROW

01363   0 "14023503

MEN ARE IN CRISIS, whereas he is not. He does not know the meaning of "crisis." Or perhaps he does, but he pretends otherwise. He is Austrian, after all, and some things do not translate easily between cultures. (Lederhosen, for instance.) Throughout the world he is called Arnold, but that is because there are too many letters in Schwarzenegger. By now everyone has come to know that the literal meaning of Schwarzenegger is "black plowman," and like many black plowmen before him, Arnold knows exactly what it feels like when a horse falls on top of him. There is much pain, yes, but pain means little to Arnold, especially when there are stuntmen available. Anyway, Arnold is never in crisis. For this reason, it is imperative that Arnold be Arnold so that others may learn. And, from what society tells us, there has never been a more crucial epoch in history for Arnold to be alive, which is, at the very least, pretty convenient.

[EXCERPT FROM RS 611 COVER STORY
BY BILL ZEHME]

*   *   *   *   *

"I JUST GOT ARRESTED," Paul said over the telephone to his sister, Abby. "I'm gonna disappear now."

A reluctant fugitive since the fateful night of July 26th, Paul Reubens has kept in touch with only three friends. He won't tell them where he is. In his house in the Hollywood Hills, an answering machine takes calls from well-wishers. Paul's secretary calls back to say thanks.

The day after he was arrested for indecent exposure in a Florida pornographic theater, the bright red door of *Pee-wee's Playhouse* – a Saturday-morning kids' show that even parents loved – was boarded up. Unsold Pee-wee Herman dolls became orphans. Disney-MGM Studios dropped him from its two-minute tour video. Executives at Disney, CBS and Toys 'R' Us had acted swiftly to protect the interests of American children.

Bad boy, Pee-wee. Rest in peace, Pee-wee Herman. *Nyah, nyah, nyah, nyah, nyah.* An adult playing a child, he needed to be punished like a child for acting like an adult. Paul's own lawyer provided an epitaph: "His career is over." It was as if redheaded Randy, the Playhouse bully, had poisoned the gestalt: no more gentle dinosaurs or anthropomorphic furniture, no more secret word.

[EXCERPT FROM RS 614 COVER STORY
BY PETE WILKINSON]

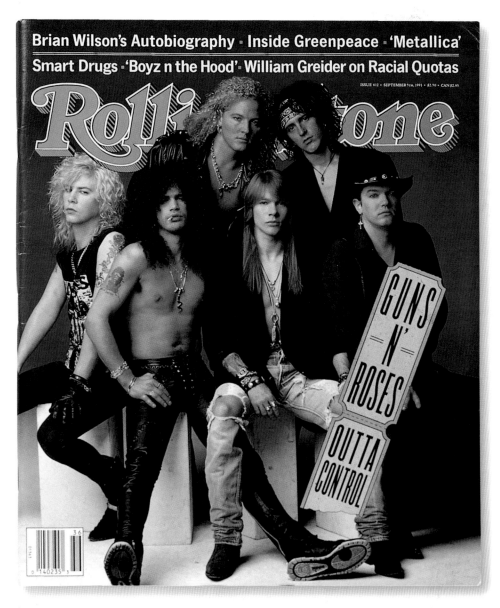

RS 612 | SEPTEMBER 5TH, 1991
GUNS N' ROSES
Photograph by HERB RITTS

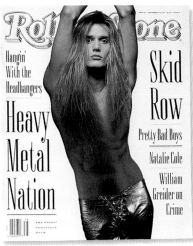

RS 613 | SEPTEMBER 19TH, 1991
SEBASTIAN BACH
Photograph by MARK SELIGER

RS 614 | OCTOBER 3RD, 1991
PEE-WEE HERMAN
Photograph by JANETTE BECKMAN

ISSUE 615 · OCTOBER 17TH, 1991 · $2.50 · CAN $2.95

Guns n'
Roses'
New LPs

Three
Days
at the
Moscow
Barricades

The
Rolling
Stone
Interview

Eric Clapton's Blues

"**AFTER MY SON** [Conor] was killed . . . it's funny, but I didn't really feel anything. I went blank. As Lori [Conor's mother] has observed, I just turned to stone, and I wanted to get away from everybody. The Italian side of the family . . . well, Italians are very dramatic, and it was all out in the open, this wailing and gnashing of teeth. But for me, from the way I was raised and being English, well, we go inside ourselves and keep a stiff upper lip. We pretend that we're okay, and we take care of business. But inside it's a different story."

~ *ERIC CLAPTON*

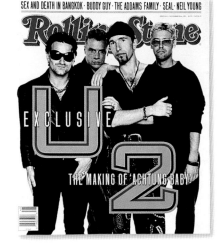

RS 616 | OCTOBER 31ST, 1991
JERRY GARCIA
Photograph by MARK SELIGER

RS 617 | NOVEMBER 14TH, 1991
METALLICA
Photograph by MARK SELIGER

RS 618 | NOVEMBER 28TH, 1991
U2
Photograph by ANTON CORBIJN

RS 622 | JANUARY 23RD, 1992
HUNTER S. THOMPSON
Illustration by RALPH STEADMAN

RS 623 | FEBRUARY 6TH, 1992
JIMI HENDRIX
Photograph by GERED MANKOWITZ

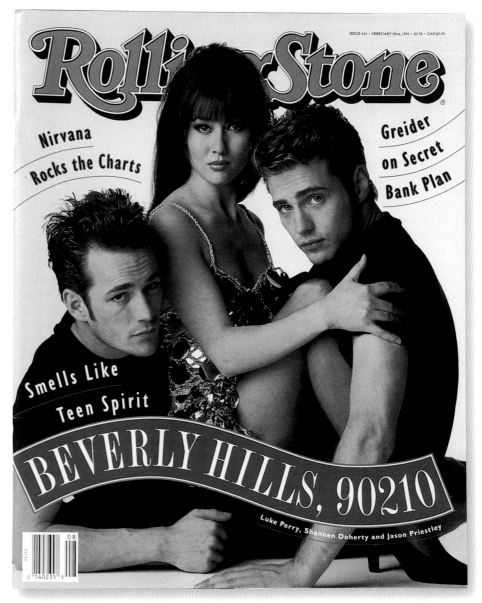

RS 624 | FEBRUARY 20TH, 1992
CAST OF 'BEVERLY HILLS, 90210'
Photograph by ANDREW ECCLES

RS 625 | MARCH 5TH, 1992
R.E.M.
Photograph by ALBERT WATSON

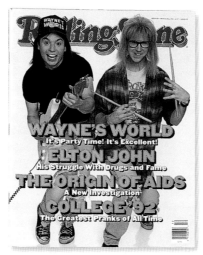

RS 626 | MARCH 19TH, 1992
MIKE MYERS & DANA CARVEY
Photograph by BONNIE SCHIFFMAN

"I'M DOWN on my elbow, and she's sitting on my kidneys, and Jason has his leg back up around her, holding her up. It looks like a wonderfully choreographed thing, but we're all in intense physical pain. I remember Jason would peek his head around her hairdo, and I'd look around the other side of her hairdo, and he'd go, 'ROLLING STONE,' and I'd go, 'I know!'"

~ LUKE PERRY

ONLY A FEW MINUTES AGO, Axl Rose, sprawled on the floor of his Las Vegas hotel villa, mentioned his lack of privacy. Now, as if to prove his point, someone knocks on the door. Rose gets up to answer it, peering out into the darkness to find two breathless, carefully made-up fans who've somehow breached Guns n' Roses' security.

"I hope you know we went to a lot of trouble just to say hello to you," the first girl says. "I'm only here because she dragged me here," says the second. "I'm not a very big Guns n' Roses fan or anything."

Given Rose's reputation as a hothead, the predictable reaction would be irritation – or at the very least a wry "see what I mean" smile. But Rose greets the giggly pair like a home owner welcoming a group of trick-or-treaters. He invites them in and, smiling, begins asking them questions: Do you live here? What are your names? How did you find out where I was? As the story unravels – it turns out the two posed as call girls to extract his room number from a tight-lipped hotel clerk – Rose seems genuinely charmed.

As do his visitors. They stick around for nearly an hour, and Rose is the perfect host – cracking jokes, offering them dinner, even laughing off their occasional barbs ("So, are you going on on time tomorrow, or what?"). By the time they leave, they've been made to feel as if it were the most natural thing in the world to barge in uninvited on a total stranger.

*   *   *   *   *   *   *

Do you want to talk about your childhood in a little more detail?

Sure.

What's your earliest memory?

. . . I've done regression therapy all the way back, just about to the point of conception. I kind of know what was going on then.

Can you talk about what you've learned?

Just that . . . my mom's pregnancy wasn't a welcome thing. My mom got a lot of problems out of it, and I was aware of those problems. That would tend to make you real fucking insecure about how the world felt about your ass. My real father was a pretty fucked-up individual. I didn't care too much for him when I was born. I didn't like the way he treated me before I was born. I didn't like the way he treated my mother. So when I came out, I was just wishing the motherfucker was *dead*.

Talking about being conscious of things that happened before you were born might throw a few people.

I don't really care, because that's regression therapy, and if they've got a problem with it, they can go fuck themselves. It's major, and it's legit, and it all fits together in my life. Everything is stored in your mind. And part of you is aware from very early on and is storing information and reacting. Every time I realize I have a problem with something, and I can finally admit it to myself, then we go, "Okay, now what were the earliest stages?" and we start going back through it.

[EXCERPT FROM AXL ROSE INTERVIEW BY KIM NEELY]

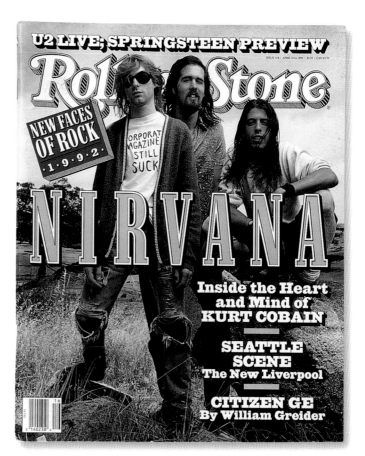

RS 628 | APRIL 16TH, 1992
NIRVANA
Photograph by MARK SELIGER

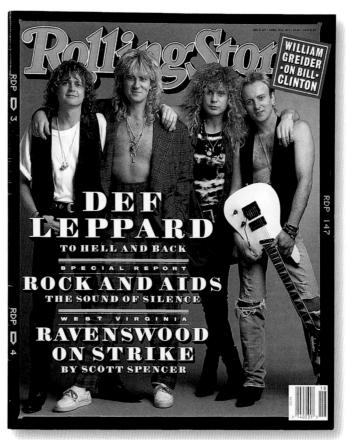

RS 629 | APRIL 30TH, 1992
DEF LEPPARD
Photograph by MARK SELIGER

"I SAID, 'I think that's a great shirt. I think that's *great*. That's a great shirt! – but let's shoot a couple, with and without it.' [Kurt Cobain] said, 'No, I'm not going to take my shirt off.'" ~ MARK SELIGER

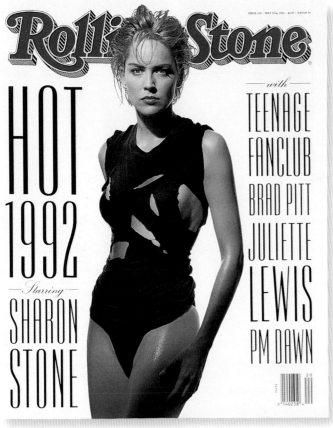

RS 630 | MAY 14TH, 1992
SHARON STONE
Photograph by ALBERT WATSON

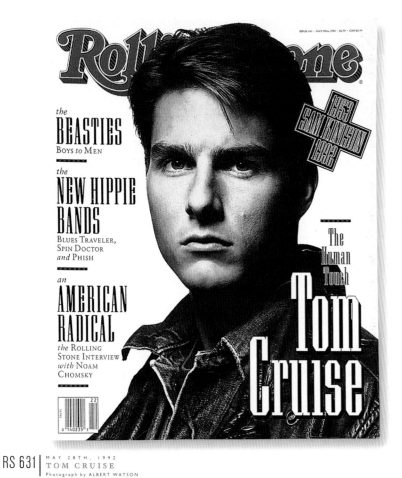

RS 631 | MAY 28TH, 1992
TOM CRUISE
Photograph by ALBERT WATSON

A LETTER FROM THE EDITOR

We see this issue as a kind of impressionistic history of the past quarter century. We started by choosing thirty of our best stories, then asked the writers to speak about themselves, about the reporting of their story and about the context of the work – i.e., what it's like to work at ROLLING STONE. . . .

The paths that led editors and writers to ROLLING STONE are a part of [the] story. They came from all kinds of places in all kinds of ways. Some got assignments after sending a letter with a good idea; David Harris wrote from prison, where he was serving two years for refusing the draft (and in his first visit to the office was advised to hunch over, since I was supposedly intimidated by tall people); Eric Ehrmann wrote from his fraternity in Ohio. Joe Eszterhas was thought to be a narc by the mailroom guys when he first came to buy back issues (and went on to write major exposés of narcs in ROLLING STONE).

Hunter S. Thompson's first assignment was to write about his nearly successful attempt to be elected sheriff in Aspen, Colorado. He first showed up in my office wearing a gray bubble wig, with a huge satchel full of God knows what and three six-packs in his other hand, and talked for an hour straight. After that came "Fear and Loathing in Las Vegas," then the 1972 presidential campaign, and on, and on. . . .

Within a few years we had assembled a legendary writing and reporting staff. In addition to Thompson and Eszterhas, there were Tim Cahill, Jonathan Cott, Tim Crouse, David Felton, Ben Fong-Torres, Howard Kohn, Michael Rogers, to name a few. At just that time, I was finally able to get Tom Wolfe to write for ROLLING STONE, covering the astronauts.

Over the years many writers have come through the portals and delivered great pieces. Getting the story these days is sometimes remarkably the same and, in some cases, sadly different. Both Bill Zehme's and Mike Sager's accounts of writing about film idol Warren Beatty and porn icon John Holmes deliciously dissect the showbiz gauntlet.

ROLLING STONE reporting and writing in the Eighties and the beginning of the Nineties has also leaned heavily on the talents of P.J. O'Rourke and William Greider. . . . For P.J., the pen is the sword, and he has used it to drive liars, cheats, thieves and scoundrels out into the open. P.J.'s conservatism is his need to conserve common sense.

Bill Greider has been articulating his own and ROLLING STONE's political conscience with eloquence since he joined us from the *Washington Post* more than a decade ago. His essay concludes this issue and recalls our sometimes lonely political mission through the Reagan-Bush years. What Bill writes, about where we are at now, is what I would also like to say to our readers on our twenty-fifth anniversary.

I am immensely proud of all the talent that has worked at ROLLING STONE over the years – in Lawrence Wright's words, "literary hellcats who brushed aside journalistic conventions and social taboos to get at new ways of telling the truth." Larry, who joined us in 1985, goes on to write in his piece here: "One accepts a ROLLING STONE assignment knowing that not only must it be the final word on a subject, it must be freshly seen and powerfully told."

~ JANN S. WENNER

[RS 632]

ISSUE 632 · JUNE 11TH, 1992 · $3.50 · CANADA $3.95

1967 · THE GREAT STORIES · 1992

A TWENTY · FIFTH ANNIVERSARY SPECIAL

ROLLING STONE®

25

'All the News That Fits'

34790

RS 632 | TWENTY-FIFTH ANNIVERSARY: THE GREAT STORIES | Typography by DENNIS ORTIZ-LOPEZ | JUNE 11TH, 1992

To celebrate its twenty-fifth anniversary, ROLLING STONE published three special issues, beginning with this one, "The Great Stories," followed by "The Interviews" in October and "The Photographs" in November. ○

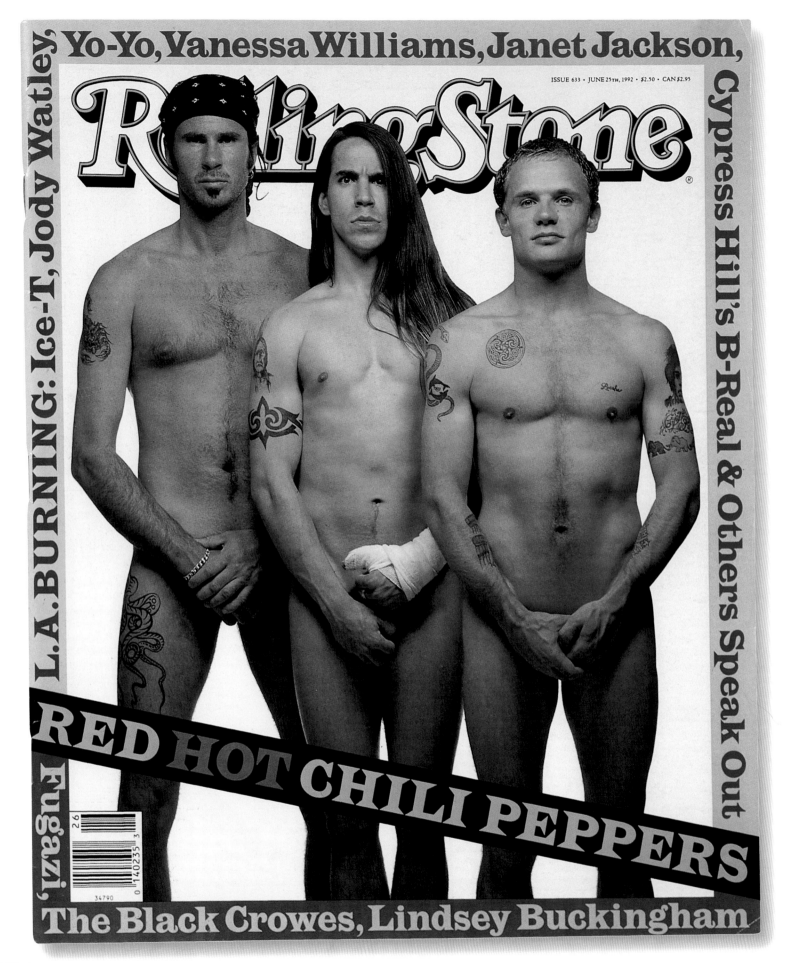

"**THEY** [the Red Hot Chili Peppers] walked off the set, they got into a little huddle, and the next thing I know, they're buck naked." ~ *MARK SELIGER*

SPECIAL DOUBLE ISSUE

Rolling Stone

ISSUE 634/635 · JULY 9TH-23RD, 1992 · $3.50 · CAN $3.95

P.J. O'ROURKE: ON THE ROAD IN VIETNAM

SOUNDGARDEN: ROCK'S HEAVY ALTERNATIVE

INSIDE BATMAN

THE ROLLING STONE INTERVIEW WITH

DIRECTOR TIM BURTON BY DAVID BRESKIN

BEN & JERRY: THE CARING CAPITALISTS

PAULY SHORE: TOTALLY HIP COMEDY

GEARHEADS: THE BIRTH OF MOUNTAIN BIKING

RINGO STARR, SOCIAL DISTORTION,

HAMMER & LINDSEY BUCKINGHAM

RS 634/635 | BATMAN'S SUIT | Photograph by HERB RITTS | JULY 9TH - JULY 23RD, 1992

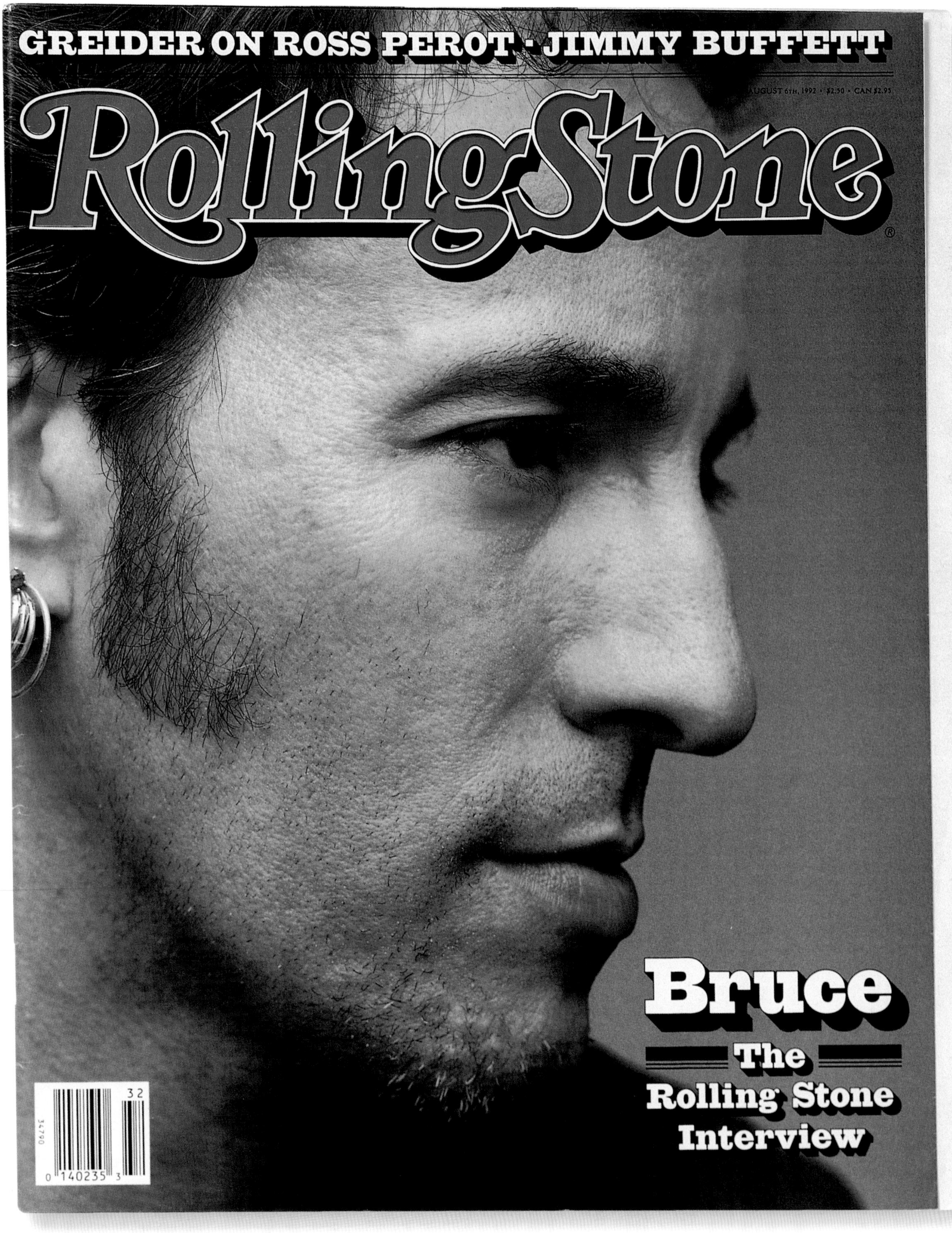

GREIDER ON ROSS PEROT · JIMMY BUFFETT

AUGUST 6TH, 1992 · $2.50 · CAN $2.95

RollingStone

Bruce

The
Rolling Stone
Interview

32

0 140235 3

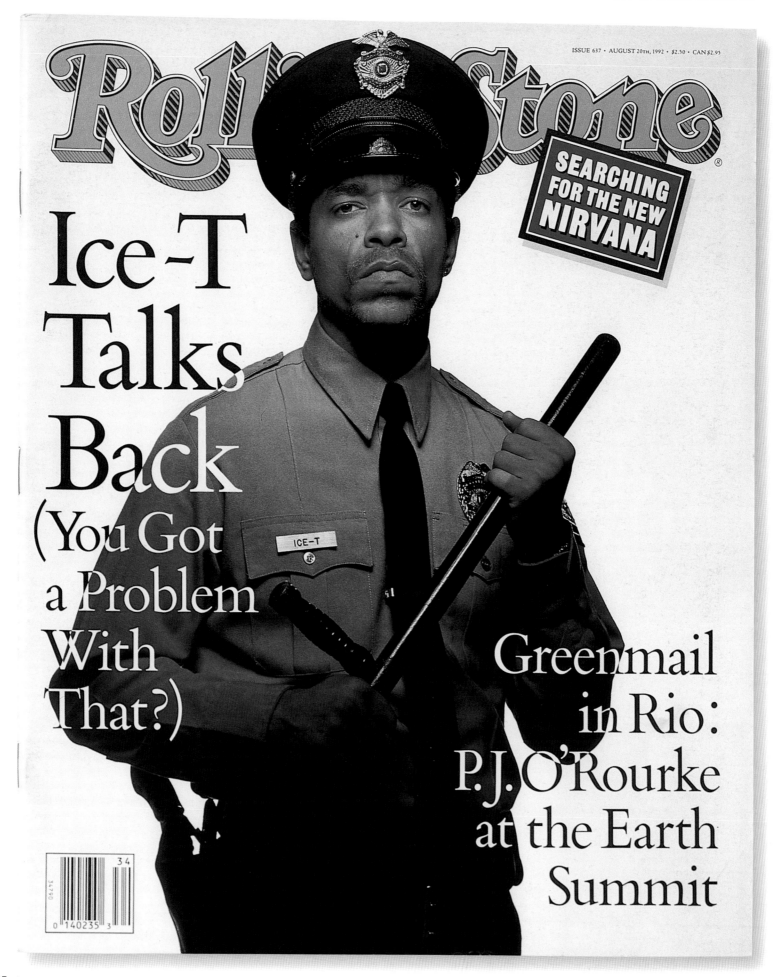

ISSUE 637 • AUGUST 20TH, 1992 • $2.50 • CAN $2.95

Rolling Stone

SEARCHING FOR THE NEW NIRVANA

Ice-T Talks Back (You Got a Problem With That?)

ICE-T

Greenmail in Rio: P.J. O'Rourke at the Earth Summit

RS 638 | SEPTEMBER 3RD, 1992
MICHELLE PFEIFFER
Photograph by HERB RITTS

MEMO FROM THE NATIONAL AFFAIRS DESK
DATE: August 4th, '92
From: Dr. Hunter S. Thompson
Subject: THE THREE STOOGES GO TO LITTLE ROCK

I have just returned, as you know, from a top-secret Issues Conference in Little Rock with our high-riding Candidate, Bill Clinton – who is also the five-term Governor of Arkansas and the only living depositor in the Grameen Bank of Bangladesh who wears a ROLLING STONE T-shirt when he jogs past the hedges at sundown. Ah, yes – the hedges. How little is known of them, eh? And I suspect, in fact, that the truth will never be known. . . . I wanted to check them out, but it didn't work. My rented Chrysler convertible turned into a kind of Trojan Horse in reverse – and frankly, I was deeply afraid to stay for even one night in Little Rock, by myself, for fear of being tracked and seized and perhaps even jailed and humiliated, on instructions from some nameless Clinton factotum.

*   *   *   *   *   *   *

MAYBE WEIRD POLITICS RUNS in twenty-year cycles. The last time I became ensnared in Dr. Hunter S. Thompson's delusional reality was on the campaign trail in 1972, when Richard Nixon was trashing George McGovern and the Constitution. The Doctor's apocalyptic rumblings turned out to be the only accurate account of that doomed presidential election. This time around, the year had already turned strange by the time I found myself in the back room of a Little Rock, Arkansas, restaurant, sitting around a checker-clothed table with ROLLING STONE's political team. . . . HST brought various exotic equipment to the table: a laser pointer, a plastic fetish wand, a battery-powered hand that undulated suggestively. He appeared to believe that this meeting constituted a high-level political parley in which we would deliver the "ROLLING STONE vote" to Bill Clinton. P.J. O'Rourke, meanwhile, determined to play the right-wing hit man, had loaded up with hard facts from the *Statistical Abstract* to zing Clinton and unmask his mush-headed liberalism. Jann Wenner, our always wise and generous leader, seemed blissfully oblivious to the potential for humiliation.

~ *WILLIAM GREIDER*

*   *   *   *   *   *   *

SO WHAT DID WE LEARN HERE? Bill Clinton's favorite Beatle is Paul McCartney. He voted for the skinny Elvis stamp (which doesn't show much self-knowledge). Also, he bites his nails – though they're bitten in a tidy, thoughtful manner, not gnawed to the raw quick the way crazy people do it. I'm sure this is all valuable information. I mean, *eeeeyew, Paul?* Especially at a moment in history when America cries out for a president whose favorite Beatle is Ringo.

~ *P.J. O'ROURKE*

[EXCERPTS FROM RS 639 COVER STORY]

RS 639 | SEPTEMBER 17TH, 1992
BILL CLINTON
Photograph by MARK SELIGER

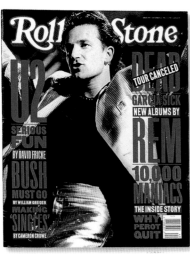

RS 640 | OCTOBER 1ST, 1992
BONO
Photograph by NEAL PRESTON

RS 641 | OCTOBER 15TH, 1992
TWENTY-FIFTH ANNIVERSARY:
THE INTERVIEWS

RS 642 | OCTOBER 29TH, 1992
SINÉAD O'CONNOR
Photograph by ALBERT WATSON

RS 643 | NOVEMBER 12TH, 1992
TWENTY-FIFTH ANNIVERSARY: THE PORTRAITS
ELVIS'S GOLD LAMÉ NUDIE SUIT
Photograph by ALBERT WATSON

RS 644 | NOVEMBER 26TH, 1992
DENZEL WASHINGTON
Photograph by ALBERT WATSON

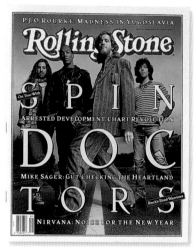

RS 647 | JANUARY 7TH, 1993
SPIN DOCTORS
Photograph by MARK SELIGER

RS 648 | JANUARY 21ST, 1993
NEIL YOUNG
Photograph by MARK SELIGER

"**IF YOU'RE CHARGED** up and have all this experience, what else is there? When you're young, you don't have any experience – you're charged up, but you're out of control. And if you're old and you're not charged up, then all you have is memories. But if you're charged and stimulated by what's going on around you and you also have experience, you know what to appreciate and what to pass by. And then you're really cruising."

~ *Neil Young*

RS 649 | FEBRUARY 4TH, 1993
NENEH CHERRY
Photograph by ELLEN VON UNWERTH

ISSUE 650 • FEBRUARY 18TH, 1993 • $2.50 • CAN $2.95

SCREAMING TREES • VAN HALEN • HENRY ROLLINS

Heeeeeeeerrre's Dave!

RS 650 | DAVID LETTERMAN | Photograph by MARK SELIGER | FEBRUARY 18TH, 1993

What does David Letterman (who's appeared beneath the ROLLING STONE logo more than any other nonmusician) recall of his six cover shoots? (RS 650 is his fourth.) "I always enjoyed the makeup."

RS 651 | BONO | Photograph by ANDREW MacPHERSON | MARCH 4TH, 1993

RS 652 | MARCH 18TH, 1993
NATALIE MERCHANT
Photograph by JEFFREY THURNHER

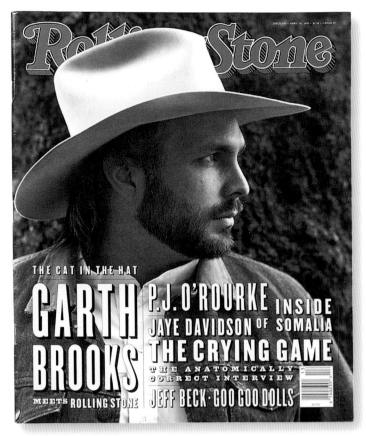

RS 653 | APRIL 1ST, 1993
GARTH BROOKS
Photograph by KURT MARKUS

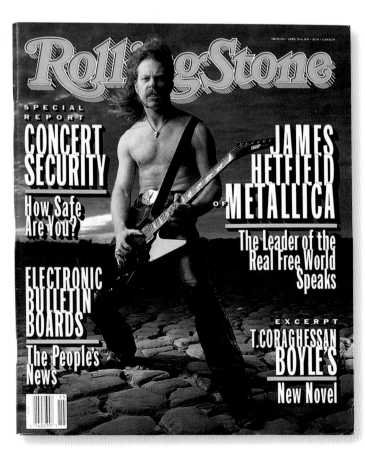

RS 654 | APRIL 15TH, 1993
JAMES HETFIELD
Photograph by MARK SELIGER

RS 655 | APRIL 29TH, 1993
ERIC CLAPTON
Photograph by ALBERT WATSON

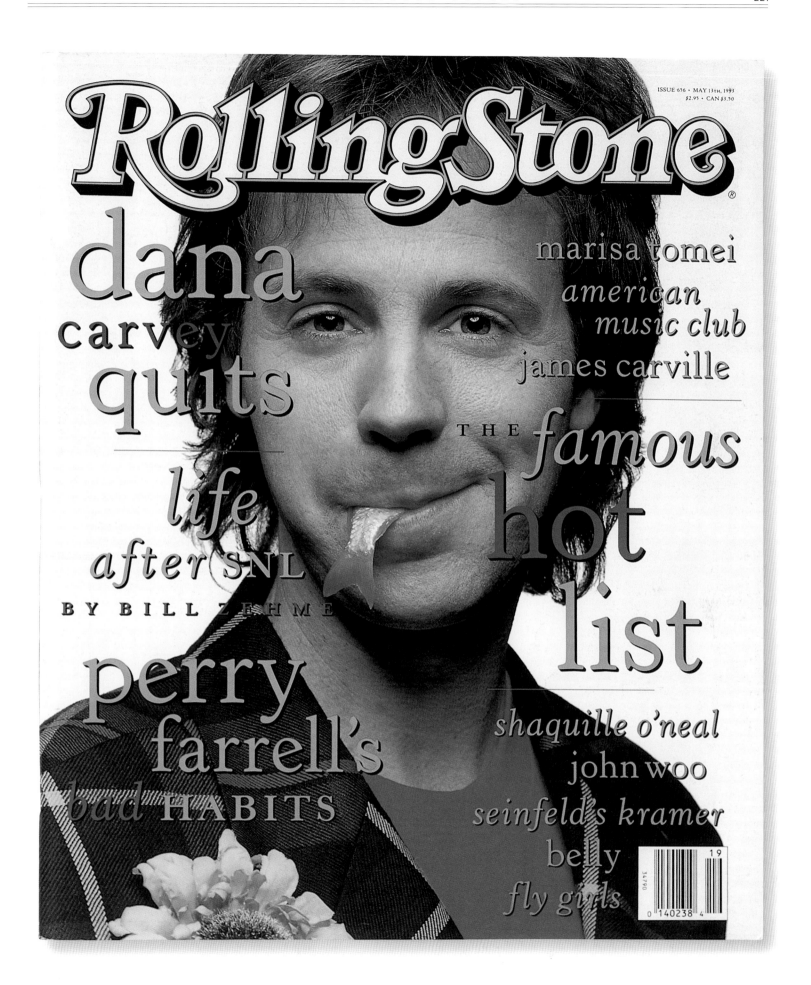

ISSUE 656 · MAY 13TH, 1993
$2.95 · CAN $3.50

RollingStone

dana
carvey
quits

life
after SNL
BY BILL ZEHME

perry
farrell's
bad HABITS

marisa tomei
american music club
james carville

THE *famous*
hot
list

shaquille o'neal
john woo
seinfeld's kramer
belly
fly girls

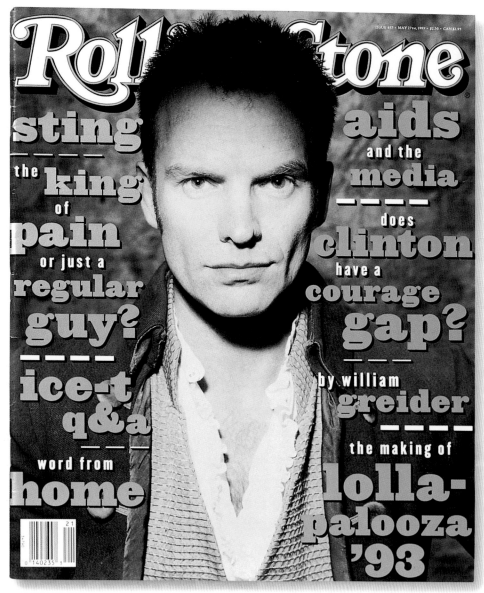

RS 657 | MAY 27TH, 1993
STING
Photograph by ANDREW MacPHERSON

RS 658 | JUNE 10TH, 1993
WHITNEY HOUSTON
Photograph by ALBERT WATSON

RS 659 | JUNE 24TH, 1993
LAURA DERN
Photograph by KURT MARKUS

BUT WHAT ABOUT these *Seinfeld* people? Yes, they do Nothing on television, do it in a way all others envy. But what about in life? To sate our curiosity, the four principal cast mates agreed to let themselves be watched doing not very much. By name and role, they are Michael Richards, as the peculiar neighbor Kramer; Jason Alexander, as the desperate friend George Costanza; Julia Louis-Dreyfus, as the platonic heroine Elaine Benes; and Jerry Seinfeld, as himself, more or less, the calm center around which all manner of Nothing revolves. What follow are details of how each of them rose to a pronounced lack of occasion.

Says Richards, "I work very hard to make this character three-dimensional." [Producer Larry] Charles concurs: "He's not a simplistic character at all. Kramer is full of facets and contradictions; he's real and unreal; he's like an adult and a child; he's like neutered yet very sexual; he's very light yet very dark; he can be idiotic and yet very wise."

Alexander frets: "There are times when George walks the line of really being kind of hateful, but ultimately his heart's in the right place." Indeed, Seinfeld has said that a George spinoff could only be titled *This Poor Man.* Even so, "George is not a loser," says Charles. "People inaccurately pigeon-hole him. He's struggling, but he's definitely not a loser."

As one of the boys, Elaine is unprecedented on television. "It's not a gender-specific kind of comedy," [Louis-Dreyfus] says. Her husband, Brad Hall, says this: "It doesn't matter whether or not Elaine's a woman – she has the same lusts and feelings that all guys have. The only woman-specific thing about her is her genitalia."

"[Jerry's] image is that of the perfect catch. He's a nice Jewish boy, very content with what he has. He's not in a rush or desperate; he's like this placid lake whose surface is never broken. Onstage or off, he's never in character, or *on* – he's just *him,*" says Charles. Seinfeld attributes this to his discomfort with acting: "Actors love to extend themselves. As a comedian, I don't want to do anything. I'm like *'Can I just wear my own pants in this scene?'*"

[EXCERPT FROM RS 660/661 COVER STORY
BY BILL ZEHME]

RS 662 | AUGUST 5TH, 1993
SOUL ASYLUM
Photograph by MARK SELIGER

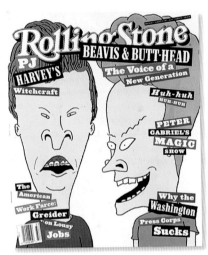

RS 663 | AUGUST 19TH, 1993
BEAVIS & BUTT-HEAD
Illustration by MIKE JUDGE

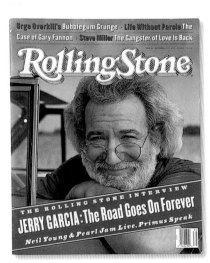

RS 664 | SEPTEMBER 2ND, 1993
JERRY GARCIA
Photograph by MARK SELIGER

I WANT TO TALK ABOUT SEX. It would seem like a simple thing to do after listening to Janet Jackson's new album and looking at her new videos. Sex is the theme. Sex is obviously on her mind, on my mind, on the minds of her fans who are consuming her record in mass quantities. Yet when Janet arrives at her dressing room, when she's standing before me in leather and suede form-fitting pants and tight halter top, when she slides into an easy chair next to me, I find myself backing off. What gives? . . .

Here with Janet, I'm reluctant to bring up sex. As silly as it sounds, I sense myself protecting her from the brashness of my own balls-out approach. What is it? Wholesomeness – that's what it is. Femininity. Up close, in the flesh, she's being so damn sincere, I question my own sincerity; Janet Jackson gives off a good-girl vibe that only a cad would challenge.

[EXCERPT FROM RS 665 COVER STORY BY DAVID RITZ]

*   *   *   *   *   *   *

"THE THING that excites me isn't becoming a bigger star but a better artist, deeper, truer to the things I find exciting. If right now, I find sex exciting, if I'm looking at physical love in a beautiful light, I put that in my art. If next year, I'm depressed or confused or angry, I hope to have the courage to express those feelings. I hope to be an honest artist – no more, no less."

~ Janet Jackson

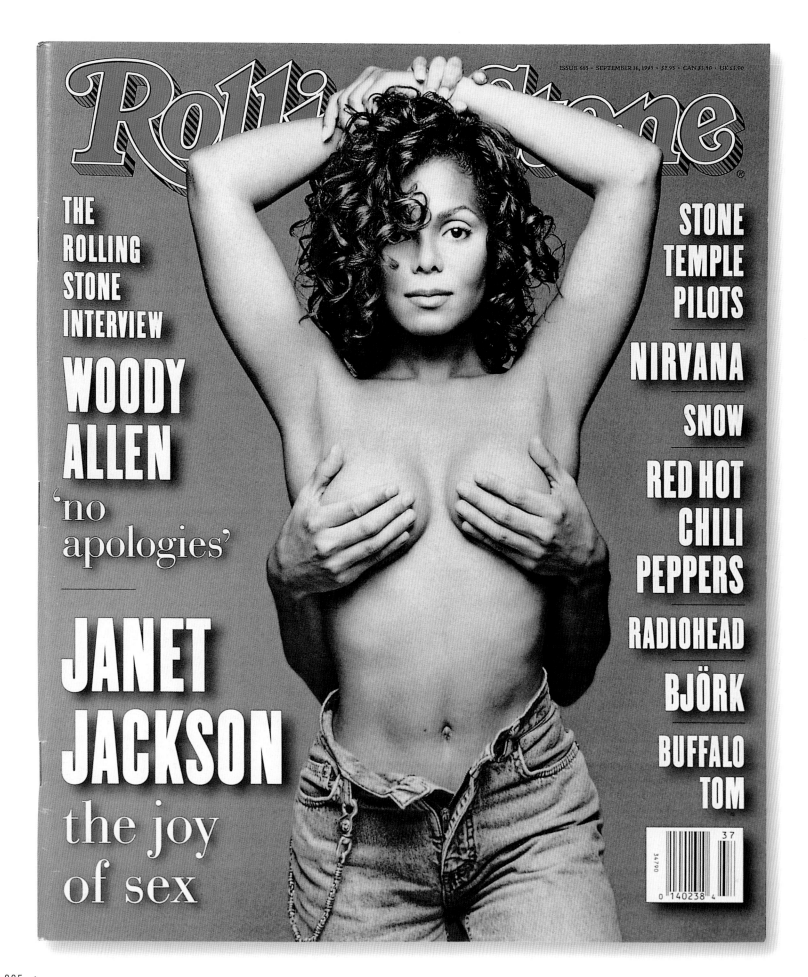

ISSUE 665 · SEPTEMBER 16, 1993 · $2.95 · CAN $3.50 · UK £3.00

Rolling Stone

THE
ROLLING
STONE
INTERVIEW

WOODY
ALLEN

'no
apologies'

JANET
JACKSON

the joy
of sex

STONE
TEMPLE
PILOTS

NIRVANA

SNOW

RED HOT
CHILI
PEPPERS

RADIOHEAD

BJÖRK

BUFFALO
TOM

RS 665 | JANET JACKSON | Photograph by PATRICK DEMARCHELIER | SEPTEMBER 16TH, 1993

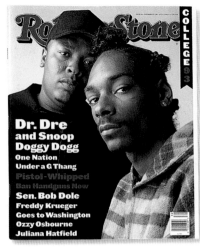

RS 666 | SEPTEMBER 30TH, 1993
DR. DRE & SNOOP DOGGY DOGG
Photograph by MARK SELIGER

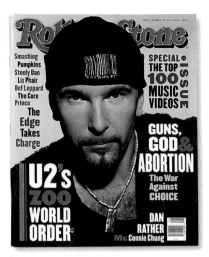

RS 667 | OCTOBER 14TH, 1993
THE EDGE
Photograph by ANDREW MacPHERSON

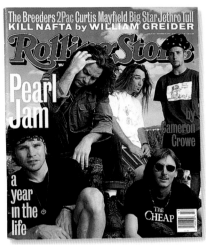

RS 668 | OCTOBER 28TH, 1993
PEARL JAM
Photograph by MARK SELIGER

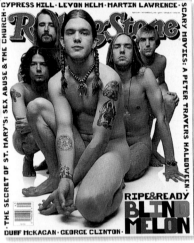

RS 669 | NOVEMBER 11TH, 1993
BLIND MELON
Photograph by MARK SELIGER

RS 670 | NOVEMBER 25TH, 1993
SHAQUILLE O'NEAL
Photograph by MARK SELIGER

RS 671 | DECEMBER 9TH, 1993
BILL CLINTON
Photograph by MARK SELIGER

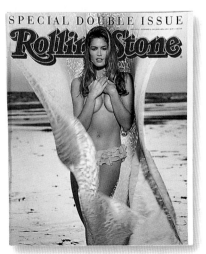

RS 672/673 | DECEMBER 23RD, 1993 – JANUARY 6TH, 1994
CINDY CRAWFORD
Photograph by HERB RITTS

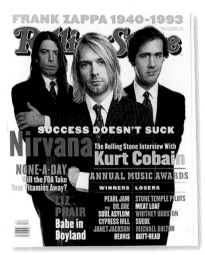

RS 674 | JANUARY 27TH, 1994
NIRVANA
Photograph by MARK SELIGER

RS 675 | FEBRUARY 10TH, 1994
HOWARD STERN
Photograph by MARK SELIGER

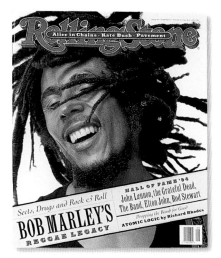

RS 676 | FEBRUARY 24TH, 1994
BOB MARLEY
Photograph by ANNIE LEIBOVITZ

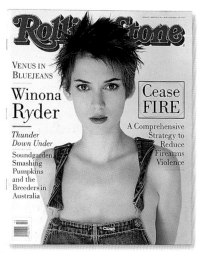

RS 677 | MARCH 10TH, 1994
WINONA RYDER
Photograph by HERB RITTS

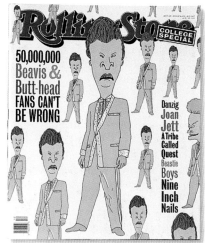

RS 678 | MARCH 24TH, 1994
BEAVIS & BUTT-HEAD
Illustration by MIKE JUDGE

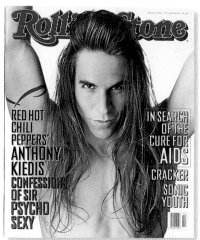

RS 679 | APRIL 7TH, 1994
ANTHONY KIEDIS
Photograph by MATTHEW ROLSTON

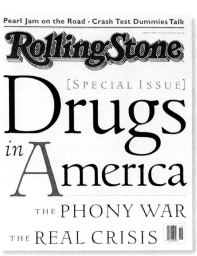

RS 681 | MAY 5TH, 1994
DRUGS IN AMERICA

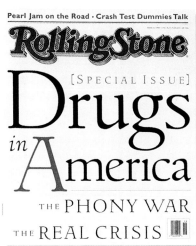

RS 680 | APRIL 21ST, 1994
SMASHING PUMPKINS
Photograph by GLEN LUCHFORD

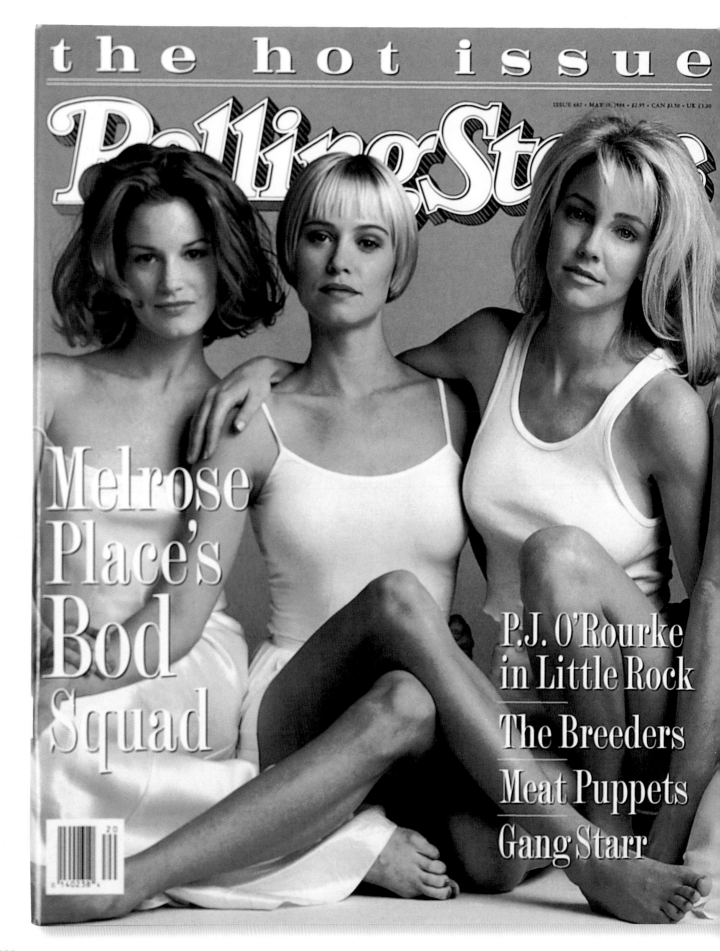

the hot issue

Rolling Stone

ISSUE 682 · MAY 19, 1994 · $2.95 · CAN $3.50 · UK £3.00

Melrose
Place's
Bod
Squad

P.J. O'Rourke
in Little Rock

The Breeders

Meat Puppets

Gang Starr

The Famous Hot List

STARRING

Leonardo DiCaprio
Gwyneth Paltrow
Green Day
Janeane Garofalo
Jon Stewart
Cassandra Wilson
The Mavericks

I HAVEN'T FELT the excitement of listening to as well as creating music, along with really writing for too many years now. I feel guilty beyond words about these things. For example, when we're backstage and the lights go out and the manic roar of the crowd begins, it doesn't affect me the way in which it did for Freddie Mercury, who seemed to love and relish in the love and admiration from the crowd which is something I totally admire and envy. The fact is, I can't fool you, any one of you. It simply isn't fair to you or to me. The worst crime I can think of would be to rip people off by faking it and pretending as if I'm having 100 percent fun."

~ *KURT COBAIN'S SUICIDE NOTE*

LAST SPRING, Kurt Cobain sat at his kitchen table at 3 a.m., chain-smoking and toying with one of the medical mannequins he collected. "It's hard to believe that a person can put something as poisonous as alcohol or drugs in their system and the mechanics can take it – for a while," he said to me, absently removing and inserting the doll's lungs, liver, heart.

At five feet seven inches, 125 pounds, Kurt was slight, painfully thin; he'd wear several layers of clothes under his usual cardigan and ripped jeans just to appear a little more substantial. He knew well just how much abuse, self-inflicted and otherwise, that fragile frame could withstand.

~ *MICHAEL AZERRAD*
[EXCERPT FROM RS 683]

SOME KIDS don't make it out of high school alive. They give up before they even try. Others stick around, wounded, just to see what happens. Introverted and depressed, Cobain maybe was born with a morbid disposition. Maybe he had a chemical imbalance that made him too sensitive to live in the world, so that even true love, a beautiful daughter, a brilliant band, detox, family life and his wholesome Northwestern community rootedness couldn't fill the hole in his soul. At twenty-seven, Cobain was tired of being alive.

~ *DONNA GAINES*
[EXCERPT FROM RS 683]

On April 8th, shortly before 9 a.m., Kurt Cobain's body was found in a greenhouse above the garage of his Seattle home. Across his chest lay the twenty-gauge shotgun with which the twenty-seven-year-old singer, guitarist and songwriter ended his life. Cobain had been missing for six days.

An electrician installing a security system in the house discovered Cobain dead. Though the police, a private investigation firm and friends were on the trail, his body had been lying there for two and a half days, according to a medical examiner's report. A high concentration of heroin and traces of Valium were found in Cobain's bloodstream. He was identifiable only by his fingerprints.

~ *NEIL STRAUSS*
[EXCERPT FROM RS 683]

KURT COBAIN NEVER WANTED to be the spokesman for a generation, though that doesn't mean much: Anybody who did would never have become one. It's not a role you campaign for. It is thrust upon you, and you live with it. Or don't.

People looked to Kurt Cobain because his songs captured what they felt before they knew they felt it. Even his struggles – with fame, with drugs, with his identity – caught the generational drama of our time. Seeing himself since his boyhood as an outcast, he was stunned – and confused, and frightened, and repulsed, and, truth be told, not entirely disappointed (no one forms a band to remain anonymous) – to find himself a star. If Cobain staggered across the stage of rock stardom, seemed more willing to play the fool than the hero and took drugs more for relief than pleasure, that was fine with his contemporaries. For people who came of age amid the greed, the designer-drug indulgence and the image-driven celebrity of the Eighties, anyone who could make an easy peace with success was fatally suspect.

Whatever importance Cobain assumed as a symbol, however, one thing is certain: He and his band Nirvana announced the end of one rock & roll era and the start of another. In essence, Nirvana transformed the Eighties into the Nineties.

~ *ANTHONY DECURTIS*
[EXCERPT FROM RS 683]

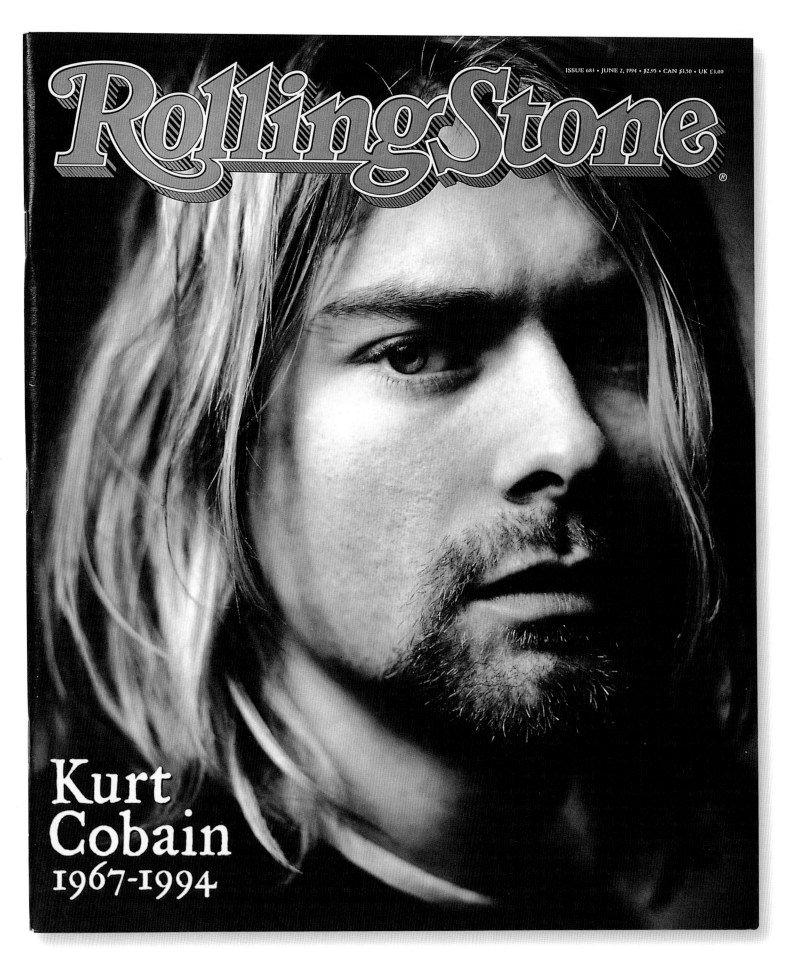

ISSUE 683 • JUNE 2, 1994 • $2.95 • CAN $3.50 • UK £3.00

RollingStone

Kurt Cobain
1967-1994

RS 683 | KURT COBAIN | Photograph by MARK SELIGER | JUNE 2ND, 1994

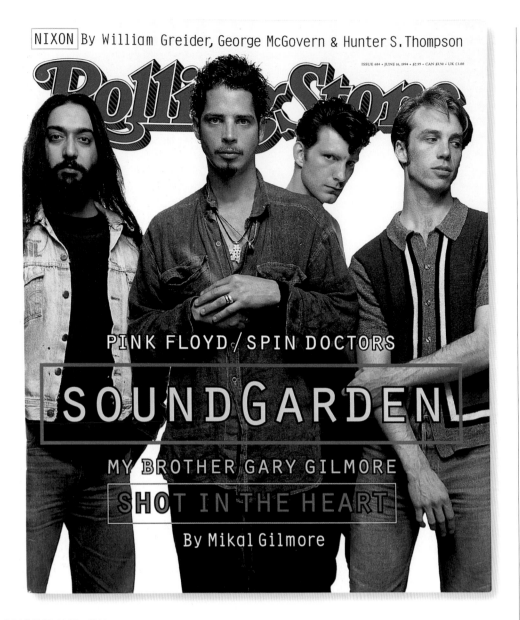

NIXON By William Greider, George McGovern & Hunter S. Thompson

ISSUE 684 · JUNE 16, 1994 · $2.95 · CAN $3.50 · UK £3.00

PINK FLOYD / SPIN DOCTORS

SOUNDGARDEN

MY BROTHER GARY GILMORE

SHOT IN THE HEART

By Mikal Gilmore

RS 684 | JUNE 16TH, 1994
SOUNDGARDEN
Photograph by MARK SELIGER

RS 685 | JUNE 30TH, 1994
COUNTING CROWS
Photograph by MARK SELIGER

RS 686/687 | JULY 14TH – JULY 28TH, 1994
JULIA ROBERTS
Photograph by HERB RITTS

THE STORY you're about to read is true. Three grown men – officially known by nicknames and wearing clothes that look like they've been handed down by much bigger brothers – are leading a cult that is threatening to suck our culture back into the 1970s. Please be aware of the warning signs. To demonstrate their loyalty, not to mention the magnitude of their sheer groovitude, the group's devotees – indie-rock gurus, legions of faceless hipsters and annoyingly ubiquitous barely celebs – are donning the garments of their chosen leaders. Puma, baggy pants and Fila tennis shirts abound. When they're not sporting knit stocking caps, their baseball hats, invariably, point backward.

This alliance – based in a Los Angeles enclave known as Grand Royal – exists ostensibly to make music under the moniker Beastie Boys. Other activities, however, persist.... It's a record label. It's a magazine. It's a way of life.

[EXCERPT FROM RS 688 COVER STORY BY CHRIS MUNDY]

* * * * *

"IT'S JUST SUCH cool chemistry between the three of us [Beastie Boys]. I don't even completely understand how it all interconnects. It's just that the three of us together is much stronger than any one of us working individually. We've been together for so long and care about each other so much, it's really like brothers."

~ADAM YAUCH

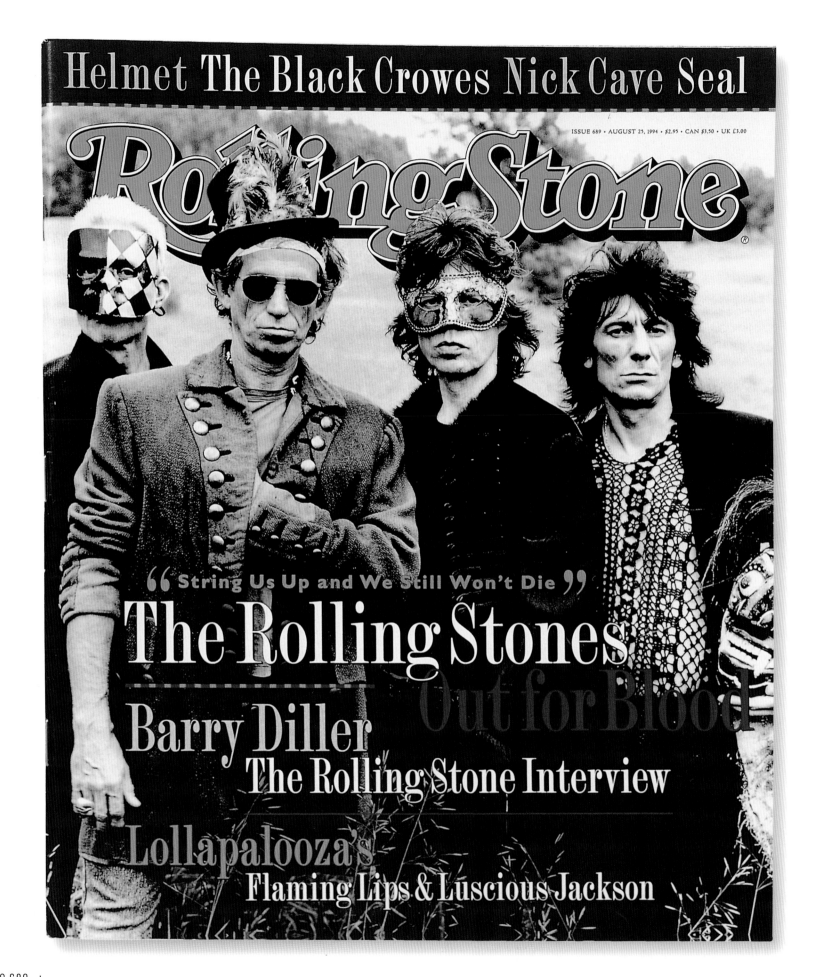

Helmet The Black Crowes Nick Cave Seal

ISSUE 689 • AUGUST 25, 1994 • $2.95 • CAN $3.50 • UK £3.00

RollingStone

"String Us Up and We Still Won't Die"

The Rolling Stones

Out for Blood

Barry Diller
The Rolling Stone Interview

Lollapalooza's
Flaming Lips & Luscious Jackson

RS 689 | THE ROLLING STONES | Photograph by ANTON CORBIJN | AUGUST 25TH, 1994

"THIS COVER worked out quite madly. The Rolling Stones don't enjoy photo sessions as a band. Because with the band, you have to get everyone in the mood, and I've found that's very difficult. People get bored. You have a good half-hour and someone else is having a bad one. So you get very, very few pictures."

– MICK JAGGER

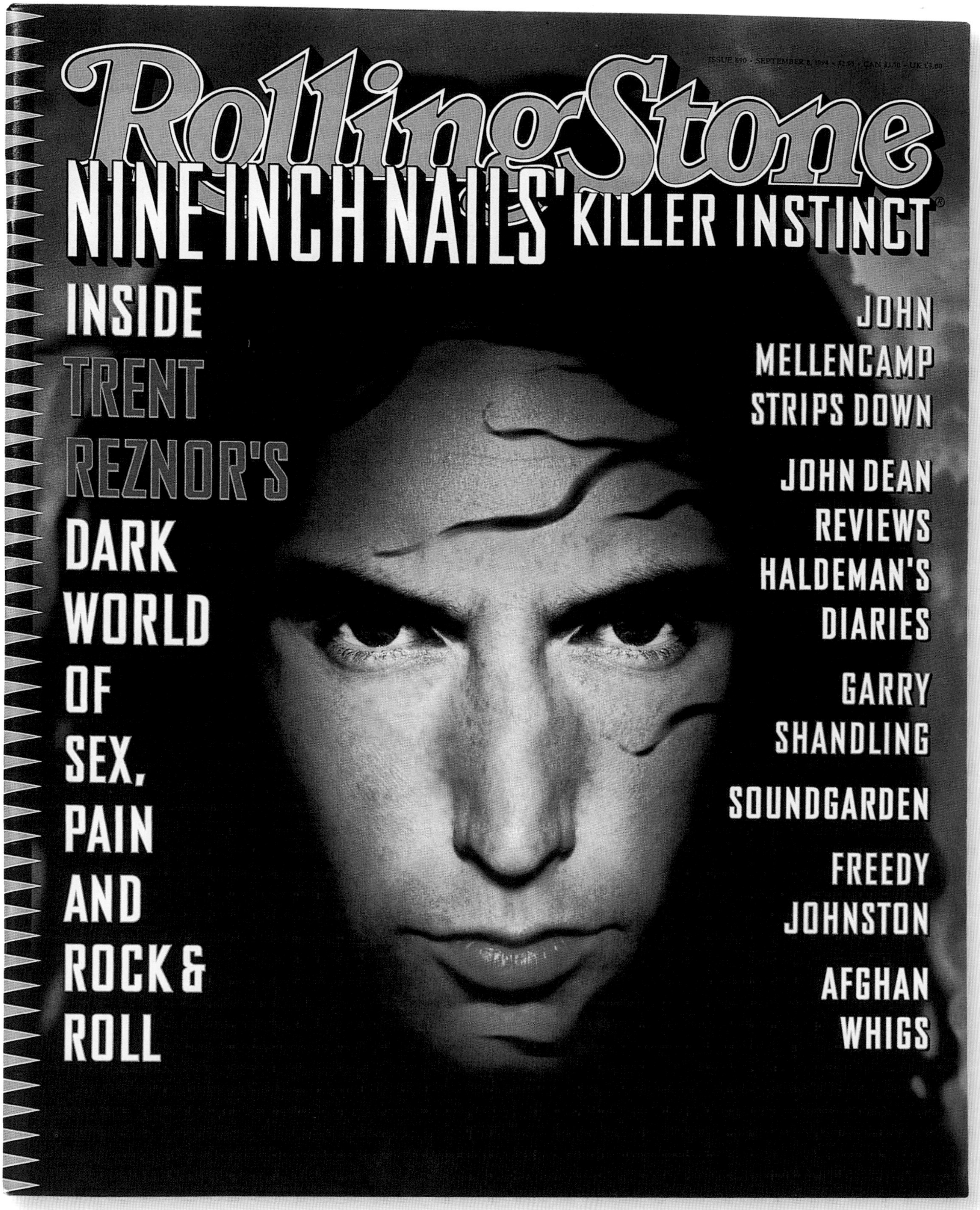

RollingStone

NINE INCH NAILS' KILLER INSTINCT

ISSUE 690 · SEPTEMBER 8, 1994 · $2.95 · CAN $3.50 · UK £3.00

INSIDE
TRENT
REZNOR'S
DARK
WORLD
OF
SEX,
PAIN
AND
ROCK &
ROLL

JOHN
MELLENCAMP
STRIPS DOWN

JOHN DEAN
REVIEWS
HALDEMAN'S
DIARIES

GARRY
SHANDLING

SOUNDGARDEN

FREEDY
JOHNSTON

AFGHAN
WHIGS

RS 690 | TRENT REZNOR | Photograph by MATT MAHURIN | SEPTEMBER 8TH, 1994

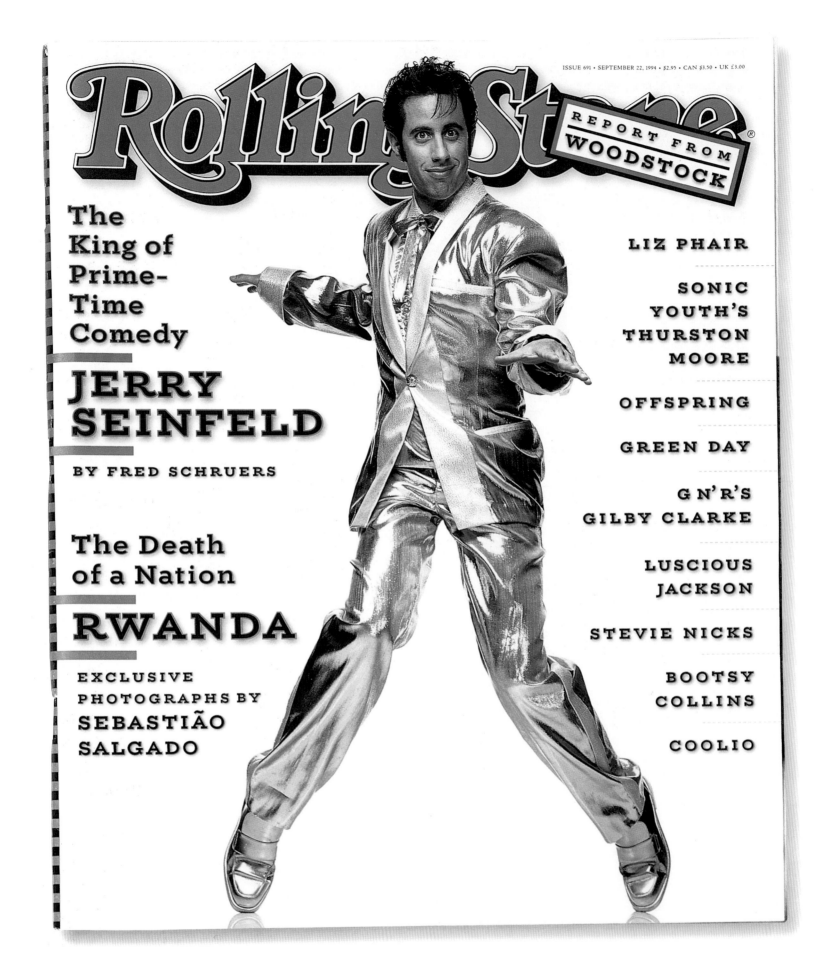

ISSUE 691 • SEPTEMBER 22, 1994 • $2.95 • CAN $3.50 • UK £3.00

REPORT FROM WOODSTOCK

The King of Prime-Time Comedy

JERRY SEINFELD

BY FRED SCHRUERS

The Death of a Nation

RWANDA

EXCLUSIVE PHOTOGRAPHS BY SEBASTIÃO SALGADO

LIZ PHAIR

SONIC YOUTH'S THURSTON MOORE

OFFSPRING

GREEN DAY

G N' R'S GILBY CLARKE

LUSCIOUS JACKSON

STEVIE NICKS

BOOTSY COLLINS

COOLIO

RS 691 | JERRY SEINFELD | Photograph by MARK SELIGER | SEPTEMBER 22ND, 1994

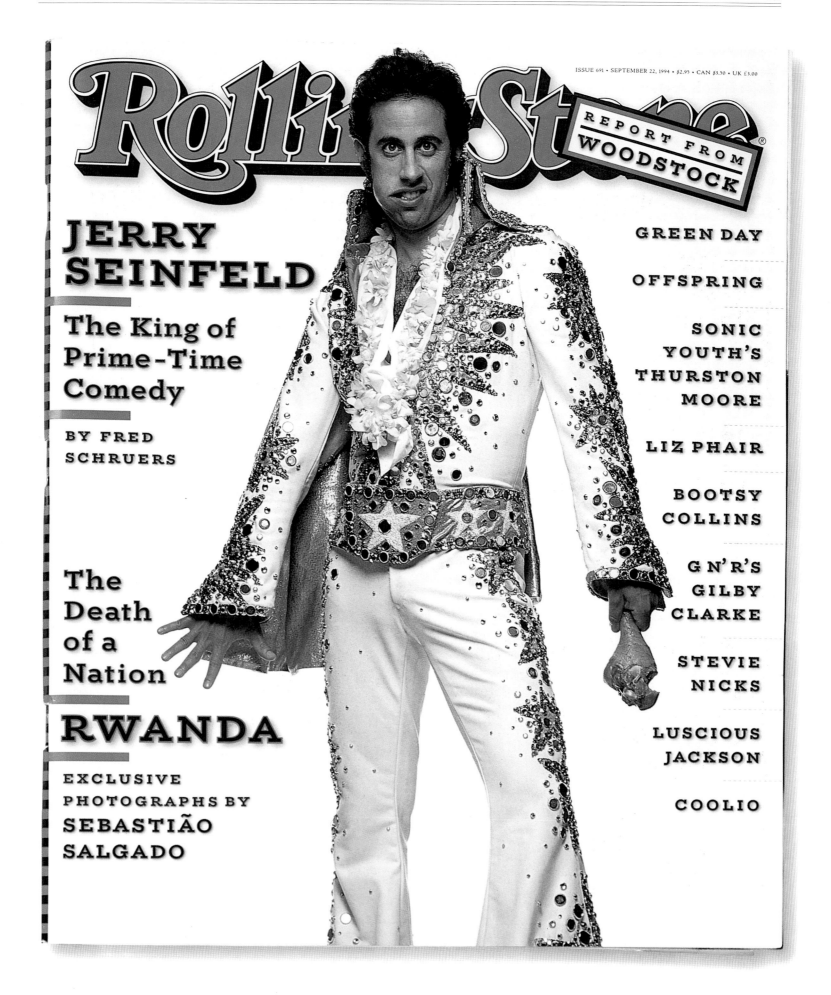

ISSUE 691 • SEPTEMBER 22, 1994 • $2.95 • CAN $3.50 • UK £3.00

REPORT FROM
WOODSTOCK

JERRY
SEINFELD

The King of
Prime-Time
Comedy

BY FRED
SCHRUERS

The
Death
of a
Nation
RWANDA

EXCLUSIVE
PHOTOGRAPHS BY
SEBASTIÃO
SALGADO

GREEN DAY

OFFSPRING

SONIC
YOUTH'S
THURSTON
MOORE

LIZ PHAIR

BOOTSY
COLLINS

GN'R'S
GILBY
CLARKE

STEVIE
NICKS

LUSCIOUS
JACKSON

COOLIO

The Editor's Note for RS 691 tells this story: "So we're looking at these two pictures of Jerry Seinfeld, and in one he's wearing a gold lamé suit, and in the other he's got on this scary white jumpsuit, and we're saying to ourselves, 'Which do you think the readers will like – Jerry as the young Elvis or Jerry as the old Elvis?' Then we say to ourselves, 'Hey, ROLLING STONE is a democratic kind of place – let the readers decide.' So we put both pictures on the cover and sent it out random-like. But it's all the same magazine inside – take our word for it." ○

RS 692 | OCTOBER 6TH, 1994
LIZ PHAIR
Photograph by FRANK W. OCKENFELS 3

RS 693 | OCTOBER 20TH, 1994
R.E.M.
Photograph by MARK SELIGER

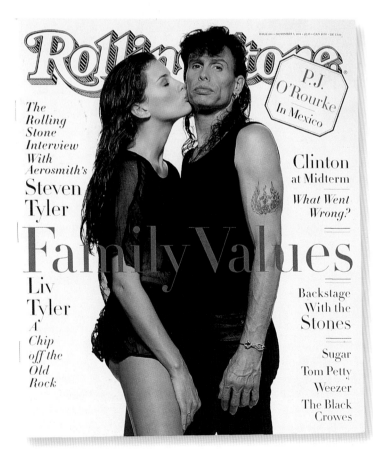

RS 694 | NOVEMBER 3RD, 1994
LIV & STEVEN TYLER
Photograph by ALBERT WATSON

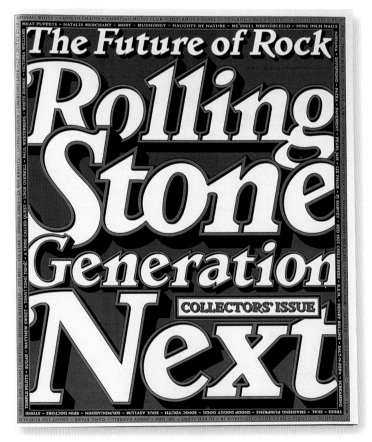

RS 695 | NOVEMBER 17TH, 1994
GENERATION NEXT
Typography by ERIC SIRY

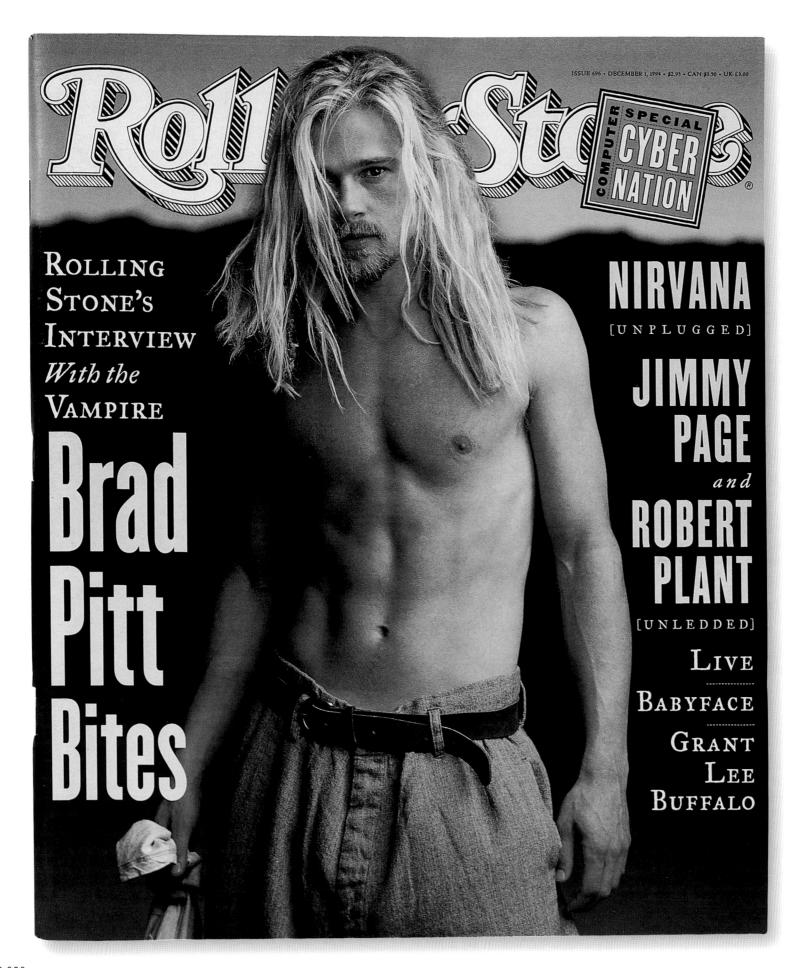

ISSUE 696 · DECEMBER 1, 1994 · $2.95 · CAN $3.50 · UK £3.00

SPECIAL COMPUTER CYBER NATION

Rolling Stone

ROLLING STONE'S INTERVIEW *With the* VAMPIRE

Brad Pitt Bites

NIRVANA [UNPLUGGED]

JIMMY PAGE *and* **ROBERT PLANT** [UNLEDDED]

LIVE

BABYFACE

GRANT LEE BUFFALO

RS 696 | BRAD PITT | Photograph by MARK SELIGER | DECEMBER 1ST, 1994

SHERYL CROW | PEARL JAM | THE JAYHAWKS | BOB DYLAN | OASIS

ISSUE 697 • DECEMBER 15, 1994 • $2.95 • CAN $3.50 • UK £3.00

EXCLUSIVE

Courtney Love

Talks About Music, Madness and the Last Days of Kurt Cobain

By
David Fricke

The O.J. Simpson Story

By
Randall Sullivan

FEAR AND LOATHING IN HORSE COUNTRY

Hunter S. Thompson

Polo Is My Life

"**SOMETIMES I WANT** to just wear regular clothes onstage. Then I wonder. If by not being so extreme can I still pull it off? I need my costume, my thing. Because my thing is a message." ~ *COURTNEY LOVE*

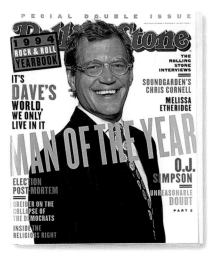

RS 698/699 | DECEMBER 29TH, 1994 – JANUARY 12TH, 1995
DAVID LETTERMAN
Photograph by FRANK W. OCKENFELS 3

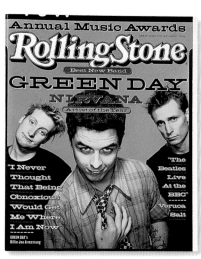

RS 700 | JANUARY 26TH, 1995
GREEN DAY
Photograph by DAN WINTERS

RS 701 | FEBRUARY 9TH, 1995
DEMI MOORE
Photograph by MATTHEW ROLSTON

RS 702 | FEBRUARY 23RD, 1995
ROBERT PLANT & JIMMY PAGE
Photograph by ANTON CORBIJN

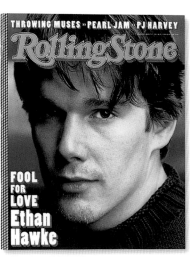

RS 703 | MARCH 9TH, 1995
ETHAN HAWKE
Photograph by MARK SELIGER

RS 704 | MARCH 23RD, 1995
DOLORES O'RIORDAN
Photograph by CORRINE DAY

RS 705 | APRIL 6TH, 1995
EDDIE VAN HALEN
Photograph by MARK SELIGER

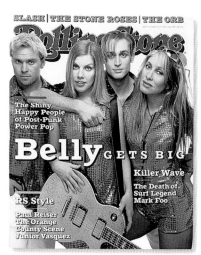

RS 706 | APRIL 20TH, 1995
BELLY
Photograph by MARK SELIGER

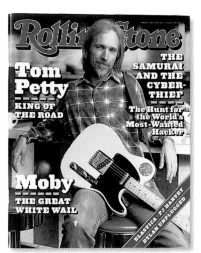

RS 707 | MAY 4TH, 1995
TOM PETTY
Photograph by MARK SELIGER

OASIS ★ METALLICA ★ BABES IN TOYLAND

Rolling Stone

ISSUE 708 • MAY 18, 1995 • $2.95 • CAN $3.50 • UK £3.00

FAST 'FRIENDS'

No Sex
Bad Jobs
Hit Show
Go Figure

Where's the Monkey?

RS 708 | CAST OF 'FRIENDS' | Photograph by MARK SELIGER | MAY 18TH, 1995

Rolling Stone

ISSUE 709 · JUNE 1, 1995 · $2.95 · CAN $3.50 · UK £3.00

On Tour

Mike Watt
Dave Grohl
Eddie Vedder

The NRA Menace 2 Society

Mudhoney

Finger-Licking Good

Melissa
Etheridge

She's the Boss

ISSUE 710 • JUNE 15, 1995 • $2.95 • CAN $3.50 • UK £3.00

RollingStone

· ROCK & ROLL SUMMER ·

Wild Thing
Drew Barrymore

Hootie
and the
Blowfish
Nice Guys
Finish First

Stone
Temple
Pilots'
Weiland
Talks

Faces of
Violence
Guns and
the Right

The
Return of
Soul
Asylum

"BETRAYAL": THE CIA'S DEADLIEST TRAITOR

Rolling Stone

ISSUE 711 · JUNE 29, 1995 · $2.95 · CAN $3.50 · UK £3.00

SMASHING PUMPKINS In the Studio

Late Nights With Dave Pirner

Scott Weiland Busted

Bad Brains
Morphine
Björk

SOUL ASYLUM
The Good, The Bad and The Lonely

RS 711 | JUNE 29TH, 1995
SOUL ASYLUM
Photograph by MATT MAHURIN

PICTURE, IF YOU WILL, a hotel lounge. [Soul Asylum singer Dave] Pirner sits on a sofa, engaged in what seems to be a heated conversation with a reporter. Drummer Sterling Campbell sits on a chair to their right, leaning in closely.

PIRNER: But look, Socrates was fucking Greek, man. I mean, what influence has that culture had on us as a people now? Those wrapped-up leaves with rice in them . . .

[*Soul Asylum's publicist arrives.*]

PIRNER: I mean, that shit doesn't taste that good, but it tastes pretty good. And you kind of sit there, and you eat it, and you go, "All right, these motherfuckers, they ate this shit, and they made a bunch of motherfuckers drag fucking rocks up a hill to build some big old colossal thing. And they tried to create this whole society." And what was the food left over from that? These fucking grape leaves wrapped around rice.

PUBLICIST: I have a recommendation to make as a publicist. You guys could stay up all night talking, but the on-the-record portion of the interview should be over at this point.

CAMPBELL: No, no, no, no.

PIRNER: I think I can be held accountable for anything that I should say. I'll tell you what I want to know, though. What's ROLLING STONE's angle here? Do they think we're rock stars and suck or what? What do they want to know about us, just between me and you?

PUBLICIST [*coughs*]: What would be the most natural, obvious question to answer that? The new record? Coming off the tremendous success of *Grave Dancers Union?*

PIRNER: I mean, what the fuck could possibly be interesting about us?

[*The publicist is silent.*]

PIRNER: Exactly. That's the right answer.

PUBLICIST [*flustered*]: Is the tape recorder running? Could you turn it off?

[EXCERPT FROM RS 711
COVER STORY BY NEIL STRAUSS]

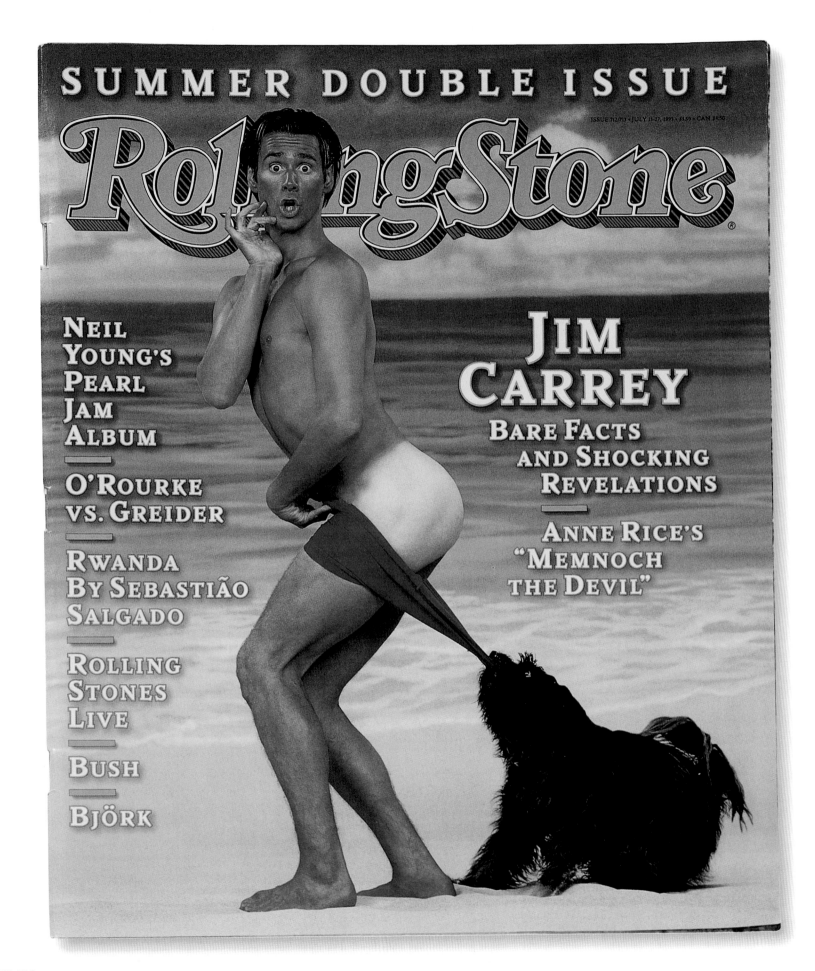

SUMMER DOUBLE ISSUE

ISSUE 712/713 • JULY 13-27, 1995 • $3.95 • CAN $4.50

NEIL
YOUNG'S
PEARL
JAM
ALBUM

O'ROURKE
VS. GREIDER

RWANDA
BY SEBASTIÃO
SALGADO

ROLLING
STONES
LIVE

BUSH

BJÖRK

JIM
CARREY
BARE FACTS
AND SHOCKING
REVELATIONS

ANNE RICE'S
"MEMNOCH
THE DEVIL"

Finding a dog that could pull the skivvies off of Jim Carrey was no simple task. A casting call went out across the land and canines galore showed up. The only one with the necessary credentials was a crafty fellow named Poundcake. Unfortunately, he was white – and for the setup to mirror the classic Coppertone ad, the assertive doggie had to be black. After weeks of intensive training, Poundcake consented to having his snowy coat dyed black (reportedly with shoe polish). Poundcake, now ebony, had risen to the occasion when Mr. Carrey's handlers called to say he couldn't make the shoot that day. Unfortunately, rescheduling took a month, and poor Poundcake had to go through boot camp once again – not to mention having his roots touched up. A trouper to the end, Poundcake came through, putting that Coppertone mutt to shame with his briefs-snatching antics. ○

*   *   *   *   *

ALICIA SILVERSTONE is a kittenish eighteen-year-old movie star whom lots of men want to sleep with. "That part's not me," Silverstone says. "What people think about me, of doing with me – it can be gross." Along with many other celebrities, has-beens, will-be's and wanna-be's, Silverstone lives in the Hollywood Hills, in California, where she pads around the house in gym socks, doing nothing more exciting than her laundry. Meanwhile she tries to balance the inaudible pangs of adolescence *(Let's get crazy)* with the audible pangs of agents *(You can't get crazy, you have a photo shoot)* and saves her good looks and enthusiasm for a party that has never been thrown. Can you believe it? Alicia Silverstone, the prettiest girl in town, the next big thing, the star of nine movies in the past two years (including *The Crush,* in which she played a young woman who kisses and then tries to kill an older man, a movie that fixed her in the minds of many as a lustful, murderous, wildcat teen), an actress who with her appearance in Aerosmith's recent videos helped revive the band, the star of three upcoming films *(The Babysitter, True Crime* and *Le Nouveau Monde)* and the summer smash *Clueless,* and she's stranded on a hill – a knocked-out, dreamy-eyed little Rapunzel waiting for some spectacle grand enough to allow her to let her hair down. "If this is the life of a starlet," she says, sighing, "it's a yawn."

[EXCERPT FROM RS 716 COVER STORY BY RICH COHEN]

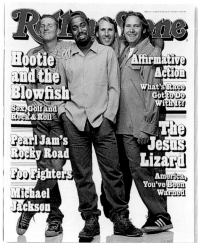

RS 714 | AUGUST 10TH, 1995
HOOTIE & THE BLOWFISH
Photograph by MARK SELIGER

RS 715 | AUGUST 24TH, 1995
HOLE
Photograph by MARK SELIGER

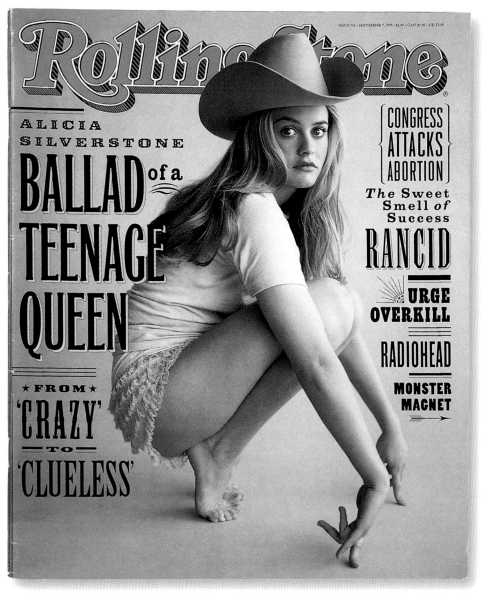

RS 716 | SEPTEMBER 7TH, 1995
ALICIA SILVERSTONE
Photograph by PEGGY SIROTA

On August 9th, 1995, Jerry Garcia died in his sleep at Serenity Knolls drug treatment center, in the Marin County community of Forest Knolls, north of San Francisco. He was fifty-three. . . . The memorial service transformed into a festive, open-air Grateful Dead theme park. . . . As the waft of marijuana and incense intensified, fans gathered at the altar and danced. . . .

~ ALEC FOEGE

[EXCERPT FROM RS 717]

IN ROCK & ROLL, there is Grateful Dead music – and then there is everything else. No other band has been so pure in its outlaw idealism, so resolute in its pursuit of transcendence onstage and on record, and so astonishingly casual about both the hazards and rewards of its chosen, and at times truly lunatic, course. . . .

~ DAVID FRICKE

[EXCERPT FROM RS 717]

HE WAS THE UNLIKELIEST of pop stars and the most reticent of cultural icons.

Onstage he wore plain clothes – usually a sacklike T-shirt and loose jeans to fit his heavy frame – and he rarely spoke to the audience that watched his every move. Even his guitar lines – complex, lovely and rhapsodic, but never flashy – as well as his strained, weatherworn vocal style had a subdued, colloquial quality about them. Offstage he kept to family and friends, and when he sat to talk with interviewers about his remarkable music, he often did so in sly-witted, self-deprecating ways. "I feel like I'm sort of stumbling along," he said once, "and a lot of people are watching me or stumbling along with me or allowing me to stumble for them." It was as if Jerry Garcia – who, as the lead guitarist and singer of the Grateful Dead, lived at the center of one of popular culture's most extraordinary epic adventures – was bemused by the circumstances of his own renown.

~ MIKAL GILMORE

[EXCERPT FROM RS 717]

FOR OUR VERY FIRST ISSUE – published in November 1967 – we lucked, journalistically speaking, into a story for the ages: the Grateful Dead getting busted at their Haight-Ashbury digs. The police had had it up to their badges with freaks flaunting various laws. Inviting local media along for the roust, they barged into the house at 710 Ashbury Street, where most of the Dead and their old ladies lived, and arrested two band members and nine associates and friends on dope charges (Jerry Garcia wasn't one of them; he was out at the time).

Baron Wolman, ROLLING STONE's first photographer, snapped shots of Bob Weir walking down the front steps, cuffed to Phil Lesh's girlfriend, and Ron "Pigpen" McKernan and Phil Lesh outside their bail bondsman's office across from the Hall of Justice. The next day, after a festive press conference at the house, Wolman shot photographs of a band of unrepentant freaks – now joined by Garcia, posing in front of 710, with Pigpen brandishing a rifle. The photos took up most of a two-page spread.

The lead, by an uncredited Jann S. Wenner, was textbook hook-'em news writing: " 'That's what ya get for dealing the killer weed,' laughed state narcotics agent Gerritt Van Raam at the eleven members of the Grateful Dead household he and his agents had rounded up into the Dead's kitchen."

The band and the magazine always had a special relationship, despite the occasional negative album review or report on an unpleasant incident or ROLLING STONE's move to New York in 1977. Our common roots transcended trivia; our love of great music kept us bonded.

~ BEN FONG-TORRES

[EXCERPT FROM RS 717]

JERRY GARCIA · 1942-1995

ISSUE 717 · SEPTEMBER 21, 1995 · $2.95 · CAN $3.50 · UK £3.00

RollingStone

RS 717 | JERRY GARCIA | Photograph by HERBIE GREENE | SEPTEMBER 21ST, 1995

RS 718 | OCTOBER 5TH, 1995
FOO FIGHTERS
Photograph by DAN WINTERS

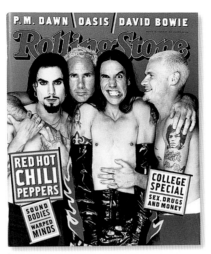

RS 719 | OCTOBER 19TH, 1995
RED HOT CHILI PEPPERS
Photograph by ANTON CORBIJN

RS 720 | NOVEMBER 2ND, 1995
ALANIS MORISSETTE
Photograph by FRANK W. OCKENFELS 3

RS 721 | NOVEMBER 16TH, 1995
SMASHING PUMPKINS
Photograph by MARK SELIGER

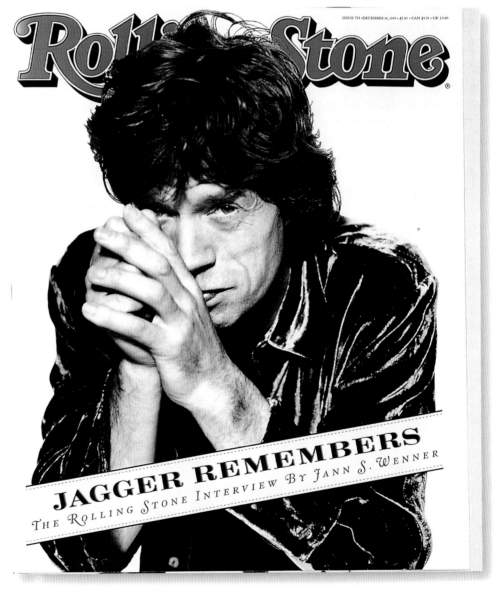

RS 723 | DECEMBER 14TH, 1995
MICK JAGGER
Photograph by PETER LINDBERGH

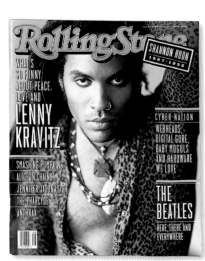

RS 722 | NOVEMBER 30TH, 1995
LENNY KRAVITZ
Photograph by MATTHEW ROLSTON

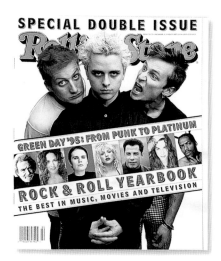

RS 724/725 | DECEMBER 28TH, 1995 – JANUARY 11TH, 1996
GREEN DAY, VARIOUS
Photographs by MARK SELIGER, VARIOUS

RS 729 | MARCH 7TH, 1996
JENNIFER ANISTON
Photograph by MARK SELIGER

RS 726 | JANUARY 25TH, 1996
LIVE
Photograph by JULIAN BROAD

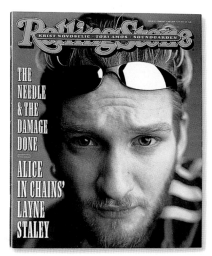

RS 727 | FEBRUARY 8TH, 1996
LAYNE STALEY
Photograph by MARK SELIGER

RS 728 | FEBRUARY 22ND, 1996
JOHN TRAVOLTA
Photograph by MARK SELIGER

RS 730 | MARCH 21ST, 1996
JOAN OSBORNE
Photograph by MARK SELIGER

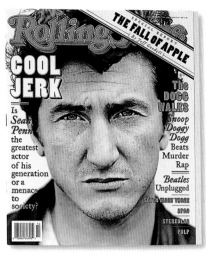

RS 731 | APRIL 4TH, 1996
SEAN PENN
Photograph by MARK SELIGER

RS 732 | APRIL 18TH, 1996
GAVIN ROSSDALE
Photograph by MARK SELIGER

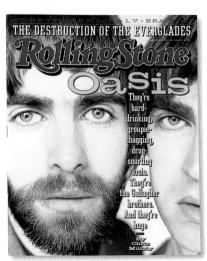

RS 733 | MAY 2ND, 1996
LIAM & NOEL GALLAGHER
Photograph by NATHANIEL GOLDBERG

What's the secret for the heat between Mulder and Scully?

We have a kind of furtive understanding that it's me and her against the world. That's kind of sexy regardless of whether or not you want to fuck them all the time.

Do you play it like Fox has impure thoughts about Scully?

No, what I tend to play is that I always want to check with her. Whenever I hear something interesting, I'll look at her. That's sexy to people. I don't play it like Fox wants to fuck her. But there's some tension between us whenever there's another woman around.

Apart from the rare vampire fling and his porno collection, Fox is pretty asexual.

He's not asexual. Sex is just not high on his list of priorities. It's weird because most of the time women don't register with this guy, then there'll be an episode where he's led around by his dick.

How many times has Fox gotten laid?

Once. The one time with the vampire.

What did you think of posing in bed together?

I thought the photos were great.

[EXCERPT FROM DAVID DUCHOVNY INTERVIEW BY DAVID WILD]

*   *   *   *   *   *   *

There's a certain powerful sexuality in your characters' interaction even though you don't do it.

We don't do it?

You don't have sex. Except on our cover. Was it good for you, by the way?

They just happened to show up in our hotel room. Was it good for me? Yes. I think what makes the relationship between Scully and Mulder sexy is the respect they have for one another. They don't manipulate or take advantage of one another. I'm sure that's very intriguing for the audience.

Sometimes it feels like a relationship out of a Forties movie.

It's that tension. We've done some incredibly intimate scenes that have nothing to do with sex. Beginnings of relationships are always the most exciting – that period when you're courting and you get near each other and start breathing heavily. The hottest stuff is before you ever touch the other person. Or the first touch. So Mulder and Scully's first touch in an episode or first touch in many episodes becomes more exciting.

Do you think Scully has thought about Mulder in a sexual way?

I think there have been times when she has been completely charmed and touched by him. I don't know if she's ever actually imagined him naked.

[EXCERPT FROM GILLIAN ANDERSON INTERVIEW BY DAVID WILD]

SPACEHOG | FUGEES | SCREAMING TREES | NICK CAVE

Rolling Stone

ISSUE 734 • $3.00
MAY 16, 1996
UK £3.00

P.J. O'Rourke
IN SWEDEN
ON THE ROAD AGAIN

X FILES

UNDER COVER

By David Wild

NEW ALBUMS

HOOTIE
AND THE
BLOWFISH

SPIN DOCTORS

DAVE MATTHEWS BAND

Lost in Space

ROCK STARS AND UFOs

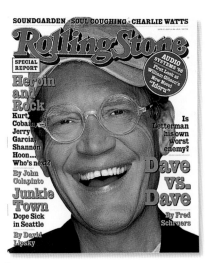

RS 735 | MAY 30TH, 1996
DAVID LETTERMAN
Photograph by ALBERT WATSON

RS 736 | JUNE 13TH, 1996
ROCK & ROLL SUMMER
VARIOUS PHOTOGRAPHERS

RS 737 | JUNE 27TH, 1996
METALLICA
Photograph by ANTON CORBIJN

RS 738/739 | JULY 11TH – JULY 25TH, 1996
JENNY McCARTHY
Photograph by MARK SELIGER

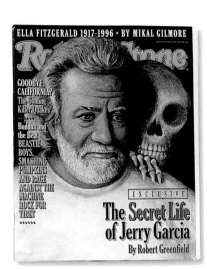

RS 740 | AUGUST 8TH, 1996
JERRY GARCIA
Illustration by PAUL DAVIS

RS 741 | AUGUST 22ND, 1996
CAMERON DIAZ
Photograph by MARK SELIGER

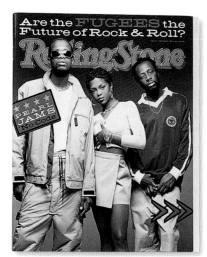

RS 742 | SEPTEMBER 5TH, 1996
THE FUGEES
Photograph by MATTHEW ROLSTON

RS 743 | SEPTEMBER 19TH, 1996
CONAN O'BRIEN
Photograph by MARK SELIGER

RS 744 | OCTOBER 3RD, 1996
BROOKE SHIELDS
Photograph by MARK SELIGER

RS 745 | OCTOBER 17TH, 1996
R.E.M.
Photograph by ANTON CORBIJN

YOU CAN CALL IT FATE or you can call it breaking and entering. The differences are marginal. The time was the late Eighties, a simpler period somewhere before the fall of the Berlin Wall but after Billy Squier had taught us "The Stroke," a time when the phrase "late-night wars" had yet to be invented.

Back then, while David Letterman was quietly building an empire in the hours past midnight, a young Harvard grad named Conan O'Brien was making his way as a writer for the recently resuscitated *Saturday Night Live*. Every now and then, to get a break from the all-night writing binges, O'Brien would sneak downstairs, pick the lock to Studio 6A, pull the tarp off the host's chair and attempt to write comedy while sitting at Letterman's desk.

"It wasn't like, 'Someday I will sit here,' says O'Brien. "It was more like, 'This is where he sits? Cool.'" He laughs – you know the sound: high-pitched, slightly braying – and continues. "Really, the point of the story is that NBC has terrible security, and I'm sure now every night there will be a different weird person sitting at my desk."

[EXCERPT FROM RS 743 COVER STORY BY CHRIS MUNDY]

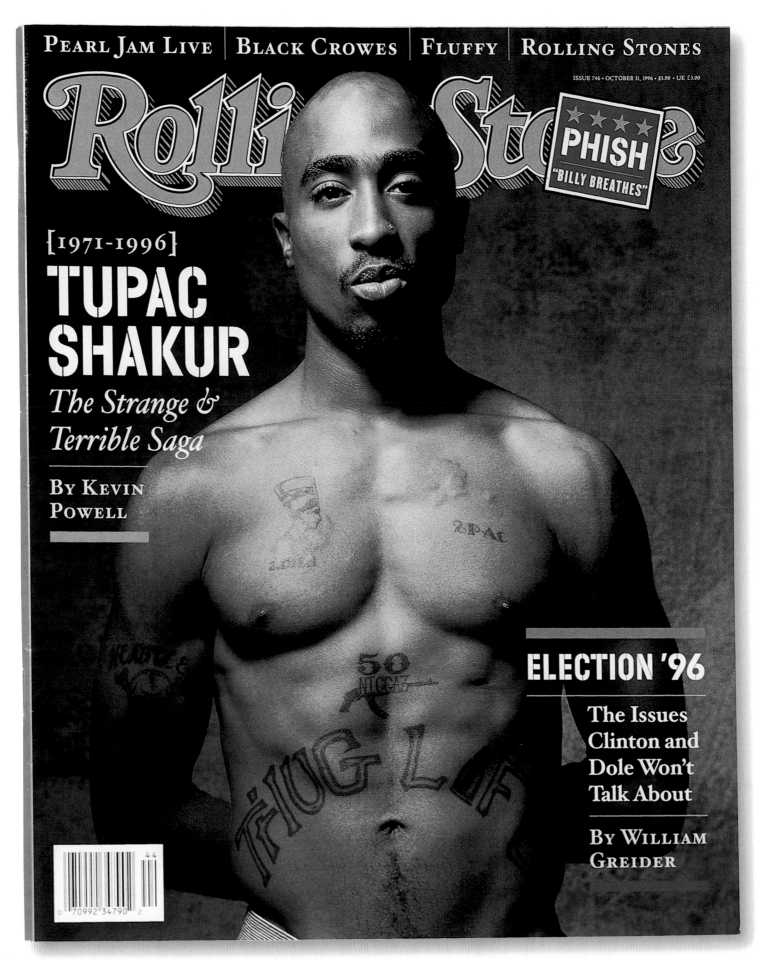

At 4:03 p.m. on September 13th, Tupac Amaru Shakur, rapper and actor, died at the University of Nevada Medical Center in the Wild West gambling town of Las Vegas, the result of gunshot wounds he had received six days earlier in a drive-by shooting near the glittery, hotel-studded strip. Shakur, a.k.a. 2Pac, was twenty-five. The rapper is survived by his mother, Afeni Shakur, his father, Billy Garland, and a half sister, Sekyiwa.

*   *   *   *   *

LIKE KURT COBAIN before him, Tupac Shakur had become a living symbol of his generation's angst and rage, and for that he is now looked upon as a martyr. But his fame and the controversy and misunderstanding that surrounded his life have also rendered Shakur – like Cobain, Marvin Gaye, James Dean, Jimi Hendrix, Jim Morrison and even Malcolm X – an enigma.

[EXCERPT FROM RS 746 ESSAY BY KEVIN POWELL]

*   *   *   *   *

I DON'T KNOW whether to mourn Tupac Shakur or to rail against all the terrible forces – including the artist's own self-destructive temperament – that have resulted in such a wasteful, unjustifiable end. I do know this, though: Whatever its causes, the murder of Shakur, at age twenty-five, has robbed us of one of the most talented and compelling voices of recent years. He embodied just as much for his audience as Kurt Cobain did for his. That is, Tupac Shakur spoke to, and for, many who had grown up within hard realities – realities that mainstream culture and media are loath to understand or respect. His death has left his fans feeling a doubly sharp pain: the loss of a much-esteemed signifier and the loss of a future volume of work that, no doubt, would have proved both brilliant and provocative.

[EXCERPT FROM RS 746 ESSAY BY MIKAL GILMORE]

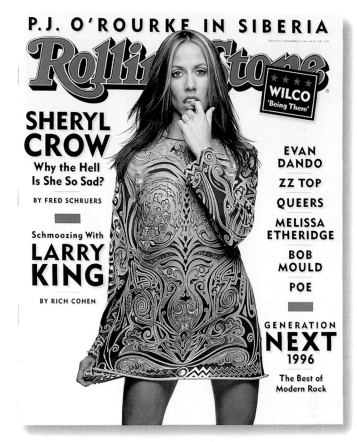

RS 747 | NOVEMBER 14TH, 1996
SHERYL CROW
Photograph by MARK SELIGER

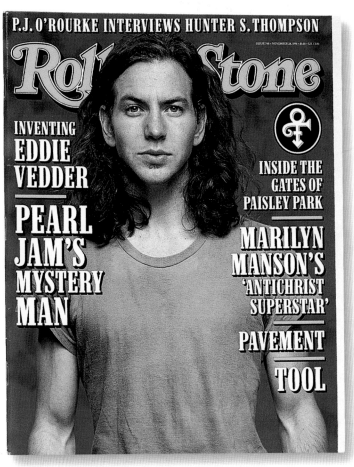

RS 748 | NOVEMBER 28TH, 1996
EDDIE VEDDER
Photograph by ROSS HALFIN

THIS IS A JOURNEY into the mind of Dennis Rodman. Think twice before volunteering to go further. Sometimes it will be funny, but sometimes it will be scary. Sometimes the paranoia and craziness will seep out of the page to get you. Sometimes you won't quite understand what Dennis Rodman is saying. Sometimes you will and wish you didn't. There will be casualties. Logic, love, basketball, fashion… these will all take a battering. You will not be lied to, but sometimes the truth will seem elusive. This trip will take in an array of guests, and not all of them will be pleased to find themselves in Rodman-land. It will be fun, in a way, but the kind of fun that gets all mixed up with trouble and sadness and never quite untangles itself. In the end, life won't seem simpler, and the world won't seem a safer place.

Don't forget: We are just tourists here. We will be going home. But Dennis Rodman can't leave. This is where he lives. . . .

RS 750/751 | DECEMBER 26TH, 1996 – JANUARY 9TH, 1997
BEAVIS & BUTT-HEAD WITH PAMELA ANDERSON LEE
Photograph by MARK SELIGER Illustration by MIKE JUDGE

DENNIS RODMAN lies back on the bus bed, the evening sunlight shining off his nose rings. "I totally feel like a rock star more than a basketball player. I totally think: Have I got to go and play basketball now?"

[EXCERPT FROM RS 749 COVER STORY BY CHRIS HEATH]

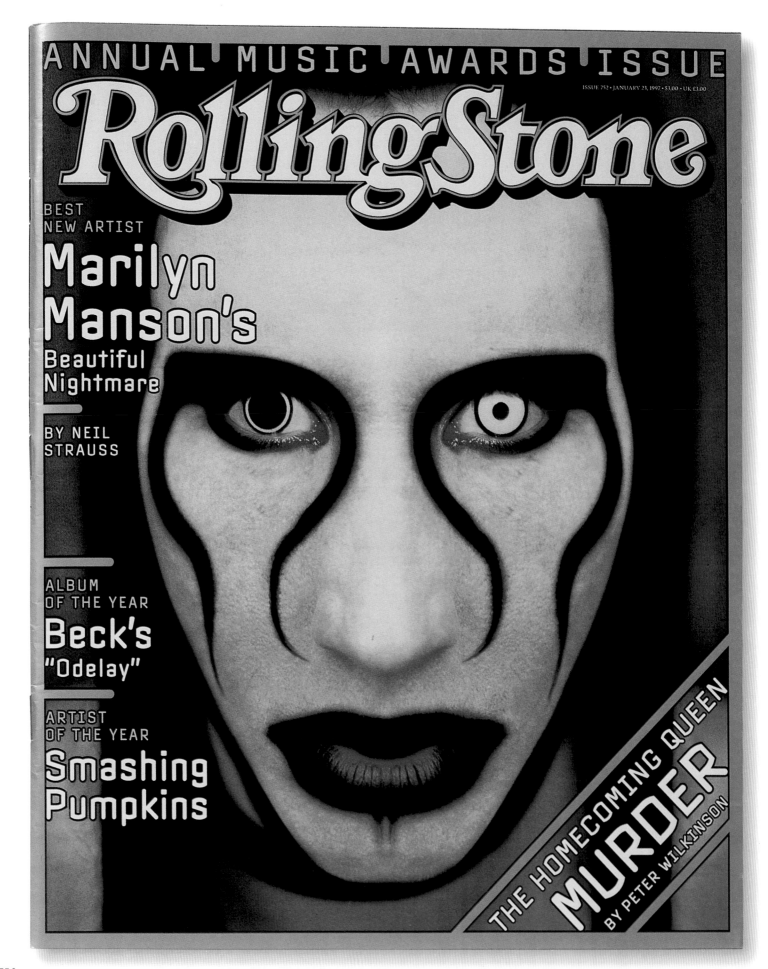

ANNUAL MUSIC AWARDS ISSUE

ISSUE 752 · JANUARY 23, 1997 · $3.00 · UK £3.00

RollingStone

BEST
NEW ARTIST

Marilyn Manson's
Beautiful
Nightmare

BY NEIL
STRAUSS

ALBUM
OF THE YEAR

Beck's
"Odelay"

ARTIST
OF THE YEAR

Smashing
Pumpkins

THE HOMECOMING QUEEN
MURDER
BY PETER WILKINSON

BE CAREFUL when you gossip: A little rumor can go a long way. Especially when the subject is Marilyn Manson. "For a solid year, there was a rumor that I was going to commit suicide on Halloween," says Manson. He is sitting in a hot tub (yes, a hot tub!) in his hometown of Fort Lauderdale, Florida. "I started to think, Maybe I *have* to kill myself, maybe that's what I was supposed to do. Then, when we were performing on Halloween, there was a bomb threat. I guess someone thought they would take care of the situation for me. It was one of those moments where chaos had control." He pauses, raises his tattoo-covered arm from the water and stares nervously through a pair of black wraparound sunglasses at the spa door. It opens a crack, then closes. No one enters. "Sometimes I wonder if I'm a character being written, or if I'm writing myself," Manson continues. "It's confusing."

Never has there been a rock star quite as complex as Marilyn Manson, frontman of the band of the same name. In the current landscape of reluctant rock stars, Manson is a complete anomaly: He craves spectacle, success and attention. And when it comes to the traditional rock-star lifestyle, he can outdo most of his contemporaries. Manson and his similarly pseudonymed band mates – bassist Twiggy Ramirez, drummer Ginger Fish, keyboardist Madonna Wayne Gacy and guitarist Zim Zum – have shat in Evan Dando's bathtub and, just last night, they coaxed Billy Corgan into snorting sea monkeys. When it comes to getting serious about his work, Manson is among the most eloquent and artful musicians. And among the most misunderstood. The rumor-hungry fans who see him as a living demon who's removed his own ribs and testicles know just as little about Manson as the detractors who dismiss him as a Halloween-costumed shock rocker riding on [Nine Inch Nails mastermind] Trent Reznor's coattails.

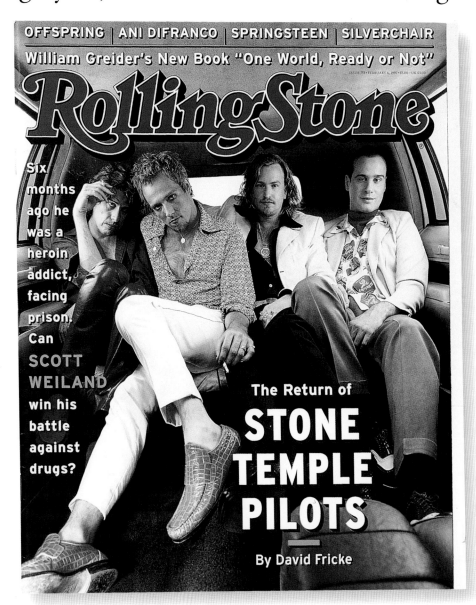

OFFSPRING | ANI DIFRANCO | SPRINGSTEEN | SILVERCHAIR
William Greider's New Book "One World, Ready or Not"

ISSUE 753 · FEBRUARY 6, 1997 · $3.00 · UK £3.00

RollingStone

Six months ago he was a heroin addict, facing prison. Can SCOTT WEILAND win his battle against drugs?

The Return of
STONE TEMPLE PILOTS

By David Fricke

[EXCERPT FROM RS 752 COVER STORY BY NEIL STRAUSS]

RS 753 | FEBRUARY 6TH, 1997
STONE TEMPLE PILOTS
Photograph by MARK SELIGER

HELMET · HENRY ROLLINS · VAN MORRISON · L7

RollingStone

Betrayal, Sex, Murder, Deception and **NINE INCH NAILS**

SPECIAL REPORT

Trent Reznor TAKES DAVID LYNCH'S 'Lost Highway'

Hillary J. Johnson Investigates **The New AIDS Drugs**

U2 Goes 'Pop'

Joni Mitchell Talks to Morrissey

BY MIKAL GILMORE

RS 755 | MARCH 6TH, 1997
TRENT REZNOR & DAVID LYNCH
Photograph by DAN WINTERS

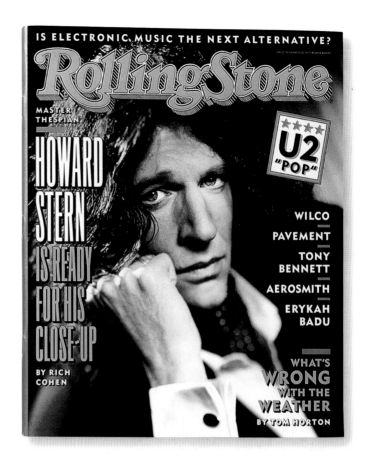

IS ELECTRONIC MUSIC THE NEXT ALTERNATIVE?

RollingStone

MASTER THESPIAN

U2 "POP"

HOWARD STERN IS READY FOR HIS CLOSE-UP

BY RICH COHEN

WILCO
PAVEMENT
TONY BENNETT
AEROSMITH
ERYKAH BADU

WHAT'S **WRONG** WITH THE **WEATHER** BY TOM HORTON

RS 756 | MARCH 20TH, 1997
HOWARD STERN
Photograph by MARK SELIGER

REBEL HOLLYWOOD

RollingStone

THE ACTORS

THE **DEFIANT ONES**

LEADER OF THE PACK

BRAD PITT TALKS TOUGH

THE STUDIO

THE **BIG BAD WOLVES** OF **MIRAMAX**

CUBA GOODING JR.
BILLY **BOB** THORNTON & EMILY **WATSON** **CRASH** THE OSCARS AND A WOMAN SCORNED **COURTNEY LOVE**

THE DIRECTOR

'SEVEN' WHIZ DAVID **FINCHER**

THE 30 GREAT REBEL **MOVIES**

RS 757 | APRIL 3RD, 1997
BRAD PITT
Photograph by MARK SELIGER

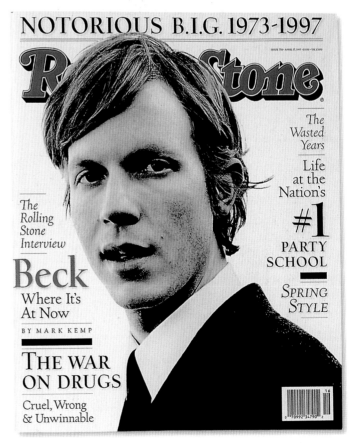

NOTORIOUS B.I.G. 1973-1997

RollingStone

The Wasted Years

Life at the Nation's **#1** PARTY SCHOOL

SPRING STYLE

The Rolling Stone Interview

Beck Where It's At Now

BY MARK KEMP

THE WAR ON DRUGS Cruel, Wrong & Unwinnable

RS 758 | APRIL 17TH, 1997
BECK
Photograph by ANTON CORBIJN

RS 759 | MAY 1ST, 1997
NO DOUBT
Photograph by NORBERT SCHOERNER

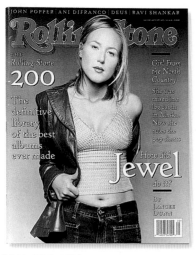

RS 760 | MAY 15TH, 1997
JEWEL
Photograph by MATTHEW ROLSTON

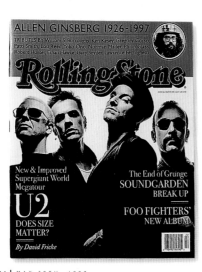

RS 761 | MAY 29TH, 1997
U2
Photograph by ALBERT WATSON

MUCH OF TONIGHT'S AUDIENCE has no idea who Jakob's father is; everyone I've talked to couldn't care less: *Bob Dylan's just a guy in my social studies book.*

"*Jaaaaaaaykob!*"

So handsome, with those sharp Armani shoulders, the startling, Samoyed-blue eyes, that cool, funky hat destined to become a video talisman . . .

"Jaaaaaykob! *Tell it!*"

What the recordmen don't know, the little girls understand. Jakob Dylan is a young man of certain passion, singing his own words with a shy, fitful intensity that seems, sometimes, to take him out and above this big, hot room. It's not the raspy, unremarkable voice so much as the delivery that draws them, some strain of the ageless troubadour DNA that goosed vestal virgins in the shadows of Stonehenge.

[EXCERPT FROM RS 762 COVER STORY BY GERRI HIRSHEY]

"IF I WAS IN A PUBLIC PLACE with my dad and people noticed, I'd cross the street. Stand next to somebody else. It was instinct. My picture was not to be in magazines. It was unsaid. I understood. It's something I spent twenty years doing a certain way – then I went completely the opposite. It's hard to figure out how that makes any sense. You find ways to rationalize it – like it's some character up there, it's not you."

~ *JAKOB DYLAN*

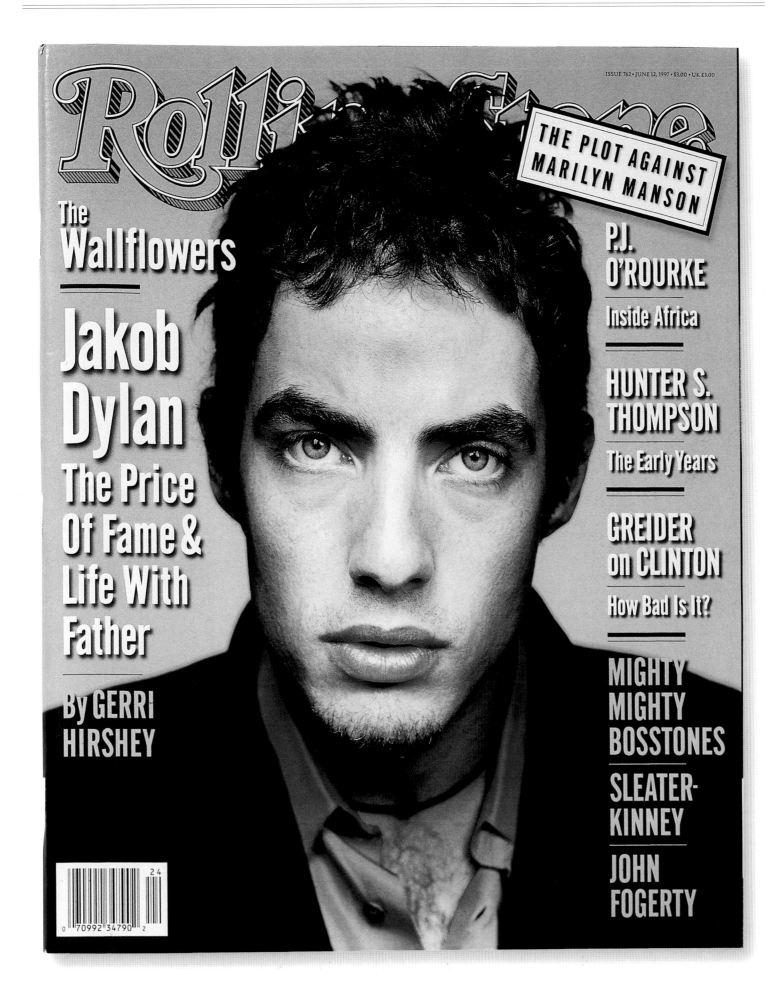

ISSUE 762 • JUNE 12, 1997 • $3.00 • UK £3.00

Rolling

THE PLOT AGAINST MARILYN MANSON

The Wallflowers

Jakob Dylan

The Price Of Fame & Life With Father

By GERRI HIRSHEY

P.J. O'ROURKE
Inside Africa

HUNTER S. THOMPSON
The Early Years

GREIDER on CLINTON
How Bad Is It?

MIGHTY MIGHTY BOSSTONES

SLEATER-KINNEY

JOHN FOGERTY

0 70992 34790 2   24

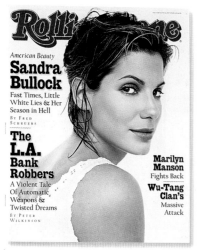

RS 763 | JUNE 26TH, 1997
SANDRA BULLOCK
Photograph by BRIGITTE LACOMBE

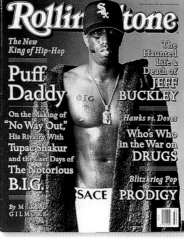

RS 766 | AUGUST 7TH, 1997
PUFF DADDY
Photograph by MATTHEW ROLSTON

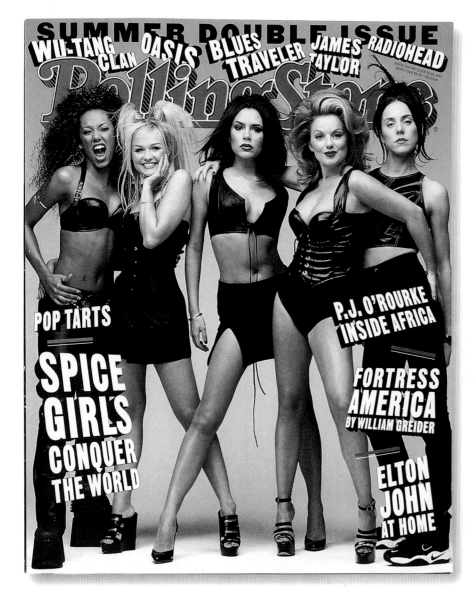

RS 764/765 | JULY 10TH – JULY 24TH, 1997
SPICE GIRLS
Photograph by MARK SELIGER

HERE, BEFORE THINGS get too silly and agitated, is a cut out 'n' keep guide to the five Spice Girls. This is what you will need to know:

Geri Haliwell is 24. She is known as Ginger Spice. . . . When Geri was young, she once poohed in the bath with her brother and sister. She is the most talkative Spice Girl and the one who is generally first to shout "girl power," the key concept in Spice Girl philosophy.

Melanie Brown (Mel B) is 22. She is known as Scary Spice. . . . When she was young, Mel B used to have a boogie collection behind her bunk bed. Now she has a pierced tongue.

Emma Bunton is 21. She is known as Baby Spice. She has blond hair, which she often wears in bunches. . . . When she was young, she was a child model. She recently announced, as a joke, "I don't want to be a cutie – I want to be a hot, sexy bitch," but she's now rather perturbed that the statement has been taken seriously.

Victoria Aadams is 22. She is known as Posh Spice. . . . When she was young, Victoria used to beg her father not to take her to school in the Rolls-Royce. She was teased for that and for her nose. She likes to dress in Prada and Gucci, and hates the way she looks when she smiles.

Melanie Chisholm is 23. She is known as Sporty Spice. . . . When she was young, Melanie used to eat cat food. She wears lots of Adidas sportswear. A tattoo on her upper right arm is of two Japanese symbols: woman and strength. Girl power, in other words.

These names – Ginger, Scary, Baby, Posh, Sporty – have been a successful part of the Spice Girls package: a perfect simultaneous pop express of heterogeneity (they're each their own person) and homogeneity (they're all disciples in the Church of Spice).

[EXCERPT FROM RS 764/765
COVER STORY BY CHRIS HEATH]

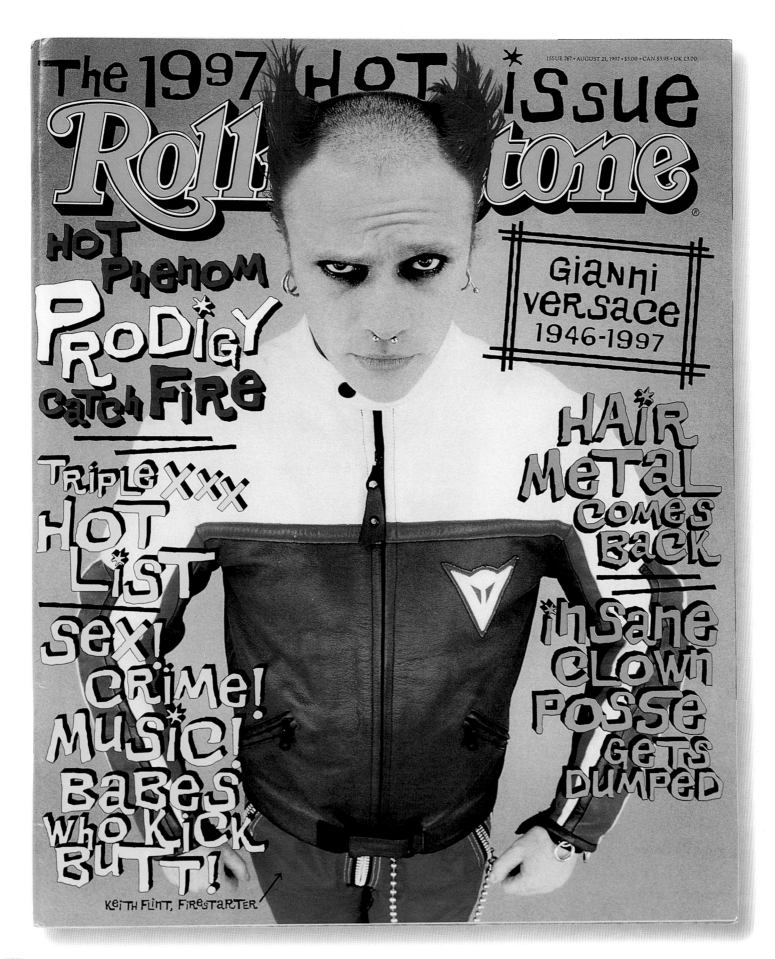

RS 767 | THE PRODIGY'S KEITH FLINT | Photograph by PETER ROBATHAN | AUGUST 21ST, 1997

RS 768 | SEPTEMBER 4TH, 1997
RZA & ZACK DE LA ROCHA
Photograph by MARK SELIGER

RS 769 | SEPTEMBER 18TH, 1997
NEVE CAMPBELL
Photograph by MATTHEW ROLSTON

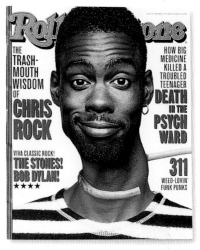

RS 770 | OCTOBER 2ND, 1997
CHRIS ROCK
Photograph by MARK SELIGER

RS 771 | OCTOBER 16TH, 1997
SALT-N-PEPA
Photograph by PEGGY SIROTA

RS 772 | OCTOBER 30TH, 1997
FLEETWOOD MAC
Photograph by MARK SELIGER

RS 773 | NOVEMBER 13TH, 1997
THIRTIETH ANNIVERSARY: COURTNEY LOVE, TINA TURNER & MADONNA
Photograph by PEGGY SIROTA

1997

RS 1	John Lennon	*'How I Won the War' Film Still*
RS 2	Tina Turner	*Baron Wolman*
RS 3	The Beatles & Friends on Location for *Magical Mystery Tour: (from left, top row)* Jeni Crowley, John Lennon, Spencer Davis, Jesse Robins, Paul McCartney, Maggie Right, Mel Evans, Alex Mardes, Bill Wall, Neil Aspinal, Shirley Evans, Ringo Starr; *(from left, second row)* Sylvia Nightingale, Pauline Davis & baby, Derek Royal, Mandy West, Linda Lawson, Amy Smedley, unknown couple; *(from left, third row)* Freda Kelley, Barbara Icing, Loz Harvey, George Claydon, Alf Mandos; *(from left, front row)* Michael Gladden, George Harrison, Nat Jackly, Leslie Cavendish, Ivor Cutler	*Photographer Unknown*
RS 4	Donovan Jimi Hendrix, Otis Redding	*Baron Wolman* *Photographer Unknown*
RS 5	Jim Morrison	*Baron Wolman*
RS 6	Janis Joplin, San Francisco's Gathering of the Tribes Be-In	*Baron Wolman*
RS 7	Jimi Hendrix	*Baron Wolman*
RS 8	Monterey Pop Festival Organizers John Phillips & Lou Adler	*Photographer Unknown*
RS 9	John Lennon & Paul McCartney in *Yellow Submarine*	*Heinz Edelmann*
RS 10	Eric Clapton	*Linda Eastman*
RS 11	Rock Fashion – Julianna Wolman	*Baron Wolman*
RS 12	Bob Dylan	*Photographer Unknown*
RS 13	Tiny Tim	*Baron Wolman*
RS 14	Frank Zappa	*Baron Wolman*
RS 15	Mick Jagger	*Dean Goodbill*
RS 16	The Band	*Elliott Landy*
RS 17	Zap Comix Mouse	*Rick Griffin*
RS 18	Pete Townshend	*Baron Wolman*
RS 19	Mick Jagger	*Ethan Russell*
RS 20	Ringo Starr, Paul McCartney, John Lennon & George Harrison	*Photographs from '16' magazine, Courtesy Gloria Stavers*
RS 21	Drugs in the Army	*Jack Warren*
RS 22	John Lennon & Yoko Ono	*John Lennon*
RS 23	Doug & Sean Sahm	*Baron Wolman*
RS 24	The Beatles	*Photographer Unknown*
RS 25	Rob Tyner	*Photographer Unknown*
RS 26	Jimi Hendrix	*Baron Wolman*
RS 27	Groupies – Karen Seltenriech	*Baron Wolman*
RS 28	Japanese Rock – Unidentified & Kenji "Julie" Sawada of Julie & the Tigers	*Naoko Lash*
RS 29	Janis Joplin	*Photographer Unknown*
RS 30	American Revolution 1969	*Nacio Brown*
RS 31	Sun Ra	*Baron Wolman*
RS 32	Stevie Winwood	*David Dalton*
RS 33	Joni Mitchell	*Baron Wolman*
RS 34	Jimi Hendrix	*Franz Maier*
RS 35	Chuck Berry	*Baron Wolman*
RS 36	Nudie	*Baron Wolman*
RS 37	Elvis Presley	*Photographer Unknown*
RS 38	Jim Morrison	*Photographer Unknown*
RS 39	Brian Jones	*Jim Marshall*
RS 40	Jerry Garcia	*Baron Wolman*
RS 41	Joe Cocker	*Steven Shames*
RS 42	Woodstock	*Baron Wolman*
RS 43	The Underground Press	*Steven Shames*
RS 44	David Crosby	*Robert Altman*
RS 45	Tina Turner	*Robert Altman*
RS 46	The Beatles	*Photographer Unknown*
RS 47	Bob Dylan	*Illustrator Unknown*
RS 48	Miles Davis	*Photographer Unknown*
RS 49	Mick Jagger	*Baron Wolman*
RS 50	Altamont	*Michael Maggia (Photographies West)*
RS 51	John Lennon & Yoko Ono	*Annette Yorke*
RS 52	Creedence Clearwater Revival	*Baron Wolman*
RS 53	Mark Frechette & Daria Halprin	*'Zabriskie Point' Film Still*
RS 54	Sly & the Family Stone	*Stephen Paley*
RS 55	Abbie Hoffman	*Bill Myers (Praxis)*
RS 56	Dennis Hopper	*Michael Anderson Jr.*
RS 57	Paul McCartney	*Linda Eastman*
RS 58	Captain Beefheart	*John Williams*
RS 59	Little Richard	*Baron Wolman*
RS 60	Antiwar Demonstrators	*Annie Leibovitz*
RS 61	Charles Manson	*Photographer Unknown*
RS 62	Van Morrison	*Photographer Unknown*
RS 63	David Crosby	*Ed Caraeff*
RS 64	Janis Joplin	*Tony Lane*
RS 65	Mick Jagger & Anita Pallenberg	*'Performance' Film Still*
RS 66	The Grateful Dead	*Jim Marshall*
RS 67	Felix Cavaliere & the Rascals	*Stephen Paley*
RS 68	Jimi Hendrix	*Jim Marshall*
RS 69	Janis Joplin	*Jim Marshall*
RS 70	Grace Slick	*Annie Leibovitz*
RS 71	Meher Baba	*Photographer Unknown*
RS 72	Leon Russell	*Ed Caraeff*
RS 73	Rod Stewart	*Annie Leibovitz*
RS 74	John Lennon	*Annie Leibovitz*
RS 75	John Lennon & Yoko Ono	*Annie Leibovitz*
RS 76	James Taylor	*Baron Wolman*
RS 77	Bob Dylan	*Photographer Unknown*
RS 78	Muhammad Ali	*Brian Hamill*
RS 79	F.C.C. Member Nicholas Johnson	*Annie Leibovitz*
RS 80	Joe Dallesandro	*Annie Leibovitz*
RS 81	Michael Jackson	*Henry Diltz*
RS 82	Peter Fonda	*Annie Leibovitz*
RS 83	Country Joe McDonald & Robin Menken	*Annie Leibovitz*
RS 84	Elton John	*Annie Leibovitz*
RS 85	Tricia Nixon	*Photographer Unknown*
RS 86	Doug Sahm	*Baron Wolman*
RS 87	Ian Anderson	*Annie Leibovitz*
RS 88	Jim Morrison	*Photographer Unknown*
RS 89	Keith Richards	*Robert Altman*
RS 90	George Harrison	*Annie Leibovitz*
RS 91	The Incredible Hulk	*Herb Trimpe*
RS 92	Jefferson Airplane	*Annie Leibovitz*
RS 93	Ike & Tina Turner	*Annie Leibovitz*
RS 94	The Beach Boys	*Annie Leibovitz*
RS 95	Fear and Loathing in Las Vegas	*Ralph Steadman*
RS 96	Fear and Loathing in Las Vegas	*Ralph Steadman*
RS 97	Pete Townshend	*Nevis Cameron*
RS 98	Evangelist Mel Lyman	*David Gahr*
RS 99	Cat Stevens	*Annie Leibovitz*
RS 100	Jerry Garcia	*Annie Leibovitz*
RS 101	The Grateful Dead	*Annie Leibovitz*
RS 102	Narc Agent Gerritt Van Raam	*Photographer Unknown*
RS 103	Bob Dylan	*Milton Glaser*
RS 104	Bob Dylan	*Robert Grossman*
RS 105	Alice Cooper	*Annie Leibovitz*
RS 106	The Art of Sensual Massage	*Robert Foothorap*
RS 107	Texas C&W Festival, Marvin Gaye, Hubert Humphrey	*Annie Leibovitz*
RS 108	David Cassidy	*Annie Leibovitz*
RS 109	Jane Fonda	*Annie Leibovitz*
RS 110	George McGovern	*Edward Sorel*
RS 111	Van Morrison	*Annie Leibovitz*
RS 112	Mick Jagger	*Annie Leibovitz*
RS 113	Paul Simon	*Peter Simon*
RS 114	Huey Newton	*Annie Leibovitz*
RS 115	George McGovern at the 1972 Democratic Convention	*Ralph Steadman*
RS 116	Randy Newman	*Annie Leibovitz*
RS 117	Three Dog Night	*Annie Leibovitz*
RS 118	1972 Republican Convention	*Ralph Steadman*
RS 119	Sally Struthers	*Mel Traxel*
RS 120	Jeff Beck	*Herbie Greene*
RS 121	David Bowie	*Mick Rock*
RS 122	Pimp Joe Conforte & His Working Girls	*Annie Leibovitz*
RS 123	Carlos Santana	*Annie Leibovitz*
RS 124	Keith Moon	*Bob Gruen*
RS 125	James Taylor & Carly Simon	*Peter Simon*
RS 126	Apollo Astronaut	*Dugald Stermer*
RS 127	Diana Ross	*Annie Leibovitz*
RS 128	Bette Midler	*Philip Hays*
RS 129	Mick Jagger	*Annie Leibovitz*
RS 130	Robert Mitchum	*Charles E. White III*
RS 131	Dr. Hook & the Medicine Show	*Gerry Gersten*
RS 132	Truman Capote	*Henry Diltz*
RS 133	Mark Spitz	*Ignacio Gomez*
RS 134	Alice Cooper	*Annie Leibovitz*
RS 135	Crime Victim Dirk Dickenson	*James McMullan*
RS 136	Jesus Freaks	*Edward Sorel*
RS 137	Rod Stewart	*Charles Gatewood*
RS 138	Paul Newman	*Stephen Shugrue*
RS 139	Tatum O'Neal	*Steve Jaffe*
RS 140	Peter Wolf	*Annie Leibovitz*
RS 141	Elton John	*Kim Whitesides*
RS 142	Dan Hicks	*Annie Leibovitz*
RS 143	Senator Sam Ervin	*Charles Shields*
RS 144	Richard Nixon	*Ralph Steadman*
RS 145	Art Garfunkel	*Jim Marshall*
RS 146	Gene Autry	*Gary Overacre*
RS 147	Daniel Ellsburg	*Dave Willardson*
RS 148	Jerry Garcia	*Robert Grossman*
RS 149	Gregg Allman	*Gilbert Stone*
RS 150	Hugh Hefner	*Annie Leibovitz*
RS 151	Funky Chic	*Peter Palombi*
RS 152	Richard Nixon	*Robert Grossman*
RS 153	Paul & Linda McCartney	*Francesco Scavullo*
RS 154	Bob Dylan	*Barry Feinstein*
RS 155	Fear and Loathing at the Super Bowl	*Hank Woodward*
RS 156	Bob Dylan	*Paul Davis*
RS 157	P.O.W. Rick Springman	*Peter Palombi*
RS 158	Marvin Gaye	*Annie Leibovitz*
RS 159	Kris Kristofferson	*Annie Leibovitz*
RS 160	Paul Getty	*Annie Leibovitz*
RS 161	Jackson & Ethan Browne	*Annie Leibovitz*
RS 162	The Economy	*Peter Palombi*
RS 163	James Dean	*John van Hamersveld*
RS 164	Karen & Richard Carpenter	*Annie Leibovitz*
RS 165	Eric Clapton	*Philip Hays*
RS 166	Maria Muldaur	*Annie Leibovitz*
RS 167	Steely Dan	*Dave Willardson*
RS 168	Crosby, Stills, Nash & Young	*Dugald Stermer*
RS 169	Richard Milhous Nixon	*Annie Leibovitz*
RS 170	Tanya Tucker	*Doug Metzler*
RS 171	Lily Tomlin & Richard Pryor	*Annie Leibovitz*
RS 172	The Beatles	*Tom Rose*
RS 173	Evel Knievel	*Ray Domingo*
RS 174	Elton John	*Annie Leibovitz*
RS 175	Dustin Hoffman	*Steve Schapiro*
RS 176	George Harrison	*Mark Focus*
RS 177	Suzi Quatro	*Peter Gowland*
RS 178	Gregg Allman	*Pete Turner*
RS 179	Freddie Prinze	*Don Peterson*
RS 180	The Electric Muse	*Phil Carroll*
RS 181	Kenny Loggins & Jim Messina	*Annie Leibovitz*
RS 182	Jimmy Page & Robert Plant	*Neal Preston*
RS 183	Linda Ronstadt	*Annie Leibovitz*
RS 184	Roger Daltrey	*Photographer Unknown*
RS 185	Peter Falk	*Annie Leibovitz*
RS 186	John Denver	*Francesco Scavullo*
RS 187	Carly Simon	*Tony Lane*
RS 188	Phoebe Snow	*Annie Leibovitz*
RS 189	Stevie Wonder	*Milton Glaser*
RS 190	Labelle	*Hiro*
RS 191	Mick Jagger & Keith Richards	*Annie Leibovitz*
RS 192	Richard Dreyfuss	*Bud Lee*
RS 193	Neil Young	*Kim Whitesides*
RS 194	Doonesbury's Uncle Duke	*Garry Trudeau*
RS 195	Mick Jagger	*Annie Leibovitz*
RS 196	The Eagles	*Neal Preston*
RS 197	Muhammad Ali	*Bruce Wolfe*
RS 198	Patty Hearst	*Jamie Putnam*
RS 199	Rod Stewart & Britt Ekland	*Annie Leibovitz*
RS 200	The Patty Hearst Story, Part Two	*Tony Lane*
RS 201	Jack Nicholson	*Kim Whitesides*
RS 202	Bonnie Raitt	*Bill King*
RS 203	Marty Balin, Paul Kantner & Grace Slick	*Greg Scott*
RS 204	Joan Baez & Bob Dylan	*Ken Regan (Camera 5)*
RS 205	Pat Boone	*Bruno of Hollywood*
RS 206	David Bowie	*Steve Schapiro*
RS 207	Grace Slick, Jerry Garcia, Steve Miller, John Cipollina & Dan Hicks	*Jim Marshall*
RS 208	Donny Osmond	*Annie Leibovitz*
RS 209	Louise Lasser	*Bill Eppridge*
RS 210	Robert Redford & Dustin Hoffman	*Stanley Tretick*
RS 211	Peter Frampton Peter Frampton *(second cover)* Inset: SLA Hideout	*Francesco Scavullo* *Bud Lee* *Alison Weir*
RS 212	Carlos Santana	*Annie Leibovitz*
RS 213	Marlon Brando	*Mary Ellen Mark*
RS 214	Jimmy Carter	*Greg Scott*
RS 215	Paul & Linda McCartney	*Annie Leibovitz*
RS 216	Paul Simon	*Annie Leibovitz*
RS 217	The Beatles	*John Zimmerman*
RS 218	Jack Ford	*Annie Leibovitz*
RS 219	Bob Marley	*Annie Leibovitz*
RS 220	Steven Tyler	*Annie Leibovitz*
RS 221	Doonesbury's Ginny Slade & Jimmy Thudpucker	*Garry Trudeau*
RS 222	Neil Diamond	*Annie Leibovitz*
RS 223	Elton John	*David Nutter*
RS 224	Richard Avedon's Portfolio The Family 1976	*Elizabeth Paul*
RS 225	Brian Wilson	*Annie Leibovitz*
RS 226	Janis Joplin	*David Gahr*
RS 227	Linda Ronstadt	*Annie Leibovitz*
RS 228	Jackson Browne	*Daniel Maffia*
RS 229	Wild Things	*Maurice Sendak*
RS 230	Rod Stewart	*David Montgomery (Radio Times)*
RS 231	Jeff Bridges	*Annie Leibovitz*
RS 232	Peter Frampton	*Annie Leibovitz*
RS 233	Boz Scaggs	*Annie Leibovitz*
RS 234	Princess Caroline	*Norman Parkinson (Sygma)*
RS 235	Fleetwood Mac	*Annie Leibovitz*
RS 236	Lily Tomlin	*Annie Leibovitz*
RS 237	Daryl Hall & John Oates	*Annie Leibovitz*
RS 238	Mark Fidrych	*Annie Leibovitz*
RS 239	Hamilton Jordan & Jody Powell	*Annie Leibovitz*
RS 240	Crosby, Stills & Nash	*Robert Grossman*
RS 241	Robert De Niro	*Leonard De Raemy (Sygma)*
RS 242	Diane Keaton	*Hiro*
RS 243	The Bee Gees	*Francesco Scavullo*
RS 244	Ann & Nancy Wilson	*Eric Meola*
RS 245	Diana Ross	*Annie Leibovitz*
RS 246	Mark Hamill, Carrie Fisher, Chewbacca & Harrison Ford	*Terry O'Neill*
RS 247	O.J. Simpson	*Annie Leibovitz*
RS 248	Elvis Presley	*Photographer Unknown*
RS 249	Bella Abzug	*Andy Warhol*
RS 250	Johnny Rotten *(left)* Johnny Rotten *(right)*	*Bob Gruen* *Dennis Morris*
RS 251	Ron Wood	*Annie Leibovitz*
RS 252	Pete Townshend	*Daniel Maffia*
RS 253	Steve Martin	*Annie Leibovitz*
RS 254	Tenth Anniversary	*Jim Parkinson*
RS 255	James Taylor, Peter Asher & Linda Ronstadt	*Annie Leibovitz*
RS 256	Fleetwood Mac	*Annie Leibovitz*
RS 257	Bob Dylan	*Annie Leibovitz*
RS 258	Doonesbury's Jimmy Thudpucker	*Garry Trudeau*
RS 259	Rita Coolidge & Kris Kristofferson	*Francesco Scavullo*
RS 260	Jane Fonda	*Annie Leibovitz*
RS 261	Donna Summer	*Brian Leatart*
RS 262	Brooke Shields	*Maureen Lambray ©1977*
RS 263	The Bee Gees & Peter Frampton	*Bruce Wolfe*
RS 264	Muhammad Ali	*Annie Leibovitz*
RS 265	Jefferson Starship	*Annie Leibovitz*
RS 266	Carly Simon	*Hiro*
RS 267	John Travolta	*Annie Leibovitz*
RS 268	Mick Jagger	*Annie Leibovitz*
RS 269	Willie Nelson	*Photograph by Beverly Parker, Painted by Jack Doonan*
RS 270	Patti Smith	*Annie Leibovitz*
RS 271	John Belushi	*Hiro*
RS 272	Bruce Springsteen	*Lynn Goldsmith*
RS 273	Mick Jagger & Keith Richards	*Lynn Goldsmith*
RS 274	Gary Busey as Buddy Holly	*Gemma Lamana*
RS 275	The Who	*Robert Grossman*
RS 276	Linda Ronstadt	*Francesco Scavullo*
RS 277	Gilda Radner	*Francesco Scavullo*
RS 278	Bob Dylan	*Morgan Renard*
RS 279	Linda Ronstadt, Steve Martin & Gilda Radner	*Annie Leibovitz*
RS 280	Cheech & Chong with Kareem Abdul-Jabbar	*David Alexander*

RS 281/282	Richard Dreyfuss	Julian Allen
RS 283	The Cars	Jim Houghton
RS 284	Neil Young	Julian Allen
RS 285	Dan Aykroyd & John Belushi	Annie Leibovitz
RS 286	Ted Nugent	Bill King
RS 287	Johnny Carson	Annie Leibovitz
RS 288	Michael & Cameron Douglas	Annie Leibovitz
RS 289	The Village People	Bill King
RS 290	Richard Pryor	David Alexander
RS 291	The Bee Gees	Richard Avedon
RS 292	Jon Voight	Annie Leibovitz
RS 293	Cheap Trick	Annie Leibovitz
RS 294	Blondie	Annie Leibovitz
RS 295	Paul McCartney	Julian Allen
RS 296	Joni Mitchell	Norman Seeff
RS 297	Rickie Lee Jones	Annie Leibovitz
RS 298	Robin Williams	Richard Avedon
RS 299	James Taylor	Annie Leibovitz
RS 300	The Doobie Brothers	Annie Leibovitz
RS 301	Jimmy Buffett	Annie Leibovitz
RS 302	Sissy Spacek	Annie Leibovitz
RS 303	Martin Sheen	Annie Leibovitz
RS 304	Bonnie Raitt, Bruce Springsteen, Carly Simon, James Taylor, Jackson Browne, Graham Nash & John Hall	Annie Leibovitz
RS 305	The Eagles	Norman Seeff
RS 306	Bette Midler	Annie Leibovitz
RS 309	Teva Ladd, Bryan Wagner, Connie Burns, James Warmoth, Karen Morrison, Peter Bowes, Jacqueline Eckerle, Phillip Snyder, David Heck, Stephan Preston, Walter Adams Jr.	Photographers Unknown
RS 310	Stevie Nicks & Mick Fleetwood	Richard Avedon
RS 311	Tom Petty	Annie Leibovitz
RS 312	Richard Gere	Terry O'Neill
RS 313	Bob Hope	Richard Avedon
RS 314	Linda Ronstadt	Annie Leibovitz
RS 315	Joe Strummer & Mick Jones	Annie Leibovitz
RS 316	Bob Seger	Annie Leibovitz
RS 317	Ann & Nancy Wilson	Annie Leibovitz
RS 318	The Pretenders	Annie Leibovitz
RS 319	Edward Kennedy	Annie Leibovitz
RS 320	Pete Townshend	Annie Leibovitz
RS 321	John Travolta	Annie Leibovitz
RS 322	Billy Dee Williams, Mark Hamill, Carrie Fisher & Harrison Ford	Annie Leibovitz
RS 323	Jackson Browne	Annie Leibovitz
RS 324	Keith Richards & Mick Jagger	Julian Allen
RS 325	Billy Joel	Kim Whitesides
RS 326	Rodney Dangerfield	Annie Leibovitz
RS 327	Robert Redford	Annie Leibovitz
RS 328	Pat Benatar & Neil Geraldo	Annie Leibovitz
RS 329	The Cars	Annie Leibovitz
RS 330	Mary Tyler Moore	Annie Leibovitz
RS 331	Jill Clayburgh & Michael Douglas	Annie Leibovitz
RS 332	Dolly Parton	Richard Avedon
RS 335	John Lennon & Yoko Ono	Annie Leibovitz
RS 336	Bruce Springsteen	Annie Leibovitz
RS 337	The Police	Klaus Lucka
RS 338	Goldie Hawn	Denis Piel
RS 339	Warren Zevon	Annie Leibovitz
RS 340	Roman Polanski	Julian Allen
RS 341	Jack Nicholson	Albert Watson
RS 342	Ringo Starr	Michael Childers (Sygma)
RS 343	Gun Control/Inset: John Lennon	Annie Leibovitz
RS 344	Susan Sarandon	Albert Watson
RS 345	James Taylor	Aaron Rapoport
RS 346	Harrison Ford	Bill King
RS 347	Margot Kidder	Denis Piel
RS 348	Tom Petty	Aaron Rapoport
RS 349	Rickie Lee Jones	Annie Leibovitz
RS 350	Bill Murray	Andrea Blanch
RS 351	Stevie Nicks	Annie Leibovitz
RS 352	Jim Morrison	Gloria Stavers
RS 353	Yoko Ono	Annie Leibovitz
RS 354	Meryl Streep	Annie Leibovitz
RS 355	Elvis Presley	Rudolf Paulini
RS 356	Keith Richards	Annie Leibovitz
RS 357	William Hurt	Annie Leibovitz
RS 358	Carly Simon	Jim Varriale
RS 359/360	The Rolling Stones at Madison Square Garden	Lynn Goldsmith
RS 361	John Belushi	Annie Leibovitz
RS 362	Timothy Hutton	Annie Leibovitz
RS 363	Steve Martin	Annie Leibovitz
RS 364	Peter Wolf	Annie Leibovitz
RS 365	Art Garfunkel & Paul Simon	Annie Leibovitz
RS 366	Warren Beatty	Jack Mitchell (Outline)
RS 367	Mariel Hemingway	Annie Leibovitz
RS 368	John Belushi	Annie Leibovitz
RS 369	Sissy Spacek	Annie Leibovitz
RS 370	Nastassia Kinski	Richard Avedon
RS 371	David Letterman	Herb Ritts (Visages)
RS 372	Pete Townshend	Julian Allen
RS 373	Sylvester Stallone	Annie Leibovitz
RS 374	E.T.	Aaron Rapoport
RS 375	The Go-Go's	Annie Leibovitz
RS 376	Jeff Bridges	Annie Leibovitz
RS 377	Elvis Costello	Annie Leibovitz
RS 378	Robin Williams	Bonnie Schiffman
RS 379	Richard Gere	Herb Ritts
RS 380	John Lennon & Yoko Ono	Allan Tannenbaum
RS 381	Billy Joel	Annie Leibovitz
RS 382	The Who	Annie Leibovitz

RS 383	Matt Dillon	Annie Leibovitz
RS 384	Bette Midler	Greg Gorman
RS 387	Paul Newman	Jim Varriale
RS 388	Dustin Hoffman	Richard Avedon
RS 389	Michael Jackson	Bonnie Schiffman
RS 390	The Stray Cats	Richard Avedon
RS 391	Jessica Lange	Jim Varriale
RS 392	Dudley Moore	Bonnie Schiffman
RS 393	Joan Baez	David Montgomery
RS 394	Prince & Vanity	Richard Avedon
RS 395	David Bowie	David Bailey
RS 396	Sean Penn	Mary Ellen Mark
RS 397	Christie Brinkley & Michael Ives	E.J. Camp
RS 398	Men at Work	Aaron Rapoport
RS 399	Eddie Murphy	Richard Avedon
RS 400/401	Darth Vader, Ewok, Carrie Fisher & Gamurian Guard	Aaron Rapoport
RS 402	John Travolta	Richard Avedon
RS 403	Sting	Lynn Goldsmith (LGI)
RS 404	Jackson Browne	Aaron Rapoport
RS 405	Annie Lennox	E.J. Camp
RS 406	Chevy Chase	Bonnie Schiffman
RS 407	Sean Connery	David Montgomery
RS 408	Boy George	David Montgomery
RS 409	Mick Jagger	William Coupon
RS 410	Michael Jackson & Paul McCartney	Vivienne Flesher
RS 413	Eric Clapton, Jeff Beck, Jimmy Page, Joe Cocker, Charlie Watts, Bill Wyman, Kenney Jones, Paul Rodgers & Ronnie Lane	Bonnie Schiffman
RS 414	Duran Duran	David Montgomery
RS 415	The Beatles	John Launois (Black Star)
RS 416	The Police	David Bailey
RS 417	Michael Jackson	Matthew Rolston
RS 418	Jack Nicholson	Richard Avedon
RS 419	Eddie Murphy	Richard Avedon
RS 420	Daryl Hannah	E.J. Camp
RS 421	Marvin Gaye	Neal Preston (Camera 5)
RS 422	Cyndi Lauper	Richard Avedon
RS 423	Culture Club	Richard Avedon
RS 424	Bob Dylan	Ken Regan (Camera 5)
RS 425	The Go-Go's	Albert Watson
RS 426/427	Tom Wolfe	Annie Leibovitz (Contact Press Images)
	Steven Spielberg	Hiro
	Little Richard	Ralph Morse (Life Magazine © Time Inc.)
RS 428	Bill Murray	Barbara Walz (Outline)
RS 429	Prince	Richard Avedon
RS 430	Huey Lewis	Aaron Rapoport
RS 431	John Belushi	Gottfried Helnwein
RS 432	Tina Turner	Steven Meisel
RS 433	David Bowie	Greg Gorman
RS 434	Steve Martin	Bonnie Schiffman
RS 435	Madonna	Steven Meisel
RS 436	Bruce Springsteen	Aaron Rapoport
RS 439	Daryl Hall & John Oates	Bert Stern
RS 440	Billy Idol	E.J. Camp
RS 441	Mick Jagger	Steven Meisel
RS 442	Bruce Springsteen	Neal Preston
RS 443	U2	Rebecca Blake
RS 444	Don Johnson & Phillip Michael Thomas	Deborah Feingold
RS 445	David Lee Roth	Bradford Branson (Visages)
RS 446	Richard Gere	Herb Ritts
RS 447	Madonna & Rosanna Arquette	Herb Ritts
RS 448	Phil Collins	Aaron Rapoport
RS 449	Julian Lennon	Richard Avedon
RS 450	David Letterman	Deborah Feingold
RS 451	Clint Eastwood	Gottfried Helnwein
RS 452/453	John Travolta & Jamie Lee Curtis	Patrick Demarchelier
RS 454	Mick Jagger	Albert Watson
	Bob Dylan, Madonna	Ken Regan (Camera 5)
	Paul McCartney	Linda McCartney
	David Bowie	Greg Gorman
	Chrissie Hynde, Phil Collins	Aaron Rapoport
	Bono	Photographer Unknown
	Bob Geldof	Simon Fowler
	Ric Ocasek	William Coupon
	Sting, John Taylor	Eric Boman
	Robert Plant	Ilpo Musto
	Eric Clapton	David Montgomery
	Sade	Brian Aris (Outline)
	Pete Townshend	Davies & Starr
	Bryan Ferry	Lothar Schmid
	Tina Turner, Mark Knopfler, Bryan Adams	Deborah Feingold (Outline)
RS 455	Mel Gibson & Tina Turner	Herb Ritts
RS 456	Prince	'Raspberry Beret' Video Still © 1985 PRN Productions
RS 457	Sting	Eric Boman
RS 458	Bruce Springsteen	Neal Preston (Camera 5)
RS 459	Steven Spielberg	Moshe Brakha
RS 460	Don Johnson	Herb Ritts
RS 461	Mark Knopfler	Deborah Feingold
RS 462	Bob Geldof	Davies & Starr
RS 465	Michael Douglas	E.J. Camp
RS 466	John Cougar Mellencamp	Herb Ritts
RS 467	Elvis Presley	Springer (Bettmann Film Archive)
	Ray Charles, Buddy Holly	James J. Kriegsmann
	Fats Domino, Jerry Lee Lewis, Chuck Berry, James Brown, Little Richard, The Everly Brothers, Sam Cooke	Michael Ochs Archives
RS 468	Bruce Springsteen	Aaron Rapoport
RS 469	Jim McMahon	Ken Regan (Camera 5)
RS 470	Bruce Willis	Bonnie Schiffman

RS 471	Stevie Wonder	Mark Hanauer
RS 472	Prince with Wendy & Lisa	Jeff Katz
RS 473	Whoopi Goldberg	Bonnie Schiffman
RS 474	Michael J. Fox	Chris Callis
RS 475	Madonna	Matthew Rolston
RS 476	Tom Cruise	Herb Ritts
RS 477	Van Halen	Deborah Feingold
RS 478/479	Tom Petty & Bob Dylan	Aaron Rapoport
RS 480	Jack Nicholson	Herb Ritts
RS 481	Boy George	Norman Watson
RS 482	Paul McCartney	Harry DeZitter
RS 483	Don Johnson	E.J. Camp
RS 484	Cybill Shepherd	Matthew Rolston
RS 485	Tina Turner	Matthew Rolston
RS 486	Billy Joel	Albert Watson
RS 487	Huey Lewis	Tim Boole
RS 488	Run-D.M.C.	Moshe Brakha
RS 491	Talking Heads	Richard Corman
RS 492	Peter Gabriel	Robert Mapplethorpe
RS 493	Pee-wee Herman	Janette Beckman
RS 494	Bruce Springsteen	Albert Watson
RS 495	Michael J. Fox	Deborah Feingold
RS 496	The Bangles	Bonnie Schiffman
RS 497	Woody Allen	Brian Hamill (Photoreporters)
RS 498	Twentieth Anniversary: Style – David Bowie	Herb Ritts
RS 499	U2	Anton Corbijn
RS 500	Jon Bon Jovi	E.J. Camp
RS 501	Twentieth Anniversary: The Greatest Performances – Jimi Hendrix	Ed Caraeff
RS 502	Robert Cray	Deborah Feingold
RS 503	Paul Simon & Ladysmith Black Mambazo	Mark Seliger
RS 504/505	The Grateful Dead	Michael O'Neill
RS 506	Mötley Crüe	E.J. Camp
RS 507	The 100 Best Albums of the Last Twenty Years	Constance Hansen
RS 508	Madonna	Herb Ritts
RS 509	Michael Jackson	Anita Kunz
RS 510	Bono	Matthew Rolston
RS 511	George Harrison	William Coupon
RS 512	Twentieth Anniversary	Jim Parkinson
RS 513	Pink Floyd	Melissa Grimes
RS 514	R.E.M.	Brian Smale
RS 517	Michael Douglas	Albert Watson
RS 518	George Michael	Matthew Rolston
RS 519	Sting	Matt Mahurin
RS 520	Robin Williams	Bonnie Schiffman
RS 521	U2	Matthew Rolston
RS 522	Robert Plant	David Montgomery
RS 523	Martin Luther King Jr.	Paul Davis
RS 524	David Byrne	Hiro
RS 525	Bruce Springsteen	Neal Preston
RS 526	Lisa Bonet	Matthew Rolston
RS 527	Neil Young	William Coupon
RS 528	Terence Trent D'Arby	Matthew Rolston
RS 529	Tom Hanks	Herb Ritts
RS 530/531	Van Halen	Timothy White
RS 532	Tom Cruise	Herb Ritts
RS 533	Eric Clapton	David Bailey
RS 534	The 100 Best Singles of the Last Twenty-five Years	Steve Pietzsch
RS 535	Tracy Chapman	Herb Ritts
RS 536	Keith Richards	Albert Watson
RS 537	John Lennon	Barbara Nessim
RS 538	Johnny Carson & David Letterman	Bonnie Schiffman
RS 539	Guns n' Roses	Timothy White
RS 540	Steve Winwood	Herb Ritts
RS 543	Mel Gibson	Herb Ritts
RS 544	Roy Orbison	Ann Summa (Onyx)
RS 545	Jon Bon Jovi	Timothy White
RS 546	Sam Kinison	Mark Seliger
RS 547	Bono	Anton Corbijn
RS 548	Madonna	Herb Ritts
RS 549	James Brown	Gottfried Helnwein
RS 550	R.E.M.	Timothy White
RS 551	Lou Reed	Mark Seliger
RS 552	Uma Thurman	Matthew Rolston
RS 553	Harold Ramis, Bill Murray, Sigourney Weaver, Ernie Hudson & Dan Aykroyd	Timothy White
RS 554	Paul McCartney	Herb Ritts
RS 555	Michael Keaton	Bonnie Schiffman
RS 556/557	Pete Townshend, Roger Daltrey & John Entwistle	Davies & Starr
RS 558	Axl Rose	Robert John
RS 559	Eddie Murphy	Bonnie Schiffman
RS 560	Mick Jagger & Keith Richards	Albert Watson
RS 561	Madonna	Herb Ritts
RS 562	Roland Gift	Andrew MacPherson
RS 563	Andie MacDowell	Matthew Rolston
RS 564	Jay Leno & Arsenio Hall	Bonnie Schiffman
RS 565	The 100 Greatest Albums of the Eighties	Terry Allen
RS 566	Jerry Garcia	William Coupon
RS 569	Tom Cruise	Herb Ritts
RS 570	Billy Joel	Timothy White
RS 571	Paul McCartney	Timothy White
RS 572	Janet Jackson	Matthew Rolston
RS 573	Keith Richards & Mick Jagger	Neal Preston
RS 574	The B-52's	Mark Seliger
RS 575	Aerosmith	Mark Seliger
RS 576	The Fifties	Terry Allen & Dennis Ortiz-Lopez
RS 577	Bonnie Raitt	E.J. Camp
RS 578	Claudia Schiffer	Herb Ritts
RS 579	Warren Beatty	Herb Ritts

RS 580	Sinéad O'Connor	*Andrew MacPherson*
RS 581	Bart Simpson	*Matt Groening*
RS 582/583	Tom Cruise	*Herb Ritts*
RS 584	Julia Roberts	*Herb Ritts*
RS 585	The Sixties – John Lennon	*Richard Avedon*
RS 586	M.C. Hammer	*Frank W. Ockenfels 3*
RS 587	The Seventies – Jimmy Page & Robert Plant	*Bob Gruen (Star File)*
RS 588	Lara Flynn Boyle, Sherilyn Fenn & Mädchen Amick	*Matthew Rolston*
RS 589	Prince	*Jeff Katz*
RS 590	Living Colour	*Mark Seliger*
RS 591	The Eighties – Bruce Springsteen	*Annie Leibovitz*
RS 592	Kevin Costner	*Gwendolen Cates*
RS 595	Johnny Depp	*Herb Ritts*
RS 596	Slash	*Mark Seliger*
RS 597	Sting	*Herb Ritts*
RS 598	Robin Williams	*Mark Seliger*
RS 599	Sinéad O'Connor	*Herb Ritts*
RS 600	Jodie Foster	*Matthew Rolston*
RS 601	Jim Morrison	*Joel Brodsky*
RS 602	Chris Isaak	*Randee St. Nicholas (Visages)*
	Charlatans U.K., De la Soul, Nuno Bettencourt	*Mark Seliger*
RS 603	Wilson Phillips	*Andrew Eccles*
RS 604	Winona Ryder	*Herb Ritts*
RS 605	The Black Crowes	*Mark Seliger*
RS 606	Madonna	*Steven Meisel*
RS 607	R.E.M.	*Frank W. Ockenfels 3*
RS 608/609	Rod Stewart & Rachel Hunter	*Andrew Eccles*
RS 610	Tom Petty	*Mark Seliger*
RS 611	Arnold Schwarzenegger	*Herb Ritts*
RS 612	Guns n' Roses	*Herb Ritts*
RS 613	Sebastian Bach	*Mark Seliger*
RS 614	Pee-wee Herman	*Janette Beckman (Outline)*
RS 615	Eric Clapton	*Albert Watson*
RS 616	Jerry Garcia	*Mark Seliger*
RS 617	Metallica	*Mark Seliger*
RS 618	U2	*Anton Corbijn*
RS 621	Michael Jackson	*Herb Ritts*
RS 622	Hunter S. Thompson	*Ralph Steadman*
RS 623	Jimi Hendrix	*Gered Mankowitz*
RS 624	Luke Perry, Shannen Doherty & Jason Priestley	*Andrew Eccles*
RS 625	R.E.M.	*Albert Watson*
RS 626	Mike Myers & Dana Carvey	*Bonnie Schiffman*
RS 627	Axl Rose	*Herb Ritts*
RS 628	Nirvana	*Mark Seliger*
RS 629	Def Leppard	*Mark Seliger*
RS 630	Sharon Stone	*Albert Watson*
RS 631	Tom Cruise	*Albert Watson*
RS 632	Twenty-fifth Anniversary: The Great Stories	*Dennis Ortiz-Lopez*
RS 633	Red Hot Chili Peppers	*Mark Seliger*
RS 634/635	Batman's Suit	*Herb Ritts*
RS 636	Bruce Springsteen	*Herb Ritts*
RS 637	Ice-T	*Mark Seliger*
RS 638	Michelle Pfeiffer	*Herb Ritts*
RS 639	Bill Clinton	*Mark Seliger*
RS 640	Bono	*Neal Preston*
RS 641	Twenty-fifth Anniversary: The Interviews	
RS 642	Sinéad O'Connor	*Albert Watson*
RS 643	Twenty-fifth Anniversary: The Portraits – Elvis's Gold Lamé Nudie Suit	*Albert Watson*
RS 644	Denzel Washington	*Albert Watson*
RS 647	The Spin Doctors	*Mark Seliger*
RS 648	Neil Young	*Mark Seliger*
RS 649	Neneh Cherry	*Ellen Von Unwerth*
RS 650	David Letterman	*Mark Seliger*
RS 651	Bono	*Andrew MacPherson*
RS 652	Natalie Merchant	*Jeffrey Thurnher*
RS 653	Garth Brooks	*Kurt Markus*
RS 654	James Hetfield	*Mark Seliger*
RS 655	Eric Clapton	*Albert Watson*
RS 656	Dana Carvey	*Mark Seliger*
RS 657	Sting	*Andrew MacPherson*
RS 658	Whitney Houston	*Albert Watson*
RS 659	Laura Dern	*Kurt Markus*
RS 660/661	Jason Alexander, Jerry Seinfeld, Julia Louis-Dreyfus & Michael Richards	*Mark Seliger*
RS 662	Soul Asylum	*Mark Seliger*
RS 663	Beavis & Butt-Head	*Mike Judge*
RS 664	Jerry Garcia	*Mark Seliger*
RS 665	Janet Jackson	*Patrick Demarchelier*
RS 666	Dr. Dre & Snoop Doggy Dogg	*Mark Seliger*
RS 667	The Edge	*Andrew MacPherson*
RS 668	Pearl Jam	*Mark Seliger*
RS 669	Blind Melon	*Mark Seliger*
RS 670	Shaquille O'Neal	*Mark Seliger*
RS 671	Bill Clinton	*Mark Seliger*
RS 672/673	Cindy Crawford	*Herb Ritts*
RS 674	Nirvana	*Mark Seliger*
RS 675	Howard Stern	*Mark Seliger*
RS 676	Bob Marley	*Annie Leibovitz (Contact Press Images)*
RS 677	Winona Ryder	*Herb Ritts*
RS 678	Beavis & Butt-Head	*Mike Judge*
RS 679	Anthony Kiedis	*Matthew Rolston*
RS 680	Smashing Pumpkins	*Glen Luchford*
RS 681	Drugs in America	*I. P. Daley*
RS 682	Laura Leighton, Josie Bissett, Heather Locklear, Daphne Zuniga & Courtney Thorne-Smith	*Mark Seliger*
RS 683	Kurt Cobain	*Mark Seliger*

RS 684	Soundgarden	*Mark Seliger*
RS 685	Counting Crows	*Mark Seliger*
RS 686/687	Julia Roberts	*Herb Ritts*
RS 688	The Beastie Boys	*Matthew Rolston*
RS 689	The Rolling Stones	*Anton Corbijn*
RS 690	Trent Reznor	*Matt Mahurin*
RS 691	Jerry Seinfeld	*Mark Seliger*
RS 692	Liz Phair	*Frank W. Ockenfels 3*
RS 693	R.E.M.	*Mark Seliger*
RS 694	Liv & Steven Tyler	*Albert Watson*
RS 695	Generation Next	*Eric Siry*
RS 696	Brad Pitt	*Mark Seliger*
RS 697	Courtney Love	*Mark Seliger*
RS 698/699	David Letterman	*Frank W. Ockenfels 3*
RS 700	Green Day	*Dan Winters*
RS 701	Demi Moore	*Matthew Rolston*
RS 702	Robert Plant & Jimmy Page	*Anton Corbijn*
RS 703	Ethan Hawke	*Mark Seliger*
RS 704	Dolores O'Riordan	*Corrine Day*
RS 705	Eddie Van Halen	*Mark Seliger*
RS 706	Belly	*Mark Seliger*
RS 707	Tom Petty	*Mark Seliger*
RS 708	Jennifer Aniston, Matthew Perry, Lisa Kudrow, Courteney Cox, David Schwimmer & Matt LeBlanc	*Mark Seliger*
RS 709	Melissa Etheridge	*Peggy Sirota*
RS 710	Drew Barrymore	*Mark Seliger*
RS 711	Soul Asylum	*Matt Mahurin*
RS 712/713	Jim Carrey	*Herb Ritts*
RS 714	Hootie & the Blowfish	*Mark Seliger*
RS 715	Hole	*Mark Seliger*
RS 716	Alicia Silverstone	*Peggy Sirota*
RS 717	Jerry Garcia	*Herbie Greene*
RS 718	Foo Fighters	*Dan Winters*
RS 719	Red Hot Chili Peppers	*Anton Corbijn*
RS 720	Alanis Morissette	*Frank W. Ockenfels 3*
RS 721	Smashing Pumpkins	*Mark Seliger*
RS 722	Lenny Kravitz	*Matthew Rolston*
RS 723	Mick Jagger	*Peter Lindbergh*
RS 724/725	Green Day, Jerry Garcia, Sheryl Crow, Billy Corgan, Courtney Love	*Mark Seliger*
	John Travolta	*Richard Foreman*
	Alanis Morissette	*Frank W. Ockenfels 3*
	Coolio	*Albert Watson*
RS 726	Live	*Julian Broad*
RS 727	Layne Staley	*Mark Seliger*
RS 728	John Travolta	*Mark Seliger*
RS 729	Jennifer Aniston	*Mark Seliger*
RS 730	Joan Osborne	*Mark Seliger*
RS 731	Sean Penn	*Mark Seliger*
RS 732	Gavin Rossdale	*Mark Seliger*
RS 733	Liam & Noel Gallagher	*Nathaniel Goldberg*
RS 734	David Duchovny & Gillian Anderson	*Montalbetti/Campbell for RS Australia*
RS 735	David Letterman	*Albert Watson*
RS 736	Perry Farrell, Billy Corgan	*Kevin Mazur*
	"Independence Day"	*Film Still*
	Alanis Morissette, Beck	*Frank W. Ockenfels 3*
	Jimmy Buffett	*Randy Davey (LGI)*
	James Taylor	*Andrew Brucker*
	Sandra Bullock	*Kate Garner (Visages)*
	Chris Cornell	*Mark Seliger*
	John Popper	*Tom Wolff*
	Kiss	*Costello (Retna)*
RS 737	Metallica	*Anton Corbijn*
RS 738/739	Jenny McCarthy	*Mark Seliger*
RS 740	Jerry Garcia	*Paul Davis*
RS 741	Cameron Diaz	*Mark Seliger*
RS 742	The Fugees	*Matthew Rolston*
RS 743	Conan O'Brien	*Mark Seliger*
RS 744	Brooke Shields	*Mark Seliger*
RS 745	R.E.M.	*Anton Corbijn*
RS 746	Tupac Shakur	*Danny Clinch*
RS 747	Sheryl Crow	*Mark Seliger*
RS 748	Eddie Vedder	*Ross Halfin (Photofeatures)*
RS 749	Dennis Rodman	*Albert Watson*
RS 750/751	Beavis & Butt-Head with Pamela Anderson Lee	*Mike Judge & Mark Seliger*
RS 752	Marilyn Manson	*Matt Mahurin*
RS 753	Stone Temple Pilots	*Mark Seliger*
RS 754	Gillian Anderson	*Matthew Rolston*
RS 755	Trent Reznor & David Lynch	*Dan Winters*
RS 756	Howard Stern	*Mark Seliger*
RS 757	Brad Pitt	*Mark Seliger*
RS 758	Beck	*Anton Corbijn*
RS 759	No Doubt	*Norbert Schoerner*
RS 760	Jewel	*Matthew Rolston*
RS 761	U2	*Albert Watson*
	Inset: Allen Ginsberg	*Fred W. McDarrah*
RS 762	Jakob Dylan	*Mark Seliger*
RS 763	Sandra Bullock	*Brigitte Lacombe*
RS 764/765	Spice Girls	*Mark Seliger*
RS 766	Puff Daddy	*Matthew Rolston*
RS 767	The Prodigy's Keith Flint	*Peter Robathan (Katz/Outline)*
RS 768	Wu-Tang Clan's RZA & Rage Against the Machine's Zack de la Rocha	*Mark Seliger*
RS 769	Neve Campbell	*Matthew Rolston*
RS 770	Chris Rock	*Mark Seliger*
RS 771	Salt-n-Pepa	*Peggy Sirota*
RS 772	Fleetwood Mac	*Mark Seliger*
RS 773	Thirtieth Anniversary: Courtney Love, Tina Turner & Madonna	*Peggy Sirota*

ACKNOWLEDGMENTS

Digging through piles and piles of tattered and torn back issues of ROLLING STONE was similar to going on a fantastic treasure hunt. We'd like to thank those who shared our enthusiasm for *ROLLING STONE: The Complete Covers,* making our archaeological excavation possible: ROLLING STONE's Jann S. Wenner, Jane Wenner, Kent Brownridge, John Lagana, Fred Woodward and Robert Love; Eric Himmel, our very committed editor at Harry N. Abrams; and our energetic literary agent Sarah Lazin, herself an important part of ROLLING STONE's history. Kudos to the indomitable team who labored tirelessly making the book a reality: my superb Rolling Stone Press staff, associate editor Shawn Dahl (an RS vet since #561) and editorial assistant Ann Abel; Fred Woodward and his creative crew, Jesper Sundwall, Fredrik Sundwall, Yoomi Chong and Eric Siry; photographer Dan Baliotti who shot the 728 covers reproduced here; and our hardworking editorial colleagues, Patricia Romanowski, Tom Conroy, Rich Cohen, Corey Seymour, Peter Kenis, Greg Emmanuel, Will Rigby, Tom Soper, Andy York, Jim Duffy and Janet Wygal. ROLLING STONE staffers who were indispensable to our endeavors include: Mary MacDonald, Steve Best, Tom Worley, Rich Waldman, Kilian Schalk, Dennis Wheeler, Maury Viola, Kelly Sipos, Jodi Peckman, Fiona McDonagh, Kristin Dymitruk, Richard Skanse and Mike Guy. Our gratitude to a few others who gave us their time: David Bowie, Chrissie Hynde, Mick Jagger, David Letterman, Yoko Ono, Tom Petty, Teresa Redburn, Fran Curtis, Rebecca Rosen, Sheila Rodgers, Michael Phillips, Mary Klauzer, Denise Sfraga, Julie Claire and Tana Osa-Yande. Of the many people who've made ROLLING STONE what it is, several were indispensible to this book: Baron Wolman, Annie Leibovitz and Mark Seliger. Our hats off to longtime photo editor Laurie Kratochvil, all the previous art directors – John Williams, Robert Kingsbury, Michael Salisbury, Tony Lane, Roger Black, Bea Feitler, Mary Shanahan and Derek Ungless – and, of course, the many talented cover photographers and artists. A special thanks to the writers whose work has appeared in ROLLING STONE, especially those whose words can be found within these pages: Michael Azerrad, David Breskin, John Burks, E. Jean Carroll, Rich Cohen, Christopher Connelly, Jonathan Cott, Paul Cowan, Cameron Crowe, Anthony DeCurtis, Joe Eszterhas, David Felton, Chet Flippo, Alec Foege, Ben Fong-Torres, David Fricke, Donna Gaines, Paul Gambaccini, Mikal Gilmore, Ralph J. Gleason, Michael Goldberg, William Greider, Chris Heath, James Henke, Gerri Hirshey, Stephen Holden, Jerry Hopkins, Peter W. Kaplan, Howard Kohn, Kurt Loder, Greil Marcus, Dave Marsh, Michael McClure, Ed McCormack, Chris Mundy, Kim Neely, Robert Palmer, Steve Pond, Kevin Powell, P.J. O'Rourke, David Ritz, David Rosenthal, Scott Spencer, Neil Strauss, Harry Swift, Hunter S. Thompson, David Wild, Peter Wilkinson, Ellen Willis, Tom Wolfe, Ritchie Yorke, Charles M. Young and Bill Zehme.

What a legacy – I can only imagine what the next thirty years will bring.

~ *HOLLY GEORGE-WARREN*
[EDITOR, ROLLING STONE PRESS]